The Early Eastern
Orthodox Church

The Early Eastern Orthodox Church

A History, AD 60–1453

STEPHEN MORRIS

McFarland & Company, Inc., Publishers

Jefferson, North Carolina

Portions of "Chapter 4: Constantinople, Alexandria and the Mother of God" appeared previously in "Clothed with Scarlet, Clothed with the Sun: Patristic Thoughts on the Women of Apocalypse 11-12 and 17" in *Earth's Abominations: Philosophical Studies of Evil* (ed. Daniel Haybron) (Rodopi: Amsterdam, 2002).

Portions of "Chapter 6: Justinian and Theodora" appeared previously in "The Feminine Voice of Vice in *The Ladder of Divine Ascent*" in *The Forces of Evil* (eds. Anthony F. and Denise Crisafi) (Inter-Disciplinary Press: Oxford, 2011).

Portions of "Chapter 10: Constantinople, Rome and Leo VI" appeared previously in Stephen Morris, *When Brothers Dwell in Unity: Byzantine Christianity and Homosexuality* (McFarland, 2015).

LIBRARY OF CONGRESS CATALOGUING-IN-PUBLICATION DATA

Names: Morris, Stephen, 1958 June 18– author.
Title: The early Eastern Orthodox Church : a history, AD 60–1453 / Stephen Morris.
Description: Jefferson, North Carolina : McFarland & Company, Inc., Publishers, 2018. | Includes bibliographical references and index.
Identifiers: LCCN 2018039538 | ISBN 9781476674810 (softcover) ∞
Subjects: LCSH: Orthodox Eastern Church—History. | Orthodox Eastern Church—Doctrines.
Classification: LCC BX300 .M677 2018 | DDC 281.909—dc23
LC record available at https://lccn.loc.gov/2018039538

BRITISH LIBRARY CATALOGUING DATA ARE AVAILABLE

ISBN (print) 978-1-4766-7481-0
ISBN (ebook) 978-1-4766-3422-7

Front cover: The tiled mosaic of *The Ascension of the Lord* by Matthew Digby Wyatt in All Saints Church, London (iStock/sedmak)

Printed in the United States of America

McFarland & Company, Inc., Publishers
  Box 611, Jefferson, North Carolina 28640
  www.mcfarlandpub.com

For the monks and layfolk
on East Third Street:
"Many Years!"

For Alan:
"Memory eternal!"

Acknowledgments

I want to thank the monks, clergy, and layfolk associated with the Russian monastery on East Third Street on the Lower East Side of Manhattan who first invited me to teach a year-long course in church history. My notes for that course have become the pages of this book. A dozen of us gathered every week in the chilly refectory downstairs and got to know Ignatius of Antioch, Athanasius, Cyril of Alexandria, Maximus the Confessor, John of Damascus, and all the others who appear in these pages. I want to thank those monks, clergy, and layfolk for their patience with me and for their comments and their questions. This book would not exist if it had not been for them.

I want to thank John, Tom, Stuart, Jaana, and the others who read either this manuscript or sections of it in order to tell me what was clear, what was unclear, what was confusing, or to exclaim, "How could you have left THAT out?!" Their comments have also made this a better book.

I want to thank Alan Mack, the parish priest who allowed me—then a high-school student in Seattle—to read nearly every book in his library and to fall in love with the study of theology, liturgical practice, and Church history as well as the ways in which these all intersect. May his memory be eternal!

I want to thank Tony Lewis for his friendship and prayers over the years, beginning with those long walks around the Old Campus at Yale to discuss the Big Questions of life.

There are others who have contributed to the development of this project in a variety of ways, both small and large. To them, each too generous and too numerous to mention, I give my thanks as well.

Finally, I want to thank my partner Elliot who endured—quietly for the most part—the transformation of our dining room table into my office as I spread out notecards, books, and papers around my laptop for more than a year. His ongoing support for this—and all my other projects—is truly a reflection of the love of God and means more than I can ever say.

Table of Contents

We have heard with our ears, O God,
our forefathers have told us,
    the deeds you did in their days,
    in the days of old
        [Psalm 44:1].

Lord, you have been our refuge
    from one generation to another.
        [Psalm 90:1].

Introduction

"It seemed good to the Holy Spirit and to us," the apostles declared at the conclusion of their council described in Acts 15. This apostolic council was only the first of many councils in the life of the Church as Christians sought to discern the will of God in the midst of historic challenges. Church history is the story of the people of God across time, of his interaction with humanity and human response to him. It begins with the initial act of creation, of God's saying "Let there be light" on the first day (Sunday), and will only conclude on the Last, Great Day when Christ comes again to judge the living and the dead. In the meantime, the faithful struggle to express that apostolic faith in new words, new languages, new places, new times.

This is the story of that struggle from the days of the New Testament up to the fall of the city of Constantinople (AD 1453). For our purposes, church history more particularly begins with the Ascension of Christ. The Ascension is the last of the resurrection appearances to the apostles on any kind of regular basis and it is the first step of the Christian community on the road leading to the Second Coming of "this Jesus, who was taken up from you into heaven, [and who] will come [again] in the same way as you saw him go into heaven" (Acts 1:11).

This book focuses on the story of the Christian community in the eastern Mediterranean which eventually became known as the Byzantine Empire. Much of this story necessarily involves the Christian community in Western Europe. Those who focus on the western Mediterranean area as they tell the story of church history are necessarily interested in what happens in the east as well, especially the record of the seven great ecumenical councils which were all held in Byzantine territory. But many of the great personalities of the eastern Christian world are lost or ignored when church history is told from a Western European perspective. We aim to rediscover those great personalities and the events that they shaped.

Each chapter attempts to tell "who-what-where-when" of particular episodes and then examines the "why," the theology that was at the heart of the debates and events described. The events and the theology that fueled them are inextricably entwined, as are the personalities of the people involved.

Telling the story of God's interaction with humanity and the world necessarily involves dates and asking what else was going on in the world at that time. We might suggest that the most significant pre-church history dates to know (in approximate terms) are these:

- Creation
- the foundation of Jericho, one of the first known cities (8000 BC)
- the Pyramids are built (2500 BC)
- Abraham (2000 BC)
- the Exodus from Egypt (1350–1200 BC)
- King David (1,000 BC; also Homer in Greece)
- the exile to Babylon (600 BC)
- Jesus Christ (born approx. 3 BC, due to a calendar miscalculation in the sixth century)

Beginning our exploration of church history with the Ascension and the first generations of Christian experience, we will embark on an examination of apostolic and sub-apostolic Christianity by reviewing questions dealt with in the earliest New Testament writings, church handbooks such as the *Didache* and the *Apostolic Tradition* of Hippolytus, the epistles of Ignatius of Antioch, and Justin Martyr's apologetics. We will also see the role of martyrs and martyrdom in the early Christian churches, using the *Martyrdom of Polycarp* as a guide. Irenaeus of Lyons' *Against Heresies* and the theology of recapitulation as well as a brief review of styles of biblical study and interpretation will prepare us for one ongoing theme, that of the conflict between the interpretative styles of Alexandria and Antioch.

Next, we turn to the events of the Great Persecution of Diocletian and the legalization of Christianity by Constantine, followed by examinations of the building projects of the emperor and his mother, the development of monasticism in Egypt under Antony, the conflict with the Donatists in North Africa, and the dispute between Arius and Athanasius. Finally, we will see how the decision of the council at Nicea to endorse the term *homoousias* engulfed the Christian world.

The chronology of events involving the debates with the *Pneumatomachoi* and the proclamation of the divinity of the Holy Spirit at the Second Ecumenical Council follow on the heels of the dispute with Arius. We will read about Basil the Great's life and his *On the Holy Spirit* as well as selected topics in his *Hexameron (Sermons on the Six Days of Creation)*, some of which are still surprisingly pertinent in today's world. We will also discover how the theology of Gregory Nazianzus, found in his *Theological Orations* and selected other writings, was able to contribute to the resolution of the argument with the *Pneumatomachoi*.

In Chapter 4, we spend some time with John Chrysostom, one of the most famous of the early Christian preachers. We then turn to the preaching of Nestorius and his teaching about Mary, the Mother of God, and the response of Cyril of Alexandria (especially his famous *12 Anathemas*) and the events surrounding the third ecumenical council at Ephesus.

The aftermath of the council of Ephesus results in ongoing conflict, leading to the council at Chalcedon which endorses the *Tome of Leo* and results in schisms that continue to exist in the 21st century. The terminology of *hypostasis, prosopon,* and *physis* all will be examined in context and in depth.

Justinian and Theodora's policies toward the non–Chalcedonian churches will be examined, as well as the liturgical developments (such as the *Monogenes* and Cherubic hymns) of their reign. The disputes concerning the Theopaschites, Origen, and the Three Chapters with their implications for Christian theology will be important to look at. We will also discover the articulation of the important Eastern Christian idea of the harmony ("symphony") between civil and religious authority.

Further developments of Christology will be examined in Chapter 7, especially the Monothelite controversy and the response of Maximus the Confessor. We will discover how important the idea of gnomic will and the microcosm/macrocosm nature of humanity is in Maximus' thought. Political developments in the Byzantine Empire will also be investigated, especially the Persian invasions and the Emperor Heraclius' restoration of Byzantine power, including the recovery of the relics of the Cross.

Chapters 8 and 9 deal with the appearance of Islam and its significance, leading us into the Iconoclastic attacks on Orthodox practice and the decisions of the seventh ecumenical council (AD 787). We will meet John of Damascus and discuss his *On the Holy Icons*. Charlemagne's interaction with the Byzantines and his subsequent claim to imperial authority in Western Europe is also discussed. The second wave of Iconoclasm is described and its resolution with the Triumph of Orthodoxy (AD 843).

The rivalry and divisions between Rome and Constantinople take center stage in Chapter 10. The famous schism in which the Patriarch Photius was a central figure had long-lasting consequences for church unity and policy regarding the importance of the papacy in Rome. At least some leading churchmen have suggested that the resolution of the dispute about Photius could be a model for contemporary ecumenical efforts between the Roman Catholic and Eastern Orthodox churches. The missionary work of Cyril and Methodius, the expansion of Byzantine Christianity among the Slavs, and the marital problems of Leo VI were not only contributing factors to the division between Rome and Constantinople but helped forge contemporary Orthodox practice regarding missionary work and attitudes toward marriage.

Ongoing divisions between Rome and Constantinople also played a role in Western European military support—or the lack thereof—for the Byzantine efforts to resist the growing Muslim threat. The Crusades, launched to ostensibly protect pilgrims, concluded with the overthrow of Constantinople and the Crusaders' refusal to acknowledge the Byzantines as fellow Christians. Theological issues—such as the Filioque, the use of leavened or unleavened bread in the Eucharist, the growing importance of purgatory and the material nature of hell in Western Christianity—all revealed fault lines in the Eastern and Western approaches to theology and Christian life. These issues also came to signify Byzantine political and military independence from Western Christians.

The conflict over the possibility of actual human contact with divinity was at the heart of the dispute in which Gregory Palamas played a leading role. His efforts to defend the hesychasts resulted in the final Byzantine clarification of the nature of the divine insofar as he clarified the distinction between the unknowable essence of God and the divine energies which can be known and experienced by humans. The Byzantine effort to win Western Christian military aid against the Turks in return for theological and ecclesiastical union—or submission, depending on one's point of view—failed at the Council of Ferrara-Florence and New Rome fell in AD 1453.

This journey of the People of God through time will involve many disputes and ideas that seem unfamiliar—or even unimportant—to modern readers. Some readers might wonder how such issues could become so divisive in the past. As C.S. Lewis remarked,

> Every age has its own outlook. It is specially good at seeing certain truths and specially liable to make certain mistakes. We all, therefore, need the books that will correct the characteristic mistakes of our own period.... We may be sure that the characteristic blindness of the twentieth century—the blindness about which posterity will ask, "But how could they have thought that?"—lies where we have never suspected it.... [*Introduction to "On the Incarnation"*].

There will be other issues that arose in the past—such as the interaction of science and faith, between divinity and humanity, the relationship between Church and State, how differing religious communities can learn to live together in common geographic areas and political systems—that still seem familiar and pertinent. Some might wish to resolve the discussion of these issues in different ways than they are seen to be resolved in history, but contemporary readers can see the importance of discussing them.

It is with great excitement and a sense of adventure that I invite you, my readers, to join me on this exploration of the People of God as they make their way through time and begin the work of understanding themselves and the God they worship.

1

Before Nicea

The early Christians took Jesus' command "Go therefore and make disciples of all nations, baptizing them in the name of the Father and of the Son and of the Holy Spirit" (Matthew 28:19) very seriously. Almost immediately after the Resurrection, Peter and the other apostles began preaching in Jerusalem that Jesus was the long-expected Messiah and had been raised from the dead. Christian communities sprang up across the Middle East and Asia Minor; it was in Antioch, the capital of Syria, that the followers of Jesus were first called Christians (Acts 11:26).

Missionaries and preachers, such as the Apostle Paul, would often travel to Jewish communities and preach in local synagogues until they and the circle of followers they gathered were expelled by the synagogue officials. Then they would establish distinct Christian communities and begin preaching to the non–Jews as well. Other missionaries went directly to communities that were not Jewish but were familiar in some way with the Old Testament, such as the Apostle Philip who preached to the Ethiopian eunuch (Acts 8:27). The Apostle Thomas, who had initially doubted the reports of Jesus' Resurrection, is said to have preached in India; Mark, having first served as the Apostle Peter's secretary in Rome, later preached in Egypt; the Apostle Paul intended to preach in Spain one day (Romans 15:24, 28) and might have succeeded; the Apostle James is also said to have preached in Spain. Mary Magdalene reportedly led a group of preachers to Great Britain while the Apostle Jude may have gone to Mesopotamia and the Apostle Simon made his way across North Africa.

Although these later legends claiming apostolic or nearly apostolic origins for Christian communities may not be verifiable as history, they point to the early arrival of Christian preachers and the establishment of Christian communities in far-flung areas across the Roman world and beyond; the record of persecution of Christians across the Roman Empire testifies to the rapid spread of Christianity. Outside the Roman Empire, it was Armenia that embraced Christianity in AD 304 while Georgia (in the Caucasus region where

Eastern Europe-Western Asia meet) did so in AD 319 and the kingdom of Aksum (modern Ethiopia) embraced Christianity as the official faith of The Kingdom, in AD 324.

Development of the New Testament

The first written records of this new Christian community on its way through history are the epistles of the New Testament, followed later by the Gospels, the Acts of the Apostles, and the Apocalypse or Book of Revelation. There were many more epistles, gospels, acts, and apocalypses than just the ones we know of today; different Christian communities used a variety of collections of texts that they treasured and read during liturgical celebrations. Differing communities had differing criteria that texts would be measured against; the texts that met these criteria would be preserved and handed on while those that did not would either be ignored and discarded or actively refuted in arguments with other communities that held them to be authoritative.

One of the earliest and simplest of these criteria was the question "Was this text written by an apostle?" Another was "Does this text accord with the other texts that we hold to be authentic witnesses of Christian teaching and experience?" Even these apparently easy questions that seem uncontroversial today received widely different answers in those early days of the Church's experience. For instance, the western (Latin-speaking) Christian insistence that all texts had to be written by an apostle meant that the Epistle to the Hebrews was often rejected by Latin-speaking Christians because of common doubts concerning its Pauline authorship. But that insistence on apostolic authorship meant that the Apocalypse was widely adopted among Latin-speaking Christians because of its early and accepted association with the Apostle John the Divine, the Theologian.

Greek-speaking Christians, however, came to opposite conclusions based on different answers to those questions. Greek-speaking Christians embraced the Epistle to the Hebrews because they saw its liturgical viewpoint and commentary as being at one with the rest of early Christian experience and were happy to acknowledge that it was probably written by either Apollos or even his teacher, Priscilla, rather than the Apostle Paul (Acts 18). But the Apocalypse of John was rejected throughout the early Greek-speaking Christian world, despite its association with John the apostle and evangelist, because it was thought too idiosyncratic and difficult to understand or interpret.

Disputes such as these, involving not only texts but teachings that might or might not be supported by these texts, were based on a series of choices by the early Christian leaders. Some of these choices were, at the time, considered relatively minor or even trivial; others were considered more significant, causing the Greek word *heresy*, meaning "choice," to become the label by which all such choices to differ with mainstream Christianity were known. The *heresies* that early Christians contended with were the choices made by various Christian spokesmen to set themselves up in opposition to other more *orthodox* ("right-worshipping" or "right-believing") leaders, such as those described in Titus 3:10 and 2 Peter 2:1.[1]

We can see some of these disputes and choices, these developing heresies, are present already in the New Testament itself, as early Christian writers and communities struggled to understand and live out the implications of what they had experienced of Jesus: Were the followers of Jesus obligated to keep the dietary rules that Jesus lived by (Acts 10 and 15)? Were they obligated to actually convert to Judaism before they were eligible for baptism (Acts 15)? Were they obligated to care for those in the *parish* (Greek for "community") who were from other ethnic backgrounds (Acts 6) or social classes (I Cor. 11)? Were they obligated to maintain ties with the original Christian parish in Jerusalem (Acts 8 and 11)?

Church Handbooks and St. Ignatius of Antioch

In the earliest layers of the New Testament itself we can already see the first stages of church organization developing. Bishops (lit. "overseers") were already serving in each community as authoritative teachers who presided at liturgical celebrations and were responsible for the authenticity of the community's adherence to Christian faith and practice. The deacons ("servants") were his assistants, responsible for the social welfare of community members, including insuring the hungry were fed, the sick or imprisoned were visited, the naked clothed, the homeless cared for. The deacons would know who needed to be prayed for because they were aware of the personal needs of the community members. The presbyters ("elders") were the bishop's assistants in managing any physical property that the community owned as well as assisting in the preaching and teaching ministries (Acts 15 and I Timothy 5). These roles developed early in the Christian communities; Acts 6 describes the ordination of the first deacons to oversee the Christian soup kitchens and feeding programs. Councils of presbyters or elders oversaw the life of the community; one of these was always the final authority, whether that particular community called the chief presbyter a "bishop" or not (see I Timothy 3).

One source for early Christian thought and practice is the *Didache*. It survived—but only in one manuscript—because some communities considered it worthy of inclusion in the New Testament. Apparently written in Syria, near Antioch, it is a brief handbook in Greek—only 16 chapters with most chapters only a paragraph or two—of instructions for managing a local Christian community, i.e., a parish church. Scholars continue to debate how early the *Didache* was written, but most agree it was written during the first century; I agree with those that think it was written before AD 70 since it does not mention the destruction of the Temple in Jerusalem, an incident that it would be sure to report if it had already occurred since the *Didache* is especially concerned with distinguishing the authentic faithful from "the hypocrites." Generally, such church handbooks are thought to reflect practices at least 25–50 years old by the time they are written down; this means the *Didache* is contemporaneous with much of the New Testament itself.

The first six books of the *Didache* are a set of instructions and teaching—a catechism—that the catechumens ("those being instructed," in preparing for baptism; mentioned in Galatians 6:6 as well) should receive during their period of preparation. The catechism outlines the Two Ways which are the Way of Life (behaviors and beliefs that foster love of God and neighbor, such as charitable giving, refraining from anger, embracing humility, forgiving others) and the Way of Death (behaviors and beliefs that lead to spiritual destruction, such as blasphemy, murder, adultery, hypocrisy, jealousy, deceit).

The seventh book of the *Didache* gives instruction for baptism, preferring the use of living (i.e., running) water and that the candidate for baptism ought to fast for a day or two beforehand. Book eight continues with instructions for fasting, presuming that the Christians will all fast twice a week (on Wednesdays and Fridays, unlike the hypocrites—i.e., the Jews—who fast on Mondays and Thursdays) and that the faithful should pray the Our Father thrice daily. Books nine and ten provide the instructions and prayers for the Eucharist.

Itinerant prophets and apostles should be welcomed but sent on their way if they ask for money or stay more than three days (books 11–12). Prophets-in-residence, who are known and trusted, may expect to be supported by donations (book 13). The community ought to celebrate the Eucharist weekly on the Lord's Day (book 14). Bishops and deacons should be elected by the community; they provide the same ministry as prophets and teachers but in a stable, more consistent manner (book 15). The *Didache* concludes with warning its readers to be always ready for the Second Coming and to not fall prey to false teachers and prophets or allow their faith to grow lukewarm before the Lord returns "and all his saints with him" (book 16).

What we find in the *Didache* then is that Christians were already fasting on Wednesday and Friday each week as well as celebrating the Eucharist. A bishop and a handful of deacons in each community served as both the principle of stability in the community and as apostles, prophets, and teachers. Wandering prophets and teachers might be welcomed briefly if their words accorded with the beliefs already held by the community; this concern with consistency of teaching is the same as that reflected in the Greek-speaking Christian acceptance of the Epistle to the Hebrews as a legitimate Christian text; this consistency of teaching across times and locales quickly became one of the hallmarks of "catholic" (i.e., authentic) Christianity.

Baptism in the *Didache* was a significant moment of ceremonial drama preceded by instruction and fasting. Daily prayer was to be offered on a regular schedule and the prayers of the Eucharist, although the Words of Institution were not included, already contained a prayer for the descent of the Spirit in the petition that the Church be sanctified, saved from all evil and made perfect by the Father's love. Later prayers for the Eucharist specify that the descent of the Spirit to sanctify the Gifts of bread and wine is but the first step in this process of sanctifying and perfecting the Church. All this, and the New Testament itself not yet complete.[2]

The *Didache* is our first handbook describing the organization of parish life, the first "church order manual" as such handbooks are now called. Another early church order, this one from Rome—written in Greek, indicating that the Christians in Rome were still primarily Greek-speaking rather than Latin-speaking residents—and known as the *Apostolic Tradition* is attributed to Hippolytus (a presbyter and later bishop of Rome); it was compiled perhaps early as AD 215. It covers many of the same subjects as the *Didache* but in slightly different order and in more detail.

The *Apostolic Tradition* of Hippolytus begins with instructions about electing and ordaining a bishop to serve in the community (chapters 1–3), followed by directions and prayers for celebrating the Eucharist (chapter 4). Although the eucharistic prayers in the *Apostolic Tradition* contain the Words of Institution, these Words are followed by the petition that the Father send the Spirit "to the oblation of [the] Holy Church" and "give to all those who partake of your holy mysteries the fullness of the Holy Spirit, toward the strengthening of the faith in truth, that we may praise you and glorify you." Not unlike the prayers in the *Didache*, the Eucharist is sanctified so that the Church might be sanctified by partaking of the Gifts.

Directions and prayers for blessing oil [chrism], cheese, and olives are given (chapters 5–6). Directions and prayers for choosing and ordaining presbyters and deacons (chapters 7–8) are followed by instructions concerning confessors (Christians who are arrested and tortured for their faith but not killed) and widows (elderly women who depend on the donations of the community to survive) in chapters 9 and 10. Although wandering prophets and apostles do not seem to be of much concern to Hippolytus, he is still concerned about who may or may not expect to receive support from the community and what they owe the community in return: the clergy and widows may be supported but they are obligated to serve and pray for the community in return. If they fail in their obligations, the parish is no longer obligated to support them.

The appropriate behavior and instruction of catechumens (chapters 15–19) is followed by the description of baptism (chapters 20–22). Catechumens who are employed in occupations considered inappropriate for the baptized faithful—such as artists (who make idols), teachers of children (who are expected to impart knowledge of classical mythology), government officials (who are obligated to sit in judgment and condemn criminals as well as partake in pagan sacrificial rites and military exercises),[3] or actors and actresses (whose roles often included prostitution)—are told to find new jobs before they can be baptized. The conclusion of the *Apostolic Tradition* (chapters 23–43) covers a wide range of subjects: times of daily prayer (the various practices involved with praying and the times of day appropriate for prayer both at home and at church), burials (that supplies and workmen should be paid but burial in the Christian cemeteries should not be limited to the wealthy), that deacons ought to be diligent about bringing Holy Communion to the ill, the preservation of the Eucharist (clergy should be careful that the container in which the Eucharist is kept is adequate to keep mice from nibbling at the reserved Gifts!), and fasting before the celebration of Pascha.[4] Much of the material in the *Apostolic Tradition* still looks familiar to anyone involved with managing and maintaining the integrity of a church community.

The epistles of St. Ignatius, the bishop of Antioch who was arrested and charged with being a Christian about AD 98–117, expand the picture of church life that we glimpse in the *Didache*. (We must remember that at this time there was probably only one or two parishes in any given city and that the bishop was in fact the local pastor of that parish. To be "the bishop of Antioch" does not imply a far-flung network of parishes across a large diocese; it means that Ignatius was the leader of the local, albeit small, Christian community.) He was brought to Rome for trial (just as the Apostle Paul was taken from Judea to Rome for trial) and martyred there by order of the Emperor Trajan. As he was being taken from Antioch to Rome, Ignatius sent a series of letters to the parish churches in cities that he was passing near (the Ephesians, Trallians, Magnesians, Romans, etc.). These epistles, written only 30 years or so after the *Didache*, amplify much of what we see in the *Didache* concerning church ministry and order and eucharistic fellowship.

Ignatius is especially concerned with the interconnection of the episcopacy, dogmatic orthodoxy, and the legitimacy of the Eucharist. The *Didache* says that the local bishop is the prophet and teacher of the local community; each community was evidently expected to have several prophets in their midst and the bishop was the chief of these local prophets. Ignatius himself is still known as the "God-inspired," i.e., a prophet himself. Ignatius expands on that role in his letters. The local bishop, Ignatius stresses, ought to be respected "as you respect the authority of God the Father ... who is everybody's bishop." Ignatius goes on to remind his readers: "Let the bishop preside in God's place, and the presbyters take the place of the apostolic council, and let the deacons ... be entrusted with the ministry of Jesus Christ" (Magnesians 3 and 6). He is underscoring the importance of the harmonious functioning of the Christian community under the supervision of the bishop, replicating the life of the first Christian communities gathered around the apostles.

Ignatius does not develop the idea of an apostolic succession (i.e., that each bishop must have been taught and ordained by someone who had been taught and ordained by someone who had been taught and ordained by someone that had eventually been taught and ordained by one of the apostles) but he does insist that each church (parish) that celebrates the Eucharist is a "type" or reflection of heaven, a microcosm on earth of heavenly reality (Ephesians 5) and that the bishop's role in each community is to insure the consistency of teaching across the network of parishes that constituted the worldwide Christian community (Ephesians 16–17; Magnesians 8, 10; Trallians 6, 8–10). Only the Eucharist celebrated by the local bishop is to be considered legitimate; each member of the community is to accept the authority of the bishop and to resist the bishop is to lack the true Eucharist and thus forfeit salvation (Ephesians 5; Philadelphians 4). Participation in the weekly Eucharist is the fundamental act of faith and love, without which there is no salvation (Trallians 8). As far as Ignatius is concerned, heretical or schismatic communities have—by definition—no love or charity (Smyrnaeans 6) and God only heeds those who heed the bishop (Ignatius to Polycarp 6).

In fact, Ignatius' basic rule can be summed up: stick with the bishop and avoid all heresy, error and schism. There is no good reason to ever break off fellowship with the bishop. (It was apparently inconceivable to Ignatius that a legitimate bishop might ever preach error.) Only by maintaining one's communion with the bishop (and all that such fellowship implies) can salvation be achieved.

We can also see in Ignatius' letters how important the martyrs and martyrdom are in the Christian experience. Ignatius' chains are spiritual pearls (Ephesians 11) which the faithful kiss (Polycarp 2); martyrs experience the birth pangs of heaven (Romans 6); and Ignatius is eager to take his place among the martyrs (Trallians 4), telling his readers to not interfere with the legal process (Romans 4).

Participation in the Eucharist goes hand in hand with martyrdom, Ignatius tells his readers. Martyrs are offered on the altar, just as the bread and wine are; he is himself to be ground like wheat by the teeth of the beasts he expects to confront in the amphitheater at Rome in order to make a pure loaf for Christ; to be martyred is to eat the bread which is Christ's flesh and drink the wine which is his blood, "an immortal love feast indeed" (Romans

2, 4, 7). (Ignatius' musings and meditations on the Eucharist are, in fact, some of the most beautiful written in all of Christian literature.)

But to the larger world, the disputes among Christians—such as Ignatius warned his readers to avoid—were the petty squabbles of a particularly troublesome collection of people known commonly as "the Jews" who had never quietly acquiesced to Rome's conquest and dominion of their homeland. There was constant murmuring against Rome, frequently boiling over into revolts and uprisings against Roman authority. They were so troublesome that the Emperor Claudius expelled all the Jewish residents from the city of Rome sometime between the years AD 41–54; the revolt in AD 66–70 in Judea led to the Roman destruction of the Temple and removal of its treasures to Rome in an attempt to impress on the Jews the futility of revolt; the last straw was the Bar Kokhba revolt of AD 132–136 that resulted in the complete demolition of Jerusalem and the permanent exile of the Jewish people from Jerusalem as well as from most of Judea. Jews and Jewish-Christians were dispersed across the known world.

The Romans renamed the region "Palestine" and built a Roman city known as "Aelia Capitolina" atop the ruins of Jerusalem. The Romans erected a temple for Jupiter over the ruins of the Jewish Temple and a temple for Adonis atop the hill known as Calvary, thus clearly marking the sites that would later be so important for Christian excavation and church building.

During this time of chaos, confusion, destruction, and upheaval the Christian terminology was still very fluid as Christians were still searching for an adequate vocabulary, for "words appropriate for God." Various Christian communities had a variety of titles for their leaders, as we saw in both the *Didache* and in the *Apostolic Tradition* of Hippolytus: in one place they were "prophets," in another "preachers" or "teachers," while in still other places they were called "bishops." The Christians were in the midst of adapting the earlier Jewish practices and terminology that they were familiar with, in both Greek and Aramaic.

Apologetics

There were two basic styles of Jewish Christianity that for ease of identification are most often called "West Syrian" (reflected by the *Didache* and the letters of Ignatius) and "East Syrian" because of their geographic locations. The style known as East Syrian survived until the Persian Empire conquered that territory in AD 337–344. The style of Jewish Christianity known as West Syrian survived to become what we call the Eastern Orthodox today. In addition, there were groups that identified themselves—or are identified nowadays—as Gnostics, Montanists, etc. Each of these Christian groups were missionary minded and *apologetic*, i.e., they wrote *apologies* (from the Greek *apologia*, or "speaking in defense" as might a lawyer in court) for their beliefs.

Justin Martyr wrote one of the most famous of these Christian apologies (c. AD 150). Although he had been born in Judea/Palestine, he lived as an adult in Rome. Justin developed apologetics as the attempt to explain the faith to a literate, educated audience in a way that they would understand; apologetics is thus part of the basic missionary work of the Church in every age and place and we will see this effort play out in the struggles to define and teach the faith over the ages, at the great councils of the Church, and in the missionary work, such as that of Cyril and Methodius.

In his *First Apology*, Justin begins by asking his Gentile or pagan readers to give his words a fair hearing and then goes on to describe Christian life and faith, the superiority of Christianity to paganism, how Christianity fulfills Old Testament prophecy and how pagan beliefs and practices are imitations of Christian beliefs and practices. He concludes by describing some aspects of Christian worship that his readers may have heard of and been confused about.

To counter the common rumor that Christians were plotting to overthrow the Roman political system, Justin writes:

> When you hear that we look for a kingdom, you rashly suppose that we mean something merely human. But we speak of a Kingdom with God, as is clear from our confessing Christ when you bring us to trial, though we know that death is the penalty for this confession. For if we looked for a human kingdom we would deny it in order to save our lives, and would try to remain in hiding in order to obtain the things we look for. But since we do not place our hopes on the present [order], we are not troubled by being put to death, since we will have to die somehow in any case [*First Apology* 11].

He goes on to reassure his audience about Christian intentions and to flatter them, promising them that he trusts in their intelligence and good will:

> We are in fact of all men your best helpers and allies in securing good order, convinced as we are that no wicked man ... or virtuous man either, can be hidden from God and that everyone goes to eternal punishment or salvation in accordance with the character of his actions.... [Roman attempts to exterminate Christians] seem as if you were afraid of having all men well-behaved, and nobody left for you to punish; this would be the conduct of public executioners, not of good rulers.... [And] we have not learned [to expect] any unreasonable conduct from you, who aim at piety and philosophy [*First Apology* 12].

Justin goes on to point out

> those who are found not living as [Christ] taught should know that they are not really Christians, even if his teachings are on their lips, for he said that not those who merely profess but those who also do the works will be saved. For he said this: 'Not everyone who says to me, Lord, Lord, will enter the Kingdom of Heaven, but he who does the will of my Father who is in heaven. For whoever hears me and does what I

say hears him who sent me. Many will say to me, Lord, Lord, did we not eat in your name and drink and do mighty works? And then I will say to them, Depart from me, you workers of iniquity.' Then there will be weeping and gnashing of teeth, when the righteous will shine as the sun, but the wicked will be sent into eternal fire. For many will come in my name clothed outwardly in sheep's clothing, but being inwardly ravening wolves; by their works you will know them. Every tree that does not bring forth good fruit is cut down and thrown into the fire [*First Apology* 16].

Large portions of Justin's apology are simply long quotes from the Scriptures that Christians call the Old Testament or the Gospels. Books were difficult to obtain and most Gentiles would have never heard of most of these texts before.

To help his readers understand the Christian expectations of the resurrection of the dead, Justin explains that no one would believe that a drop of male sperm could become a human being if they had not seen it happen.

In the same way unbelief prevails about the resurrection of the dead because you have never seen an instance of it. But as you at first would not have believed that from a little drop such beings [as men] could develop, yet you see it happening, so consider that it is possible for human bodies, dissolved and scattered in the earth like seeds, to rise again in due time by God's decree and be clothed with incorruption [*First Apology* 19].

Justin goes on to spend a great deal of time quoting from the prophets and other Old Testament texts to demonstrate how Christ fulfilled the expectations of Israel, albeit in perhaps unexpected ways. The prophets, i.e., the whole of the Old Testament, were still the basic Scripture of the Church during this period; even when the Nicene Creed was developed the statement that Christ rose from the dead "according to the Scriptures" meant "in fulfillment of the Old Testament prophecies and expectations." The fulfillment of and interdependence of such Scriptural texts with Christian life were crucial aspects of Christian teaching.

When Justin comes to describe Christian worship (*First Apology* 61–67), he explains how catechumens are instructed and baptized and how the newly baptized are then allowed to participate in the weekly Sunday celebration of the Eucharist for the first time. Remembering that Justin wrote his *Apology* in Rome and that Hippolytus wrote his *Apostolic Tradition* there and that church manuals generally reflect practices at least 25–50 years old, we can conclude that Justin and Hippolytus are describing the same practices of catechumenate, baptism, and Eucharist.

The Martyrs and Martyrdom

Justin was known to his contemporaries as a Christian philosopher, a "lover of wisdom," and teacher. But he is primarily known today as a martyr, like Ignatius of Antioch, one killed for his adherence to Christian belief and practice.

In the Roman world, religion was not a matter of private belief. Religion was a collection of public activities and behaviors that were thought necessary to protect the state. A handful of religions were considered suitable or appropriate to protect the state; these were *licit* or "legal to practice." The principal licit religions were the worship of the classical Greek and Roman gods, the worship of Cybele and certain Egyptian deities (Isis, Osiris), the worship of the Persian god Mithras, and the religion of the Jews. All the *illicit* or illegal religions were considered treason and labeled "magic."

As long as Christians were seen by the Romans as simply yet another sect or subdivision of Jewish practice, they were safe. But once Jewish leaders began to denounce the Christians as a differing religious practice, asserting that the Christians were not practicing an acceptable style of Judaism, then Rome turned its attention to these new *a-theists*, those without a recognizable god or gods.

The sibling rivalry between Christianity and Judaism turned deadly. There was no systematic, organized persecution of Christians until the "Great Persecution" began in AD 303. Until then, the Roman authorities simply waited for someone to denounce a person or group of people as Christian; then the Romans would arrest and torture the accused. If they agreed to burn a few grains of incense before the image of the emperor, which was the only act required and considered little more than reciting the Pledge of Allegiance in the United States, they would be released. (This offering of incense was made to "the fortune of Caesar" or the *genius* of the emperor, akin to the emperor's guardian angel rather than to the emperor personally. Also, "Caesar" was used as a title rather than a name. Every emperor was Caesar, even when the emperors later embraced Christianity.) Those who did so were outcast from the Church and forbidden to associate with other Christians or participate in the Eucharist again.

While the accused were in prison, family and friends were allowed to visit them and to bring gifts such as food and clothing or medicine as well as bribes for the guards. Clergy would visit the imprisoned and bring the Eucharist. Often, the only food or change of clothing or medical care that a prisoner could have was whatever his friends and family would bring. That is why visiting those in prison ranks so highly as an important thing to do in early Christian texts, including the New Testament.

Once arrested, the accused might be released because they burned incense before the emperor's image; these people were called *thurificati*, as they had "burned incense." Some were called *libellatici* as they bribed the authorities in exchange for a certificate (*libellus*) that said they had burned incense or offered sacrifice to an idol, even though they had not. Those that actually offered sacrifice to idols were called *sacrificati*. *Traditores* (from "hand over," the same root as *tradition*, those practices and beliefs which are "handed over") were those who handed over sacred books, liturgical objects, or the names of other Christians. All these people were considered *apostates* (from the Greek for "departure" or "revolt"), the "lapsed" who were thereafter shunned by the Christian community and refused admittance to social or liturgical fellowship; they were now *excommunicate*, having broken *communion* (fellowship) with the Church.

However, some of the accused who were subjected to interrogation (i.e., torture) and refused to deny their faith or surrender any information to the authorities and yet survived might be released; these were welcomed back into the Church's fold and held in great esteem as "confessors," those who had confessed the faith in public and survived.

But most of those arrested were executed for treason. A person executed under such circumstances was considered by the Church to be a *martyr* (Greek for "witness," as in a court case). A martyr was a witness to the power of Christ's Resurrection and his victory over death. The bodies or other remains of the martyrs were collected by family and friends to be interred in Christian burial grounds.

Martyrdom, viewed by the Church not only as an act of loyalty or heroism but as an act of communion in the death and resurrection of Christ himself, was seen by some as a highly desirable vocation and a way to attain fame and glory. But the Church was very clear that martyrdom and suicide were mutually incompatible. Anyone who offered themselves for arrest and execution was considered a suicide, not a martyr, someone who had tempted God and trusted in their own strength rather than divine aid to overcome their suffering (*Martyrdom of Polycarp* 4).

As was common Roman practice, meals were held near or atop the grave in memory of the deceased, especially on the anniversary of death which, in the case of the martyrs especially, was considered their birthday into heaven. (Remember how Ignatius used that term in his epistle to the Romans?) In the case of the martyrs, the Eucharist was celebrated at the gravesite on the anniversary of their birthday into heaven and if a martyr was especially popular in a region, even those who could not attend the graveside Eucharist might attend a celebration of the Eucharist in their local church to mark the anniversary. (This is the root of the association of saints with certain days and the celebration of the Eucharist to celebrate their memory.)

The stories of the martyrs developed from the accounts of friends and fellow-worshippers into semi-official written notices that were exchanged among various bishops and churches. These stories and reports were always told or composed in such a way as to make certain points and became as stylized as icon painting did later. Today, we often need to know how to read each report in the appropriate way so as to understand what is going on "between the lines."

[handwritten margin note:] No, I can't find reference to it in the earlier description of Ignatius's writings.

Polycarp, the bishop of Smyrna and friend of Ignatius, was one such extremely popular martyr who was arrested and executed in either AD 155–156 or AD 167. The report of the martyrdom is sent from Smyrna to the church in Philomelium "and to all those of the holy and Catholic Church who sojourn in every place" to show everyone what "a martyrdom conformable to the Gospel" looks like.

Ignatius had been the first to call the Church a "catholic" body, in his epistle to the Smyrnaeans: "Nobody must do anything that has to do with the Church without the bishop's approval. You should regard that Eucharist as valid which is celebrated either by the bishop or by someone he authorizes. Where the bishop is present, there let the congregation gather, just as where Jesus Christ is, there is the Catholic Church" (*Smyrnaeans* 8). But with Polycarp's martyrdom we see the description of the Church as Catholic becoming one of the commonly attributed marks or notes of her life. The "holy and Catholic Church which sojourns in every place" does not use "catholic" primarily to refer to the notion of universality as a geographic concept. "Catholic" here is used to mean whole, integrated, and complete. The notion of geographic universality is secondary to the notion of universality as in "for all." The Church is universal because it is for everyone. It is the same, complete, and authentic in every place because of the ministry of the bishops which we have seen was to guarantee that authenticity and catholicity.

Polycarp "waited to be betrayed, just as the Lord did," rather than volunteer for suffering (*Mart. Polycarp* 1). He was an elderly bishop (in his mid–80s), denounced as a Christian by two slaves under torture, arrested late one Friday evening as he was in hiding in a farmhouse. He offered food and drink to those who came to arrest him while he went to offer his usual midnight prayers; he prayed for "all who had met with him at any time, both small and great, both those with and those without renown, and the whole Catholic Church throughout the world" and when he was finally done "many repented that they had come to get such a devout old man."

Refusing to offer the incense and call Caesar "Lord" as only Christ was to be accorded that title, he was taken to the arena on Saturday. A great crowd was there, news of Polycarp's arrest having spread like wildfire. The proconsul urged him to swear by Caesar and to dismiss his allegiance to the Church by saying, "Away with the atheists!" Instead, we are told that Polycarp used the proconsul's own words against the mob as he "looked with earnest face at the whole crowd of lawless heathen in the arena, and motioned to them with his hand … [and] he said, 'Away with the atheists!'"

The proconsul continued to urge him to save himself by cursing Christ but Polycarp insisted, "Eighty-six years I have served him and he never did me any wrong. How can I blaspheme my king who saved me?"

Finally the crowd demanded that Polycarp be burned at the stake if he would not recant his Christian faith. The authorities capitulated to the mob and ordered the stake erected, kindling and wood for the fire gathered from the workshops and the public baths near-by, "the Jews being especially zealous, as usual, to assist with this." (We can see the ongoing rivalry between the Jews and Christians here, the boundaries of the two communities still not rigidly fixed, the local Jewish authorities apparently trying to demonstrate who was or was not a member of their licit co-religionists.) Polycarp was fixed to the stake, "like a noble ram out of a great flock ready for sacrifice, a burnt offering ready and acceptable to God." (The author here is reminding his readers of the sacrifice of Isaac as well as the sacrificial lambs offered in the Temple, the Passover lamb, and the Lamb of God.)

Just before the fire itself was lit, Polycarp prayed:

> "Lord God Almighty, Father of thy beloved and blessed servant Jesus Christ, through whom we have received full knowledge of thee, the God of angels and powers and all creation and of the whole race of the righteous who live in thy presence: I bless thee, because thou hast deemed me worthy of this day and hour, to take my part in the number of the martyrs, in the cup of thy Christ, for resurrection to eternal life of soul and body in the immortality of the Holy Spirit among whom may I be received in thy presence this day as a rich and acceptable sacrifice, just as thou has prepared and revealed beforehand and fulfilled, thou that art the true God without any falsehood. For this and for everything I praise thee, I bless thee, I glorify thee, through the eternal and heavenly high priest, Jesus Christ, thy beloved servant, through whom be glory to thee with him and the Holy Spirit both now and unto the ages to come. Amen."

This prayer would clearly not have been out of place at a celebration of the Eucharist. Polycarp offers it to the Father who has been made known by his "beloved and blessed servant Jesus Christ"; the Greek word can mean both "child" and "servant" and was the way Jewish-Christian prayers had commonly referred to Jesus since the *Didache* itself. Polycarp identifies his martyrdom with the act of receiving the Eucharist and thanks the Father for having considered him worthy of such an honor just as Hippolytus' prayer at the Eucharist thanks the Father, "who has made us worthy to stand before [him] and to serve as [his] priests." Polycarp also makes clear that he is offering his prayer to "the true God," not the false god Caesar or any of the Roman pantheon.

The soldiers lit the fire and as the conflagration grew, the flames "made the shape of a vaulted chamber, like a ship's sail filled by the wind, and made a wall around the body of the martyr." The crowd did not smell burning flesh but rather the fragrance of bread baking or incense burning, the text underlining the eucharistic and liturgical nature of the martyr's death.

After the bishop's death, we read that Jewish efforts prevented the local Christians from collecting Polycarp's remains but that they were eventually able to gather up his bones, "more precious than gems and more valuable than gold," and inter them in "a suitable place." There they intended "to gather together in joy and gladness to celebrate the day [anniversary] of his martyrdom as a birthday, in memory of those athletes who have gone before and to train and make ready those who are to come thereafter" (*Mart. Polycarp* 18).

"Against Heresies"

One of those who knew Polycarp and who no doubt celebrated his birthday into heaven was a young boy named Irenaeus (just as Polycarp himself said that he had childhood memories of knowing the Apostle John); Irenaeus may have also studied with Justin at Rome. We do know that Irenaeus became bishop of Lyons, one of the Roman capitals of Gaul. Following a large-scale persecution of the Church in Lyons, Irenaeus was made bishop there and as part of his responsibilities as bishop he wrote both a *Demonstration of the Apostolic Preaching* to instruct new converts and a work commonly known as *Against Heresies* to defend the Catholic faith against a variety of Gnostic beliefs. *Against Heresies* was evidently written in AD 189–190 and is one of our best sources about both Gnosticism and orthodox teaching at this time.

The Gnostics (who stressed the need for secret *gnosis* or "knowledge" in order to achieve salvation) were a widespread network of communities centered on a variety of teachers who each taught a slightly different theological system. The common points among all the Gnostic systems were that the material world had been created by an evil or lesser divine figure and as a result the world we know was irredeemably wicked and fallen, a prison to escape; that Christ had not truly taken on human nature or interacted with the material world or died or been raised on the third day; that Christ had imparted secret teachings to only a few, select followers who then passed that *gnosis* on to their followers; and, that the more of this *gnosis* someone knew, the higher they would rank among the "saved." Some of the Gnostic teachers stressed radical asceticism as one of the ways to help escape the prison of this fallen world while others taught that physical behavior was irrelevant to salvation. They all denied that the dead would be raised with bodies as well as souls.

Irenaeus stressed that incarnation, Eucharist, and resurrection are all interrelated and interconnected, making salvation possible.

> Vain above all are they who despise the whole dispensation of God, and deny the salvation of the flesh and reject its rebirth, saying that it is not capable of incorruption. For if this [mortal flesh] is not saved, then neither did the Lord redeem us by his blood, nor is the cup of the Eucharist the communion of his blood, and the bread which we break the communion of his body…. For when the mixed cup and the

bread that has been prepared receive the Word of God and become the Eucharist, the body and blood of Christ, and by these our flesh grows and is confirmed, how can they say that flesh cannot receive the free gift of God, which is eternal life, since it is nourished by the body and blood of the Lord, and made a member of him? So also our bodies which are nourished by [the Eucharist] and fall into the earth and are dissolved therein, shall rise at the proper time, the Word of God bestowing on them this rising again, to the glory of God the Father [*Against Heresies* 5:2].

In his *Against Heresies*, Irenaeus argues that the Faith, the Tradition which the bishops have consistently maintained through time and across geographic locations, is sufficient to refute these Gnostic teachers:

You will be able to resist [the Gnostic heretics] faithfully and boldly on behalf of the one true and life-giving faith, which the Church has received from the apostles and imparts to her children. For the Lord of all gave to his apostles the power of the gospel, and by them we also have learned the truth, that is, the teaching of the Son of God—as the Lord said to them, 'He who hears you hears me, and he who despises you despises me, and him who sent me.' [W]e appeal again to that tradition which has come down from the apostles and is guarded by the successions of elders [*presbyteroi*] in the churches.... The tradition of the apostles, made clear in all the world, can be clearly seen in every church by those who wish to behold the truth [*Against Heresies* 3:2–3].

Irenaeus delights in this succession of teachers from the days of the apostles. He names those who have served at Rome and maintained the faith there, "that very great, eldest, and well-known Church, founded and established at Rome by those two most glorious apostles Peter and Paul ... [that faith] which comes down to us through the successions of bishops...." Irenaeus and his readers share the "same life-giving faith which has been preserved from the apostles to the present, and is handed on in truth." Irenaeus urges that disputes be settled by turning "to the oldest churches, where the apostles themselves were known, and find out from them the clear and certain answer" to any current problem.

Irenaeus describes the heart of this apostolic faith and tradition, maintained and sustained by the bishops in each church, in book 5 of *Against Heresies*. He announces that salvation is only possible because the Second Adam and Second Eve recapitulated and set right what the First Adam and First Eve set awry, similar to the ideas expressed in Romans 5 and 1 Corinthians 15.

If he had appeared as man when he was not really human, the Spirit of God could not have rested on him, as was the case ... nor would there have been any truth in him, what was [then taking place] not being what it seemed to be.... He would not have had real flesh and blood, by which he paid the price [of our salvation], unless he had indeed recapitulated in himself the ancient making of Adam [*Against Heresies* 5:1].

So the Lord now manifestly came to his own, and, born by his own created order which he himself bears, he by his obedience on the tree [of the Cross] recapitulated (see Ephesians 1:10) what was done by disobedience in [connection with] a tree; and [the power of] that seduction by which the virgin Eve, already betrothed to a man, had been wickedly seduced was broken when the angel in truth brought good tidings to the virgin Mary, who already [by her betrothal] belonged to a man. For as Eve was seduced by the word of an [fallen] angel to flee from God, having rebelled against his Word, so Mary by the word of an angel received the glad tidings that she would bear God by obeying his Word. The former was seduced to disobey God [and so fell], but the latter was persuaded to obey God, so that the virgin Mary might become the advocate of the virgin Eve. As the human race was subjected to death through [the act of] a virgin, so it was saved by a virgin, and thus the disobedience of one virgin was precisely balanced by the obedience of another. Then indeed the sin of the first-formed man was amended by the chastisement of the First-begotten, the wisdom of the serpent was conquered by the simplicity of the dove, and the chains were broken by which we were in bondage to death.... As our race went down to death by a man who was conquered we might ascend again to life by a man who overcame; and as death won the palm of victory over us by a man, so we might by a man receive the palm of victory over death [*Against Heresies* 5:19, 21].

For they [the Gnostics] cannot search out the wisdom of God, by which what he had fashioned is perfected by being conformed and incorporated with the Son—or how that his offspring, the first-begotten Word, could descend into his creature, that is, into what he had fashioned, and be contained within it—and that the creature again should lay hold on the Word and should ascend to him, passing beyond the angels, and be made [anew] according to the image and likeness of God [*Against Heresies* 5:36].

These two notions, that Christ recapitulates in himself and his mother all that Eve and Adam experienced and that he does this in order to become all that we are so that we can become all that he is, become the touchstone of all later Christology articulated at the imperial, ecumenical councils. This salvation, Irenaeus proclaims against the Gnostics, is freely available to all the Church's children, especially in the celebration of the Eucharist.

Biblical Interpretation

One of the most influential of the pre–Nicene theologians was a child at Alexandria as Irenaeus was concluding his ministry in Lyons. Origen (AD 184/185–253/254) was the leading biblical scholar of the ancient world. He wrote massive numbers of commentaries and sermons, dogmatic treatises and apologies for the faith, developed theories to support the practice of prayer and Christian spirituality. He was the first to engage in "textual criticism" of biblical texts as he produced the *Hexapla* ("sixfold") version of the Old Testament, in which the Old Testament text appeared in six columns for easy comparison: Hebrew, Hebrew in Greek characters, the Septuagint (the translation produced by Greek-speaking Jewish scholars in Alexandria, early 300s BC), and the Greek versions of Theodotion (a Greek-speaking Jewish scholar in Ephesus, about AD 150), Aquila of Sinope (A Greek-speaking Jewish scholar, about AD 130), and Symmachus (a Greek-speaking convert to Judaism, from around AD 200).

Origen led a colorful life, which brought him considerable notoriety. As a young man, he received a classical education but his father Leonides, who was a Christian teacher, also taught him the Scriptures. Leonides was martyred when Origen was an adolescent; Origen wanted to be a martyr like his father and his mother was only able to stop him from turning himself in to the Roman authorities by hiding his clothes. Despite his youth, he became known as a great teacher of Christianity and was popular with the large number of catechumens enrolling for baptism, despite the persecution by the Roman officials. However, he took Jesus' words that "there be eunuchs, which have made themselves eunuchs for the kingdom of heaven's sake" (Matthew 19:12) too literally and castrated himself. He traveled around the Mediterranean world and Middle East as he continued his studies. Eventually settling in Palestine, following a political dispute with the bishop of Alexandria, he suffered "bodily tortures and torments under the iron collar and in the dungeon; and how for many days with his feet stretched four spaces in the stocks." Although he was not killed while he was under arrest, he was released and counted as a "confessor" but he did die three years later, aged 69, from the injuries he received during his arrest.

Although several of Origen's ideas were later rejected by the Church, many others continued to be very influential and were circulated under others' names in order to avoid the scandals associated with his own. One of his achievements was categorizing the principles of biblical interpretation. These basic styles of interpretation became known as literal (the historical or literal meaning of the text), allegory (a series of free associations and reminders built up around the text), anagogy (the moral meaning of the text), typology (the prophetic aspect of the text), and eschatology (the aspect of the text linked to the Last Times or End of Days).

The best way to demonstrate these styles of interpretation is to take one straightforward text and demonstrate how it might be interpreted in each style. One of the easiest examples to use is the Exodus from Egypt. Thus, it can be interpreted as follows:

Literal: the sea parted and Moses led the Israelites through the water, after which Pharaoh and his armies were drowned when the sea closed up again.

Allegory: the sea reminds the reader of passions and temptations, so passing safely through the water is like the ascetic effort to discipline oneself.

Anagogy: passing through the sea is like turning one's back on the morals and behavior of the sinful world.

Typology: Moses and the Israelites passing safely through the water is a "type," a prophetic act anticipating Christ's Death and Resurrection or of Christian baptism in which the convert dies and rises with Christ.

Eschatology: the salvation of the Israelites and the drowning of the Egyptians is like the Last Judgement of the world, in which the righteous are saved and the wicked are damned.

The use of allegory became especially popular in Alexandria, the second most important city in the Roman empire, while the literal meaning of the text was most popular in Antioch, the third most important city in the empire. This rivalry between Alexandria and Antioch and their differing interpretative stances became increasingly important throughout Church history.

The death of Origen leaves us poised on the brink of two events that would change the Christian world: the legalization of Christianity by Constantine the Great and the controversy between Arius and Athanasius at Alexandria.

SUGGESTIONS FOR FURTHER READING

Early Christian Fathers. (Cyril C. Richardson, ed.) Macmillan, 1975.

Early Christian Writings: The Apostolic Fathers. (Andrew Louth, ed.) Penguin Classics, reprinted 1987.

Eusebius, *Ecclesiastical History.* (C.F. Cruse, trans.) Hendrickson Publishers, updated edition 1998.

Gary Anderson, *The Genesis of Perfection: Adam and Eve in Jewish and Christian Imagination.* Westminster John Knox Press, 2002.

Gustaf Aulen, *Christus Victor: An Historical Study of the Three Main Types of the Idea of Atonement.* Macmillan, 1969.

Thomas A. Robinson, *Ignatius of Antioch and the Parting of the Ways: Early Jewish-Christian Relations.* Baker Academic, 2009.

2

Nicea

In the year AD 293, the Roman emperor Diocletian divided the empire into a *tetrarchy* to make it easier to govern. This meant four men were appointed as co-rulers. Diocletian ruled the eastern portion of the empire and Maximian ruled the western portion as "senior emperors." They each had an "assistant emperor": Galerius worked with Diocletian in the east and Constantius worked with Maximian in the west.

In early 303, Galerius convinced Diocletian that the sporadic toleration of Christianity was preventing the restoration of Rome's previous glory; Diocletian wanted to restore that glory at all costs. One of the best ways to restore that glory, he thought, would be the revitalization of traditional Roman religious practices; the Roman gods, pleased at the greater attention they would receive, would be sure to restore the glory and prestige of Rome. As the most senior of the tetrarchy, Diocletian insisted that all four rulers issue edicts demanding greater religious uniformity and instructing local officials that those who refused to participate in worshipping the Roman gods were to be arrested. (Up until this time, the Roman officials did not go looking for Christians to arrest; they would arrest Christians only if someone else accused them of practicing an illegal religion.) At first, Diocletian simply wanted Christian clergy arrested and fined or deprived of legal rights; Galerius, however, insisted that all Christians—layfolk as well as clergy—be arrested and executed if they refused to perform the required sacrifice.

This organized and systematic persecution came to be known as "the Great Persecution" and many of those killed during this persecution are known as "great-martyrs." Scholars estimate that anywhere from 4 to 10 percent of the empire's residents were Christian (i.e., perhaps six million out of the approximately 60 million who lived under Roman rule) but it is impossible to say with certainty how many were arrested, tortured, or martyred. Even if we cannot know for certain how many suffered in the Great Persecution, we can say for certain that the Great Persecution was horrific and that it was burned into the historic memory of the Church.

Diocletian was more interested in forcing Christians to compromise themselves by offering the incense or sacrifices; Galerius was more interested in having Christianity itself exterminated. Many local judges, especially in the eastern Roman empire, followed Galerius' example and had Christians arrested, tortured, and then executed. The historian Eusebius—who was also a bishop and advisor to the Emperor Constantine—reports:

> But we must admire those also who suffered martyrdom in their native land; where thousands of men, women, and children, despising the present life for the sake of the teaching of our Savior, endured various deaths ... numberless other kinds of tortures, terrible even to hear of, were committed to the flames; some were drowned in the sea; some offered their heads bravely to those who cut them off; some died under their tortures, and others perished with hunger. And yet others were crucified; some according to the method commonly employed for malefactors; others yet more cruelly, being nailed to the cross with their heads downward, and being kept alive until they perished on the cross with hunger.
>
> It would be impossible to describe the outrages and tortures which the martyrs ... endured.... Others being bound to the branches and trunks of trees perished. For they drew the stoutest branches together with machines, and bound the limbs of the martyrs to them; and then, allowing the branches to assume their natural position, they tore asunder instantly the limbs of those for whom they contrived this.
>
> All these things were done, not for a few days or a short time, but for a long series of years. Sometimes more than ten, at other times above twenty were put to death ... and yet again a hundred men with young children and women, were slain in one day, being condemned to various and diverse torments.
>
> We, also being on the spot ourselves, have observed large crowds in one day; some suffering decapitation, others torture by fire; so that the murderous sword was blunted, and becoming weak, was broken, and the very executioners grew weary and relieved each other [*Church History* VIII.8–9].

Many Christians, including bishops and other members of the clergy, went into hiding in order to avoid arrest. Some clergy were able to save themselves by handing over copies of heretical books instead of the scriptures in order to satisfy the demands that they hand over books; in most cases, the officials didn't know which books were scripture and which weren't.

Large churches were prominent in many cities of the empire and prominent members of society were known to have converted and been baptized. Christianity, originally a religious movement whose adherents were mostly city dwellers, had even become numerous in the countryside. (The designation "pagan" for those who believed in the old Greek and Roman gods was a Latin word that originally meant "country-dweller" or "rural person," i.e., an unsophisticated or unlearned rustic or bumpkin, indicating that the old religion was much more popular in the countryside than in the cities.)

Non-Christian philosophers and members of the religious establishment encouraged the imperial persecution of Christians, although many of the common people were upset at the extreme nature of the punishments handed down and demanded lighter sentences be imposed. Eusebius also tells us,

> Therefore it was commanded that our eyes should be put out, and that we should be maimed in one of our limbs. For such things were humane in their sight, and the lightest of punishments for us. So that now on account of this kindly treatment accorded us by the impious, it was impossible to tell the incalculable number of those whose right eyes had first been cut out with the sword, and then had been cauterized with fire; or who had been disabled in the left foot by burning the joints, and afterward condemned to the provincial copper mines, not so much for service as for distress and hardship. Besides all these, others encountered other trials, which it is impossible to recount; for their manly endurance surpasses all description.
>
> In these conflicts the noble martyrs of Christ shone illustrious over the entire world … and the evidences of the truly divine and unspeakable power of our Savior were made manifest through them. To mention each by name would be a long task, if not indeed impossible [*Church History* VIII.12.10–11].

Maximian and Constantius in the west, however, were less enthusiastic about the persecution and as time went on, did little to enforce the laws against the Christians.

During November AD 303 Diocletian celebrated the 20th year of his reign, the tenth anniversary of the tetrarchy, and a triumph in the war against Persia. Shortly thereafter, he became very ill and many people thought he had died. He recovered somewhat, however, and Galerius convinced him to became the first Roman emperor to resign. Diocletian also insisted that Maximian step down with him.

Galerius was then made the senior emperor in the east and Constantius become senior emperor in the west, with two new assistant emperors (Maximian in the east and Severus in the west). Three years later, Constantius died in AD 306. Galerius promoted the assistant emperor Severus to senior emperor but Constantius' soldiers proclaimed his son Constantine emperor instead.

In the confusion, several other men also stepped forward to claim the throne. A civil war began but in AD 312 Constantine had only one rival left in the western portion of the Roman empire, his brother-in-law Maxentius in Rome. Constantine led his army towards Rome. En route, he saw the sun with a cross of light above it and the phrase, "In this sign, conquer." Constantine reportedly was unsure what his vision of the cross and the slogan meant but the next night he dreamed that Christ told him to use the sign against his enemies. Constantine ordered the image of the Chi-Rho (a combination of the X and P which were the first two Greek letters in the word "Christ") be placed on all his armies' banners and shields.

Meanwhile, Maxentius led his army out of Rome towards Constantine. They met at a stone bridge that crossed the river Tiber north of the city. If Maxentius could stop Constantine from crossing the bridge, there was no way he could reach Rome. Maxentius would be able to declare himself the victor and the only emperor of the western Roman empire. Maxentius consulted prophets and offered sacrifices. He was certain of victory.

The next day, Constantine won the Battle at the Milvian Bridge. Maxentius was drowned in the river. Constantine was welcomed into Rome by the soldiers and people and acclaimed emperor of the west. Licinius, another brother-in-law of Constantine, remained the emperor in the east until his death in AD 324. Together, the two men issued the Edict of Milan the next year (AD 313) which made Christianity one of the legally tolerated religions of the Roman empire. It is important to understand that they did not make Christianity THE religion of the empire but simply made it one of the religions which the law allowed people to practice. All property and objects that had been confiscated by the Roman officials during the persecutions were to be returned.

Constantine did not make Christianity the religion of the empire; he simply made it one of the acceptable religions. Constantine himself does not seem to have become a Christian immediately. He seems to have attributed his success to the God of the Christians and was eventually enrolled as a catechumen. But he was not baptized until he was on his deathbed, in part because his position as emperor demanded that he perform certain duties (such as warfare) that were still seen as incompatible with Christianity.

Building Projects

Constantine did not become a Christian but he supported the Church in substantial ways, such as ordering that Sunday was to be observed as a "day of rest." His mother Helen, however, did embrace Christianity shortly after her son's victory in 312 and seems to have been a devout and pious woman. She undertook extensive building projects to support the Church: for example, she is said to have built the original basilica atop Vatican Hill over the site considered the Apostle Peter's grave. She also convinced her son to build the other major churches in Rome (St. John Lateran, St. Mary Major, St. Paul Outside the Walls).

When Constantine and his mother Helen began their church building projects they turned to Roman architects to design the new buildings. These architects turned to the familiar model of the basilica to create buildings for public assembly. "Basilica" indicates a building of a certain architectural style although later, in the Latin-speaking regions of Western Europe, the term "basilica" also came to designate churches of a certain rank that often attracted pilgrims and in Romania the word *biserica* (derived from "basilica") means a church building of any sort.

A basilica in classic Roman architecture was a public building used for public business, usually law courts. It was a rectangular building, with a semi-circular apse at one end. Inside the apse was a slightly raised dais; there was a throne on the dais for the judge or other imperial official to sit on. The central aisle was the length of the basilica and fairly wide. There was a narrower aisle along each side, separated from the main aisle by a series of columns. Lawyers could meet with clients in these side aisles and then approach the judge to argue their cases. When Christians used the basilica format for churches, they repurposed the judge's throne in the apse as the seat of the bishop and an altar-table was placed on the dais in front of the throne. (In smaller building projects, the side aisles were omitted.)

The bishop sat on his throne for the readings and to preach; additional seats were placed on either side of the throne for the assisting priests but deacons were expected to stand throughout the services. (This same seating plan is what the book of Revelation describes when it says that "surrounding the throne were twenty-four other thrones, and seated on them were twenty-four elders. They were dressed in white and had crowns of gold on their heads" [Rev. 4:4]. The word for "elder" is *presbyter* which becomes "priest" in English.)

Deacons read the lessons and cantors led the singing from the center of the central aisle, which came to be called the "nave" of the building. A platform, called a *bema* (Greek for "raised platform"), was often erected in the middle of the nave for the deacons and singers to use so that the congregation could see and hear them more easily. In some regions or in certain churches, the bishop would also come to the bema to preach so that he could be heard more easily by the congregation.

The basilica was oriented for Christian use so that the congregation stood facing east which was a long-standing custom for Christian liturgical practice. (Classical Roman practice expected the people to stand facing the west when facing pagan statues, so the architects on some imperial church building projects were confused and the building was built facing the wrong way.)

The Christians faced east to pray for several reasons. Jesus was expected to come again to judge the world "as lightning flashes from the east to the west" (Matthew 24:27). Jesus was the Dawn that enlightened the world. Basil the Great wrote that facing east to pray was among the oldest unwritten laws of the Church (*On the Holy Spirit* 27). Because everyone was expected to face east to pray, the bishop would leave his throne and come around to stand in front of the altar-table to celebrate the Eucharist itself so that he and the congregation were all facing the same direction to pray.

There were benches around the edge of the basilica for elderly or ill people to sit but most of the congregation would stand for the entire service, holding their hands either at their sides or at shoulder height. (Standing with

hands at shoulder height, palms outward, is called the *Orans* ["prayer"] position and is frequently seen in icons or fresco paintings.) Benches were used
in the naves of some Western European churches beginning in the 1200s and
became more common during the 1300–1400s but rows of seats only became
common in Western European churches during the 1500–1600s. Kneeling,
or "standing on your knees" with palms pressed together in front of the chest,
only became regular practice in Western European churches when Latin-
speaking Christians adopted the position of a knight swearing loyalty to the
king or prince as the common attitude for prayer. In earlier practice and
throughout the Greek-speaking East, the *orans* position was the standard
prayer posture although prostrations, in which the faithful would touch their
forehead, palms, and knees to the floor, would be made during certain
moments of the services. Even then, prostrations would never be made on
Sundays or festal days.

In many regions, there were also customary places for certain members
of the congregation to stand in the nave of the basilicas, just as it was expected
that the clergy—the bishop, presbyters, deacons, and deaconesses—had their
particular places to stand in the apse. Men would stand on the right side of
the nave, women on the left; children were expected to gather around the
bema so they could see and hear and a deacon or subdeacon would be in
charge of keeping them in order; widows who were supported by the parish
("community") would be standing closest to the altar. Catechumens (those
preparing for baptism) and penitents (those Faithful who had betrayed the
Church in some way, were therefore ineligible to receive Holy Communion,
and were in the process of being reconciled again into the community of the
Faithful) would stand in the back of the nave and would be prayed for but
then dismissed after the sermon as only the Faithful (a technical term, meaning the baptized who were participants in receiving the Eucharist) would
remain present for the Eucharist itself.

The Empress Helen also went on pilgrimage to Jerusalem and oversaw
the archeological expeditions there to establish the locations of events in the
life of Christ. She had the Church of the Nativity built in Bethlehem to mark
the place where Jesus was said to have been born and the Church of the
Ascension outside Jerusalem to mark Jesus' last regular appearance to his
apostles after his resurrection. She also established the location of Golgotha
(where Jesus had been crucified) as well as the location of Jesus' tomb.

The location of the crucifixion and burial of Christ were probably already
fairly well known to the local Christians in Jerusalem. When the Romans tore
Jerusalem apart in the AD 130s and replaced it with the city called Aelia Capitolina, they built a temple for Aphrodite over the cave where the Christians
said Jesus had been buried and a temple for Adonis over Golgotha. So all the
local Christians still knew where to direct the empress when she came looking

for the places of Christ's Death and Resurrection. The pagan temples were removed and excavations begun to build Christian churches atop those sites.

During the excavations on Golgotha, the empress is said to have discovered the remains of three wooden crosses but no one was sure how to identify which cross had been Jesus' and which had been used to crucify the two thieves. The bishop of the city suggested bringing the ill or the dead to touch the crosses and so the empress had three sick people brought to the site; they each touched the remains of a different cross and one was healed. The empress tested this result by having three corpses brought and each was touched to one of the crosses; the corpse that touched one of the crosses was raised from the dead. It was the same cross that had worked both miracles and that cross was acclaimed as the True Cross.

Excavations were begun around the cave associated with Christ's burial as well. Considerable amounts of rock were removed from around the tomb, without damaging the cave itself, resulting in a free-standing outcropping. This was surrounded by a small rotunda called the *Kouvouklion* in Greek or the *Aedicula* in Latin. The rotunda was enclosed in a much larger basilica which was called the "Great Church" (i.e., the cathedral of the city) or "the Church of the Resurrection" or more simply "the Anastasis." (It did not become commonly known as "the Church of the Holy Sepulchre" until the Crusaders occupied the city.) The two churches, the Anastasis and Golgotha, were built around a central courtyard which was later enclosed; thus the sprawling complex eventually become a single sprawling building.

The Church of the Resurrection was completed in AD 335. About that same time, Cyril of Jerusalem was ordained deacon; he was elected bishop of Jerusalem in AD 350. Although he was not the first bishop to serve in the great new Church of the Resurrection, he built on and expanded the liturgical practices that he inherited; he also wrote and organized much of the hymnography and liturgical material for the celebration of Lent, Holy Week, and Pascha in the new cathedral as well as events from the life of Christ in the other new churches in the area built with imperial support. He played a large part in developing the cycle of services that impressed the large number of pilgrims who came to Jerusalem to celebrate the events of Christ's life in the very places where they had occurred.

A woman named Egeria, who might have been a nun, came on pilgrimage from the Iberian peninsula in AD 381–384 and wrote detailed notes in her diary of every place she visited and how the services she attended were organized (which was copied and transcribed several times, then lost and forgotten until parts of it were rediscovered in 1884). She describes the daily and Sunday services at the Church of the Resurrection (including the variations for Lent) and she attended the services of Lent, Holy Week, and Pascha there as well.

Egeria is the first example we have of pilgrims coming to Jerusalem for Holy Week and Pascha and then telling everyone back home about how the services were organized and how the last days of Christ's ministry were celebrated, all in order to replicate these services back home as best they could. Cyril's liturgical influence is felt throughout the Christian world every year as the services of Holy Week are celebrated, among both Eastern and Western Christians but especially in the Orthodox liturgical traditions.

Egeria describes a Palm Sunday afternoon procession with palms and branches from the Mount of Olives to the Resurrection church and that on Thursday of Holy Week the bishop (almost certainly Cyril) and people celebrated the Eucharist in mid-afternoon in the Resurrection church. A procession with readings began on the Mount of Olives at midnight and slowly made its way back to the Resurrection church (arriving at sunrise), stopping to read Gospel readings about the Passion at the locations where the events occurred. Hymns were sung between the readings, many of which are still used by Byzantine Christians and attributed to Cyril. There were a series of services at the Resurrection church throughout Friday to commemorate the death and burial of Christ. She describes the baptism of the catechumens during the Paschal vigil on Saturday night and the joyous celebration of the Eucharist in the main church. She adds that the bishop and a handful of people celebrate the Eucharist a second time, actually in the Tomb of Christ itself, but this second celebration was "done quickly, because everyone is tired" by that point!

Monasticism

There was a distinctly ascetic strain in Christian practice from the beginning; the *Didache* instructed believers to fast twice a week, on Wednesdays in commemoration of Judas' agreement to betray Christ and on Fridays in commemoration of Christ's crucifixion. There were also expectations that some believers would dedicate themselves to lives of virginity, awaiting the coming of the Bridegroom, as a sign that the Last Days had begun when Christ was crucified. But there was no widely organized system of life for those (most often women) who embraced such a vocation although there do seem to be scattered groups of women who lived together in households or small communities.

That changed towards the end of the third century. Antony was born in Egypt around AD 251 and when he was 18 years old, he was left responsible for his sister and for managing the family estate when his parents died. Shortly after this happened, we are told that one Sunday he heard the Gospel read during the Eucharist: "If you would be perfect, go and sell what you have and give it to the poor and you will have treasures in heaven." He left the church, gave some land to his neighbors but sold most of it and gave the money to the poor; he gave his sister to a small local community of ascetic women, and went off himself to live a hermit in the desert.

Antony lived first in an abandoned fort and then in a tomb. He depended on donations of food from local villagers; (during the height of the Great Persecution in Egypt (around AD 311), he went into Alexandria to visit the imprisoned Christians and hoped that he might be martyred as well. But the persecution ended before that could happen and he returned to the desert.)

Antony had become known as a holy man, a wise counselor and a miracle worker. Many people came to him in the desert to ask his advice or guidance; many men settled in huts around where Antony lived. Antony kept moving, hoping to avoid the growing crowds but more people still kept coming and more communities sprang up across the desert. Three of these communities became extremely large and well-known: Kellia ("the Cells"), Scete ("community"), and Nitria (known for the alkaline nitria found in the lakes of the area). The men who embraced the radical, ascetic life either in these communities or as hermits become known as monks ("alone," as they cut themselves off from their families and all ties to their previous lives).

Although Antony was probably not the first man to actually become a hermit in the desert, he was the first to become widely known. The monks who gathered around him tended to live as hermits as well, coming together with others only for the Eucharist on Saturdays and Sundays. Another monk, Pachomius, was the first to write a "rule" to organize the life of a large community.

Whether as hermits or in communities, the monastic life focused on personal prayer, fasting, sexual abstinence, and liturgical prayer. (Singing the psalms from the Old Testament was central to monastic practice and as most monks came from poor, illiterate families that meant memorizing all 150 psalms.) Several of the more famous hermits or monastic elders became known as "fathers" and collections of "Sayings of the Desert Fathers" were widely circulated.

The monastic communities were often large villages or even small cities of monks who lived together in households of two or three monks together, often as fellow-disciples of an "elder" or "abba" ("Father"). They would often support themselves by weaving baskets that they would take into villages or cities to sell, then buy food or other supplies, and afterwards return to the monastic settlement. There might be one church for the settlement or, if it was particularly large, several churches would be built in various "neighborhoods" of the settlement.

(But monasticism was always primarily a lay movement. Monks were discouraged from seeking ordination; most of the priests in any community had been ordained and served parishes in the city before going out into the desert.)There might be only one or two priests in very large monastic settlements and part of their *ascesis* ("exercise") or discipline was the responsibility for the daily services like Matins (morning) and Vespers (evening), even though the Eucharist itself was only celebrated a few times a week.

(The demands of the monastic life attracted many who might have been martyrs earlier but, now that Christianity had been legalized, there was no more danger to embracing the faith; many felt the radical nature of Christianity seemed in danger of being lost.)Monastic life also offered a refuge to those who had held great responsibilities "in the world" but who sought a life of simplicity and calm after their conversions.)

Although it began as a movement in the desert of Egypt, monasticism quickly spread to the deserts of Syria and Palestine as well. It was also adapted to the weather conditions of Gaul and Italy, adjusting the dietary patterns and other customs that were not appropriate in colder, damper climates.

Communities of monastic women also developed but these were more likely to be closer to other villages and towns so as to reduce the danger for women living on their own in the wilderness. There are many stories, however, of ascetic women who dressed as men and lived for many years either as hermits in the desert or as members of otherwise male communities and were only discovered to be women when their corpses were prepared for burial.

The presence of eunuchs in mainstream late antique culture might have made it easier for women to pass as men in monastic contexts. Beardless men with higher range voices were not uncommon in the cities and eunuchs, although discouraged from embracing monasticism because they were seen as being too much of a sexual temptation for the "bearded men" in the community, did become monks as well.

Donatists

In AD 311, just before Constantine issued the Edict of Milan which legalized Christianity, a man named Caecilian was elected and ordained as bishop in Carthage (North Africa). One of the bishops who ordained him was Felix of Aptunga, who was thought by many to be a *traditor* (someone who surrendered the scriptures to the Roman authorities during the persecution). In the estimation of these people, Felix was therefore an unworthy bishop and no one he helped ordain as bishop—including Caecilian—was legitimate. Secundus, a senior bishop in North Africa, refused to acknowledge Caecilian as bishop and broke off communion with him; he installed his own nominee, Majorinus, as bishop of Carthage. Majorinus died shortly thereafter and was replaced by a man named Donatus.

Schism (Greek for "torn apart" or "division"; those who joined such a break-away group were known as "schismatics") broke out across North Africa as many insisted that any clergy who had given up books or church property to save themselves were morally unworthy to remain as clergy. Many others acknowledged that while handing over Church property and sacred books was wrong, it was an understandable action when facing the threat of death and that the clergy who had done so but repented were to be forgiven and allowed to continue their ministry as clergy. The schismatics who opposed this offering of forgiveness were known as "Donatists" as they sided with Donatus, the bishop of the rigid and intolerant party in Carthage. As a result, all across North Africa many cities had two bishops: one a schismatic Donatist and one recognized as the "Catholic" or "Orthodox" bishop. (Remember the use of the terms "Catholic" and "Orthodox" to describe the integrity of the faith maintained against the Gnostics and other heretical teachers.)

When Constantine issued the Edict of Milan in AD 313 and ordered that all confiscated property and objects be returned "to the Catholic Church," riots broke out across North Africa as each party claimed to be the legitimate or authentic church in a region. The value of the property and objects to be returned was vast and whichever bishop the local imperial officials returned the property to would immediately become not only extremely wealthy—and expected to oversee distribution of food and other aid to the poor—but therefore one of the leading members of society, an unimaginable change from the days of the Great Persecution.

Constantine himself wrote to Caecilian in Carthage, recognizing Caecilian as the authentic bishop there, giving his church the confiscated property and Caecilian himself became responsible for handling large amounts of cash to be distributed among the poor and needy. This started a domino effect among the other bishops across North Africa who recognized Caecilian and maintained communion with him as the recipients of the properties being returned to the Church. The schismatic Donatists continued to riot across North Africa and insisted that the emperor Constantine, who was not even a catechumen yet, depose Caecilian.

Constantine instead asked Melchiades, pope [bishop] of Rome, to examine the situation and "try" the case as in a law court. Melchiades quickly called a council of local Italian bishops to serve as a "jury" and the council, Melchiades and the other bishops together, heard arguments for both Caecilian and Donatus. Caecilian was confirmed as bishop of Carthage and Donatus condemned. All the Donatist schismatic churches and bishops were urged to reunite with the legitimate, Catholic churches; if that resulted in two legitimate bishops in one place, the younger bishop would be reassigned to a new city.

The Donatist schismatics were furious at this result and refused to acknowledge either Pope Melchiades or the council of AD 313. This infuriated the emperor who ordered another council at Arles (southern Gaul) a year later in an attempt to settle the unrest. The council at Arles confirmed the Roman council of the year before but the Donatists again appealed directly to the emperor to annul both conciliar decisions. Constantine summoned both Caecilian and Donatus to Milan in AD 315 and sat himself as judge to settle the case. The emperor declared Caecilian innocent and an excellent bishop but sent delegates to oversee the election of a new, compromise candidate as bishop of Carthage that would be acceptable to both the schismatics and the Orthodox. When the delegates arrived in Carthage, the schismatics rioted again and prevented any election of a new bishop.

Constantine decided to stop seeking compromise with the Donatists. He ordered that all Donatist property be given to the Orthodox, soldiers were sent to stop any further riots, and the Donatists were evicted from North Africa city-by-city. (As this program was carried out, it became known that some of the schismatic bishops had also been *traditors* who had surrendered church books during the persecution.) Donatists fled further afield across the empire, including other areas of North Africa.

In AD 321, the emperor built a cathedral in Cirta (modern Algeria) but local Donatists seized it and Constantine, tired of all the bickering, built a new one for the Orthodox. Large groups of Donatists survived until the mid–400s, insisting that any "unworthy" clergyman—which came to mean almost any moral failure, not just handing over church property during persecution—could not preside at an authentic celebration of the Eucharist. Many spokesmen for the Orthodox argued that schism was little different from *apostasy* (Greek for "defection"), the act of denying Christ, since schism separated schismatics from the Church, the Body of Christ. Optatus of Milevis wrote that schism is a negation of all charity as it demonstrates the schismatics' lack of love for their brethren; love of the brethren is what the New Testament insisted was the indication of true Christianity (as in Hebrews 13, I John 3–4, I Corinthians 1, and John 13). Augustine, still dealing with Donatists in North Africa in the early 400s, wrote that Christ exists in three ways at once: as the eternal Word of God, as the God-man who serves as mediator for the world, and as the Church. Embracing schism is rejecting Christ, Augustine wrote.

But the important precedent had been set in that the emperor had been asked to get involved in Church business and settle Church arguments.

Arius and Athanasius

Another dispute arose in North Africa, this time in Egypt, of critical importance to the development of the theology and polity of the Church as we know it and have received it even still today. This was the conflict over Arius' teachings concerning the nature and divinity of Jesus Christ.

The conflict among theologians about the words used to describe the humanity and divinity of Christ began long before Arius. During AD 264–269 there had been three councils in Antioch which condemned Paul of Samosata and the use of the Greek words -*ousia* and *homo-ousias* to describe the relationship between Christ and the Father. -*Ousia* was understood to mean both "person" and "nature" and was tainted by its prior use by the Sabellians, who taught that the one God had only seemed to be Father or Son at different times but was in fact the same divine person or *ousia* who only changed the manner or mode in which he interacted with the created order. Paul of Samosata had tried to use *homoousias* to mean "same nature" as a way to say that the Father and the Son shared the same divinity but the Antiochenes rejected this word as an inadequate expression of this relationship. The Antiochenes said that *homoousias* was "too materialistic" a concept to describe such immaterial realities; to share the same nature seemed to them to override or negate the assertion that the Father and the Son were distinct. Again, the dispute between Paul of Samosata and the Orthodox was so strident that it necessitated the intervention by non–Christian Roman imperial officials to award the office of bishop of Antioch to the Orthodox candidate.

Born in Libya, Arius studied in Antioch as a young man. Lucian of Antioch, a famous teacher and biblical exegete, continued to teach that *homoousias* was an inadequate expression of an inadequate concept; his students, including Arius, all abhorred the term *homoousias* and vehemently rejected it. Following his studies, Arius came to Alexandria and following a dispute with the bishop about forgiving layfolk who had denied the faith during persecution and subsequent reconciliation with him, was ordained a deacon there. Arius seems to have gotten into another dispute with the bishop—probably again about Arius' own Donatist sympathies—and was excommunicated but restored to communion by the next bishop (pope) of Alexandria and made a priest there in AD 313.[1]

As a priest, Arius' parish in Alexandria was in the oldest Christian neighborhood and contained the oldest church in the city. He is reported to have been unusually tall, serious, but polite and gracious. His sermons seem to have been popular, which meant that the next pope of Alexandria, a man named Alexander, paid attention to Arius and what he was preaching. As part of his parish ministry in Alexandria, Arius is said to have composed songs for the sailors, dockworkers, and other city laborers; these songs served as simple catechetical tools. These songs, the first examples of what we might recognize as hymns that were not simply paraphrases of scripture, explained the relationship between the Father and the Son in easy-to-understand terms and were evidently extremely popular. These hymns, which insisted that only the Father was Uncreated and Unoriginated, may have been what attracted Bishop Alexander's attention.

In AD 318, Bishop Alexander had doubts about Arius' preaching about the relationship between the Father and the Son. Arius said that Alexander was a Sabellian and taught that the Son was identical with the Father. The bishop and the priest argued and the bishop called a council in Alexandria of more than 100 local bishops from Egypt and Libya to settle the dispute in AD 321.

About this same time, Alexander ordained his young protégé Athanasius as deacon and made him his secretary. Between AD 318 and 321, Athanasius (who was only in his early 20s) wrote a book (*Against the Gentiles*) to refute classical Greek and Roman religion and philosophy and another book, *On the Incarnation*, to defend the idea that the Son is divine in the same way that the Father is divine: co-eternal and co-unoriginate. Athanasius' treatise *On the Incarnation* became extremely popular and is considered a classic theological text today.

Athanasius asserted that salvation would have been impossible if the Son had not also been "without beginning." Unless the Son is divine and uncreated in the same way that the Father is divine and uncreated, Athanasius wrote, the Son would have been unable to recreate and save the world. The heart of Athanasius' theology is worth reading in its entirety:

> If then there were only offence [the sin of Adam and Eve] and not the consequence of corruption, repentance would have been fine. But if, once the transgression had taken off, human beings were now held fast in natural corruption and were deprived of the grace of being in the image, what else needed to happen? Or who was needed for such grace and recalling except the God Word who in the beginning made the universe from non-being? For his it was once more both to bring the corruptible to incorruptibility and to save the superlative consistency of the Father. Being the Word of the Father and above all, he alone consequently was both able to recreate the universe and was worthy to suffer on behalf of all and to intercede for all before the Father.
>
> For this purpose, then, the incorporeal and incorruptible and immaterial Word of God comes into our realm, although he was not formerly distant. For no part of creation is left void of him; while abiding with his own Father, he has filled all things in every place. But now he comes, condescending towards us in his love for human beings.... For seeing the rational race perishing, and death reigning over them through corruption which was upon us, and that it was absurd for the law to be dissolved before being fulfilled, and seeing the impropriety in what had happened, that the very things of which he himself was the Creator were disappearing, and seeing the excessive wickedness of human beings, that they gradually increased it to an intolerable pitch against themselves, and seeing the liability of all human beings to death—having mercy upon our race, and having pity upon our wickedness, and condescending to our corruption, and not enduring the dominion of death, lest what had been created should perish and the work of the Father himself for human beings should be in vain, he takes for himself a body no different from our own. For he did not wish simply to

be in a body, nor did he wish merely to appear, for if he had wished only to appear he could have made his divine manifestation through some other better means. But he takes that which is ours, and that not simply, but from a spotless and stainless virgin.... Although being himself powerful and the creator of the universe, he prepared for himself in the Virgin the body as a temple, and made it his own, as an instrument, making himself known and dwelling in it. And thus, taking from ours that which is like, since all were liable to the corruption of death, delivering it over to death on behalf of all, he offered it to the Father, doing this in his love for human beings, so that, on the one hand, with all dying in him the law concerning corruption in human beings might be undone (its power being fully expended in the lordly body and no longer having any ground against similar human beings), and, on the other hand, that as human beings had turned towards corruption he might turn them again to incorruptibility and give them life from death, by making the body his own and by the grace of the resurrection banishing death from them like straw from the fire [*On the Incarnation* 7–8].

The Son would have been unable to save the world if he was not divine in the same way that the Father is divine, Athanasius argued. If the Son was only a creature, albeit a super deluxe creature far above all others, he would not have been able to save human beings who were also created entities, essentially little different from himself.

Arius claimed that he was the victim of the long-standing and well-known rivalry between the Antiochene and Alexandrian methods of theology and many outside Egypt—especially in Syria—thought this a large part of the dispute. In his preaching, Arius had said that the Son had a beginning in time (even if before the world was created) unlike (*anomoea*) the Father who was eternal in and of himself and who had generated the Son. Thus, Arius reasoned, the Father was the only uncreated entity and the Son, although far more exalted and glorious than anything or anyone else, was in fact a created being, a creature, a deluxe angel of sorts.

Arius and Athanasius both agreed that a line ought to be drawn between the Uncreated and the created; they profoundly disagreed where to draw that line.

Athanasius goes on to say, "For he [the Son] was incarnate that we might be made god; and he manifested himself through a body that we might receive the idea of the invisible Father; and he endured the insults of human beings, that we might inherit incorruptibility" (*On the Incarnation* 54). The Son could not render humans divine if he was not himself also divine and uncreated, as the Father is divine and uncreated. This idea, that God became human so that humans might become divine, became one of the two principal guide posts throughout all subsequent Orthodox theological debate.

The council in Egypt in AD 321 condemned Arius and he sought refuge in the Middle East, with a bishop who had also been a student of Lucian in Antioch.

ARIUS		ATHANASIUS
Father	**Uncreated**	Father
Son		**Son**
Holy Spirit		**Holy Spirit**
Angels		Angels
Mankind	**Created**	Mankind

Among the Arians (followers of Arius), there were two camps: those called Anomoeans, who stressed how the Son was unlike the Father because of this distinction between created and uncreated and those called Homoeans, who stressed that the Son was nevertheless similar to the Father in terms of glory and exaltation and power. The Homoeans also had a profound dislike of using any non-scriptural words to describe the Father and the Son; using any of these terms taken from Greek philosophy seemed to them to teeter on the brink of apostasy.

The dispute followed Arius from Egypt into Syria and Palestine. Arius was the center of a debate that raged across the African and eastern dioceses (administrative units) of the Roman Empire. Bishops censured and broke communion with each other over whether they taught that the Son was begotten from the Father eternally and therefore co-eternal or not.

About this same time, Constantine become the sole ruler of the empire in AD 324 when Licinius, his co-emperor in the east, lost his attempt to overthrow Constantine. Licinius had made his last stand in a city on the Bosphorus at the entrance to the Black Sea known as Byzantium; it was a small but important ancient Greek trading post. Constantine saw the value of the city's position at the intersection of Europe and Asia, surrounded by water on two of its three sides. He also realized that Rome, the historic capital of the empire for one thousand years, was no longer the geographic center of the empire; in order to maintain firmer control of the empire, he needed a more centrally located capital. He decided to move the capital to Byzantium and officially rename the small city "New Rome" but everyone called it "Constantine's city" (Constantinople). The massive construction projects necessary to turn the small town into the capital of the world began shortly after Licinius' defeat in AD 324.

But the emperor's plans for a single, united, consolidated empire seemed about to fall apart, given the massive unrest in the eastern regions about Arius and his teaching. So, having settled the dispute with the Donatists in North Africa and Gaul, the emperor decided to settle the dispute about Arius and his teaching as well. Constantine invited Hosius, the highly respected bishop of Cordova in Spain and one of the emperor's trusted advisors in dealing with church matters, to meet with both Bishop Alexander and Arius and attempt a reconciliation between them.

Hosius suggested that the term *homoousias* (which had previously been condemned in Antioch) might be redefined and used as a basis for establishing a common understanding. Hosius wanted *homoousias* (translated into Latin as "consubstantial") to be understood not as Paul of Samosata had understood it previously (as an identity that overrode any distinction) but as an identity that respected and upheld the distinction between the Father and the Son. Bishop Alexander and his deacon Athanasius embraced this new use of the term; Arius rejected it, insisting that it was still as inadequate in the AD 320s as it had been in the AD 260s.

The Council of Nicea

Constantine was furious that the dispute remained unresolved and decided to hold a council as he had held councils to settle the debate with the Donatists. As his great new city of New Rome-Constantinople was still under construction and unable to host such a meeting, he decided to hold it in the nearby town of Nicea. He sent out "invitations" to the legitimate, Orthodox bishops throughout the Roman Empire instructing them to gather for the council in Nicca in the spring of AD 325. The emperor would pay for the council. He wanted the council to be as representative of the entire church throughout the imperial territories as possible so as to settle the debate that was causing such havoc throughout the eastern imperial territories. Hosius would preside at the council as an impartial third party, although Constantine himself would also be present and take part in its meetings.

How many bishops responded to the emperor's invitation? Although nearly 2,000 were invited, the number of bishops who actually attended is difficult to know for sure but is traditionally said to have been 318. Certainly, it was an unprecedented opportunity for the bishops of the Roman world—who had all been facing the possibility of martyrdom only a dozen years before—to gather together all at one time and in one place and to have the emperor pay for it all.

The council opened in Nicea in late May or early June, AD 325 and although the deacon-secretary Athanasius came to Nicea with Bishop Alexander, he was not allowed to join the council sessions as only the bishops were to meet in the sessions. It is unclear whether Arius was allowed into the sessions but stories circulated that Nicholas of Myra (who was later identified by folklore as "Santa Claus") became so angry at Arius during one session that he punched Arius in the nose.

When the council began, there were more than 20 bishops openly supporting Arius. As the debate went on, that support began to crumble. When the bishops finally agreed to teach that the Son had been begotten by the Father in eternity and was therefore co-eternal and that Hosius' redefined *homoousias* was indeed the proper way to describe this relationship between the Father and the Son, only two bishops continued to support Arius. Those two bishops were excommunicated and banished by the emperor to the Balkans, as was Arius himself.

Each bishop had traditionally used a creed or "statement of faith" that converts recited during their baptism. The council at Nicea took the creed used during baptisms in Palestine or Syria and adapted it as their new statement of Orthodox belief. This "Nicene Creed" stated that the Son was begotten, not created or made, by the Father, "God from God, Light from Light," and that the Son was therefore *homoousias* (or "consubstantial") with the Father as well. The creed proclaimed that the Son had himself made all things, been made flesh, suffered, died, and rose again. He would come again to judge the living and the dead.

The creed concluded: "And we believe in the Holy Spirit. But those who say: 'There was a time when he was not'; and 'He was not before he was made'; and 'He was made out of nothing,' or 'He is of another substance' or 'essence,' or 'The Son of God is created,' or 'changeable,' or 'alterable'—they are condemned by the holy catholic and apostolic Church." Arius and his teachings are clearly condemned by the anathemas ("condemnations") that appear at the end of the creed. It was therefore impossible to interpret the creed in a way that any of the Arian theological parties might be comfortable with. The statement was a clear victory for Athanasius and the Alexandrian position.

In addition to resolving the controversy about Arianism, the bishops took advantage of the council to discuss a wide range of other issues that had arisen over the years and that had remained points of contention between the various churches in different regions of the empire. These "canons" (lit. "standards") affirm that men who castrate themselves or allow themselves to be castrated should not be ordained, that catechumens ("hearers," i.e., converts who are candidates for baptism) should prepare for baptism for approximately three years and then not be ordained too quickly after baptism, that the bishops in each region should meet together twice a year, that those who lapsed under persecution should be dealt with mercifully, that clergy may only be ordained by the bishop in whose region they live and will serve, that clergy may not charge interest if they loan money to anyone, and that no one should kneel or make prostrations but remain standing for prayer on all Sundays as well as on any weekday between Pascha [Easter] and Pentecost.

The council also ruled that Pascha should be celebrated by all the churches on the first Sunday after the first full moon after the vernal (spring) equinox. This was to settle a dispute with many of the churches in Asia Minor that kept Pascha on the first day of [Jewish] Passover, whether it was a Sunday or not. The churches that kept this custom, called *Quartodecimani* or "Fourteenth-ers" because they kept Pascha on the 14th day of the month called Nisan as calculated by Jewish astronomers, were ancient survivors of what had been early Jewish Christianity. (Polycarp of Smyrna had been a Fourteenth-er but neither he nor Anicetus, the bishop [pope] of Rome, had thought the disagreement worth going into schism over. Later bishops however did go into schism with each other based on this disagreement.) Some congregations of Fourteenth-ers seem to have continued to exist for another century but the majority of churches adopted the Sunday celebration of Pascha.

Also at issue in this canon was the Christian attempt to not rely on Jewish calculations to determine when to celebrate the central festival of the Christian liturgical cycle. (Later medieval disputes about calculating the proper day for celebrating Pascha were often also called Quartodeciman controversies as well, even when everyone involved agreed that Pascha should be celebrated on a Sunday but couldn't agree on which Sunday was correct; the Fourteenth-ers had simply become the grandfathers of all Paschal dating disputes.)

The Aftermath of Nicea

The Arian controversy and the chaotic aftermath of Nicea was just as cataclysmic an experience for the Church as the Great Persecution had been. Bishop Alexander died five months after the council was concluded. Athanasius was elected the next bishop of Alexandria even though he was still in his 20s and several other bishops objected to his elevation because he was so young. In AD 331 the emperor, who had taken on Eusebius (a bishop who agreed with Arian teaching) as his chief advisor for church matters, tried to arrange a reconciliation between Arius and Athanasius; Athanasius refused to meet with the condemned priest. Arius was nevertheless recalled from exile and Eusebius convinced the emperor that Athanasius had violated several canons, including the one stipulating the minimum age for ordination as a bishop. Athanasius was called to a church trial in AD 335; he was deposed and exiled to Germany where he was able to take refuge with the emperor's eldest son Constantine II (sometimes called Constantius).

Arius died in AD 336. (Later historians underscore God's rejection of him by describing him as shitting himself to death in a public latrine, defecating out huge amounts of blood as well as his small intestine, liver, and spleen.) The emperor Constantine I, "the Great," was baptized on his deathbed in AD 337 by the Arian bishop Eusebius. Constantine II was crowned emperor and he reinstated Athanasius, who was extremely popular with the people of Alexandria.

But Eusebius and his supporters pointed out to the emperor that as a church council of bishops had deposed Athanasius, it was the duty of a church council—not the emperor—to reinstate him. So, in AD 340, Constantine II sent an Arian bishop to occupy Alexandria and Athanasius went into hiding in Rome to avoid arrest. In Rome, a council declared Athanasius innocent of any wrongdoing. Athanasius went to Gaul in AD 343 to see Hosius, who had continued to uphold the Nicene understanding of *homoousias* against local Arian opposition. Together, Hosius and Athanasius went to Sardica for a council that reaffirmed the Roman decision.

The emperor's younger brother Constans was ruling the western portions of the empire; the emperor ordered Athanasius to be executed if he is found in Alexandria so he went to Italy, where Constans had invited him and promised safe passage. At this point (AD 344), the Arian bishop in Alexandria died and the emperor reappointed Athanasius to his seat in Alexandria. Although Athanasius was reluctant to trust the emperor at first, he returned to Egypt and was able to remain there for ten years.

Pope Julius of Rome, a firm supporter of Nicea, died in AD 352 and his successor, Liberius, was a supporter of Athanasius as well. But when Liberius was exiled by the emperor because of his support for Athanasius, he was convinced to sign an ambiguous statement of faith that did not include the term *homoousias*. The emperor and the Arians exerted pressure on Liberius to call a council in Milan in AD 355 which condemned Athanasius and his followers again. Hosius was sent into exile and soldiers arrested Athanasius in the middle of the Eucharist in February, AD 356. An Arian was made pope of Alexandria and Athanasius managed to escape into hiding among the monks in the deserts of Egypt; Athanasius spent time with Antony there. (He later wrote the *Life of Antony,* which was extremely influential in convincing readers to embrace monasticism; in his later life, one of Athanasius' most prized possessions was the sheepskin that Antony slept on and had bequeathed to him.)

Athanasius continued to hide with the monks until the Emperor Constantine II (Constantius) died in AD 361. Julian the Apostate became emperor next and was more interested in reviving classical Roman religion than settling the Nicene-Arian disputes among the Christians. He recalled all the bishops or other Christians who were exiled, whether Arian or Nicene, and chaos erupted across the empire. There were too many bishops in each place, each with their supporters, and each claiming to be the legitimate bishop of that place. There were riots everywhere; the Arian pope in Alexandria was so unpopular with everyone that he was killed during a riot—by the pagans! Athanasius returned to the city in AD 362 and presided at a council that condemned the *Pneumatoachoi* (see Chapter 3).

Arianism	Donatists	Arius	Athanasius
AD 264–269: 3 councils held at Antioch to condemn Paul of Samosata and *homoousias*		AD 250: Arius born; as young man, studies with Lucian of Antioch	AD 296: Athanasius born
	AD 303: Felix of Aptunga gave sacred books to Roman governor (*traditor*)		
	AD 311: Caecilian ordained bishop of Carthage by Felix	AD 306: involved in dispute with Peter of Alexandria	
AD 312: Constantine Wins Battle at the Milvian Bridge			
	Schisms, riots, etc. in Carthage; Constantine invited to resolve	AD 313: Arius ordained priest	
	AD 314: Council of Arles AD 315: Council of Milan	AD 318: songs for sailors, etc.; quarrel with Bishop Alexander re: Father/Son	AD 318: becomes secretary to Bishop Alexander
	AD 321: cathedral in Cirta	AD 321: condemned by council in Alexandria; flees Arius exiled with small band of supporters	
AD 325: Council of Nicea Hosius suggests *Homoousias* be used in new context, with new definition			
		ad 328: recalled from exile	Athanasius becomes bishop of Alexandria
		AD 336: dies just before reconciliation	AD 331: refuses to be reconciled with Arius AD 335: deposed and exiled; takes refuge in Germany with Constantine II
AD 337: Constantine The Great dies; Athanasius reinstalled in Alexandria			
			AD 340: condemned by Arian council

Later in 362, the emperor Julian expelled Athanasius again because the emperor was jealous of the bishop's popularity but Julian died the next year. Athanasius was reinstated by the emperor Jovian but Jovian died in AD 364 and Athanasius was exiled again, this time by the new emperor, Valens.

Valens had decided to attempt to restore some order by deposing and exiling everyone that had been deposed and exiled by Constantine II. Athanasius was able to hide in the countryside—in his father's tomb!—for four months. There were so many riots in Alexandria demanding that Athanasius be reinstated that Valens recalled him to avoid any further violence.

This reinstatement resulted in another decade of peace and Athanasius died in the city as pope of Alexandria in AD 373.

Arianism continued to sputter along but more and more bishops aligned themselves with Athanasius and the Nicene party. Many of the non–Roman kingdoms that arose in the West as Roman authority crumbled there embraced Arian or semi-Arian versions of Christianity; they used a translation of the scriptures made by Ulfilas, an Arian missionary in the 340s-350s. Nicene orthodoxy was only accepted in the early AD 700s by many of them and in the 12th century, one Western Christian preacher called Mohammad "the successor of Arius." In both eastern and western Christianity, Arius became the prototype of all heretical teachers.

Among his many writings, Athanasius wrote 45 "Festal Letters." (Because Alexandria was the most important astronomical observatory in the empire, it was expected that the pope of Alexandria would always send out a letter shortly after Epiphany each year, announcing when to celebrate Pascha and therefore when to begin the observance of Lent beforehand as well as celebrate the holy days that follow Pascha.) Most popes of Alexandria, Athanasius included, took the opportunity of each year's Festal Letter to discuss other matters as well. (His festal letter in AD 367 listed the 27 books he thought should be considered the "New Testament," and is the list still used today.) One of the festal letters that Athanasius wrote while in exile perhaps sums up his life and attitude best:

> I know moreover that not only this thing saddens you, but also the fact that while others have obtained the churches by violence, you are meanwhile cast out from your places. For they hold the places, but you the Apostolic Faith. They are, it is true, in the places, but outside of the true Faith; while you are outside the places indeed, but the Faith is within you. Let us consider which is the greater, the place or the Faith. Clearly the true Faith. Who then has lost more, or who possesses more? He who holds the place, or he who holds the Faith? [*Festal Letter 24,* in AD 357].

SUGGESTIONS FOR FURTHER READING

Peter Brown, *The Rise of Christendom,* 2nd edition. Blackwell, 2003.
Derwas Chitty, *The Desert a City: An introduction to the Study of Egyptian and Palestinian Monasticism Under the Christian Empire.* St. Vladimir's Seminary Press, reprinted 1977.

St. Athanasius, *On the Incarnation*. (Preface by C.S. Lewis; trans. and introd. John Behr) St. Vladimir's Seminary Press, 2011.

St. Athanasius, *Athanasius: The Life of Antony and the Letter to Marcellinus*. (Robert Gregg, ed.) Paulist Press, 1979.

John Wilkinson, *Egeria's Travels*. Aris & Phillips, 2006. [This is the most recent English translation, including supporting documents and notes. Previous editions were published in 1971, 1981, and 1999.]

3

The Pneumatomachoi
and the Second
Eumenical Council

Macedonius was archbishop of Constantinople in AD 342. He was a semi-Arian, the theological party which stressed that the Son was similar to the Father in many ways but discounted the divinity of the Holy Spirit. Macedonius preached that even if the Son was like the Father, the Holy Spirit was nevertheless a "ministering angel" (Hebrews 1:14) and in no way divine or uncreated the way the Father is divine and uncreated. Macedonius justified his teaching, in part, by the vague statement at the conclusion of the Nicene Creed: "We believe in the Holy Spirit."

Macedonius continued to serve as archbishop until he was deposed in AD 360 and was particularly vicious towards the supporters of Athanasius and the Nicene council. Macedonius' notorious tactics—one Byzantine historian said, "The exploits of Macedonius, on behalf of Christianity, consisted of murders, battles, incarcerations, and civil wars" because of vicious persecution of those who opposed him—forced the emperor to withdraw his support. But Macedonius remained in the suburbs of Constantinople, making trouble until his death in AD 364. His followers were known as both "Macedonians" and as *Pneumatomachoi* ("spirit-fighters," i.e., fighters against the Holy Spirit).

Many of the Pneumatomachoi felt more sympathetic to the Nicene use of *homoousias* than Macedonius himself did, even though they rejected any suggestion that the Spirit was anything more than a created being. The opinions of these Pneumatomachoi spread fairly quickly and the Pneumatomachoi in Rome were acknowledge by poor Pope Liberius (see Chapter 2) as being Orthodox, since they upheld the creed from Nicea.

The teaching of the Pneumatomachoi came to the attention of Athanasius while he was hiding with the monks in the deserts of Egypt; when he returned to Alexandria, he called a council that condemned the Pneumatomachoi and the teaching that the Holy Spirit is a creature. Following the council, Athanasius set out for Antioch to meet the new emperor Jovian. Athanasius brought a letter with him, addressed to the bishop and people of Antioch, in which the clergy of Egypt asked the Antiochenes to require all converts from Arianism to condemn the Pneumatomachoi. Converts should be expected to reject "those who say that the Holy Spirit is a creature and separate from the essence of Christ. For those who, while pretending to cite the faith confessed at Nicea, venture to blaspheme the Holy Spirit, deny Arianism with words only, while in thought they return to it."

Opposition to the Pneumatomachoi seemed limited to Antioch and the region of Syria. Pneumatomachoi-opinions spread throughout the Roman empire and few—outside Syria—argued in public with them. A council was held in Antioch during AD 363 to discuss the issue of the Pneumatomachoi. They were condemned but no one seemed to pay much attention to the condemnation. Finally, in AD 374 one of the leading Antiochene theologians asked Basil of Caesarea to write a defense of the Holy Spirit against the Pneumatomachoi.

Basil the Great

Basil was born in AD 329 or 330 in Pontus (a region on the south coast of the Black Sea). His family were wealthy and very pious Christians. His grandfather was a martyr. His mother and father were well-known for their piety and charity. He, and four of his siblings, are considered saints. Basil intended to be a rhetor (a teacher of persuasive, public speaking such as politicians and lawyers engaged in) and was sent to study in Cappadocia, Constantinople, and Athens. Along the way he met Gregory of Nazianzus and the two became lifelong best friends. Together, they were also fellow students with the future emperor Julian the Apostate.

Early in his career, Basil met a charismatic, monastic bishop and, as a consequence, decided to quit being a rhetorician and embrace asceticism himself. He describes his experience as awaking from a deep sleep.

> Much time had I spent in vanity, and had wasted nearly all my youth in the vain labor which I underwent in acquiring the wisdom made foolish by God. Then once upon a time, like a man roused from deep sleep, I turned my eyes to the marvelous light of the truth of the Gospel, and I perceived the uselessness of 'the wisdom of the princes of this world, who come to naught [I Cor. 2:6].... Then I read the Gospel, and I saw there that a great means of reaching perfection was the selling of one's goods, sharing them with the poor, giving up all care for this life, and the refusal to allow the soul to be turned by any sympathy to things of earth [*Epistle 223*].

He traveled throughout Palestine, Egypt, Syria, and Mesopotamia to study monastic life and principles. He gave away most of his share of the family's wealth to the poor. He attempted to live as a hermit but decided that he was better suited to communal monasticism. About AD 358, he and his sister Macrina turned the family estate into a monastic community. Their brother Peter joined, as did their mother Emelia and several other people. Basil's friend Gregory of Nazianzus lived there for a while as well.

Basil wrote about monastic life, answered letters, got involved with theology, and church politics. At first, he leaned toward the semi-Arian position that the Son was similar or like the Father but he soon allied himself with the supporters of the Nicene creed and the use of *homoousias*. He was made a deacon and then a presbyter (priest). He and his friend Gregory engaged in debates with leading Arians in the region, organized by the emperor Valens, and were successful in converting others to the Nicene position—which was not what the emperor had intended. In AD 370, Basil was made archbishop of Caesarea, which was a metropolitan see ("metropolis"=principal city; "see"=*sedes*, the chair or throne of the bishop) with five suffragan (assistant) bishops. The metropolitan archbishop of Caesarea ranked with those of Rome, Antioch, Alexandria, Ephesus, and Heraclea, having authority over all the lower bishops in his province and oversight over the appointment of all bishops in their respective provinces. When the emperor divided the diocese (i.e., cutting Basil's territory in half) in an attempt to reduce Basil's influence, Basil simply appointed more suffragan bishops (including making his brother Gregory the bishop of Nyssa and his friend Gregory Nazianzus the bishop of a tiny town called Sasima) so that in the end there were more suffragan bishops than he had started with. Valens would have been smarter to leave Basil alone.

As bishop, he was first and foremost a pastor who was primarily concerned with the poor and outcast. Basil organized soup kitchens and relief efforts as the area was suffering a famine following a drought. He gave away most of the rest of his family's money to aid the poor. He was a popular preacher, pastor, and social activist, building a hospital and hospice and relief center near Caesarea. He criticized and condemned politicians who supported unjust practices.

> Thus also at the Last Judgement, when the Lord shall call the righteous, the one who shares will occupy the first rank. The one who feeds others will be foremost among those honored; the one who gives bread will be summoned first of all; the person who is good and gives generously will enter into eternal life before the rest. But the unsociable and stingy will be the first to be given over to the eternal fire [*In Time of Famine and Drought* 7].

> Is not the person who strips another of clothing called a thief? And those who do not clothe the naked when they have the power to do so, should they not be called the same? Whosoever has the ability to remedy the suffering of others, but chooses

rather to withhold aid out of selfish motives, may properly be judged the equivalent of a murderer [*I Will Tear Down My Barns* 6, 8].

As both priest and bishop, Basil was responsible for the public prayer of the church in Caesarea. Although there were clear expectations of what each of the prayers ought to say (i.e., thanksgiving for light at sunset, thanksgiving for creation-incarnation-passion/resurrection-second coming at the Eucharist), there was still a fluidity as to what words each priest or bishop could use to say them. Basil's prayers became extremely popular and he is credited with a set of prayers still used at the Eucharist by the Orthodox during Lent and Holy Week (the most important as well as most emotionally intense times of the year, when the urge to do-it-this-year-the-same-way-we've-always-done-it-before is most powerful).

When Athanasius died in Alexandria in AD 373, Basil was the loudest and most prominent spokesman of the Nicene party. He became the "de facto" ringleader of the Orthodox throughout the Roman world, much as Athanasius had been during his lifetime. In response to the Pneumatomachoi, Basil wrote *On the Holy Spirit* in AD 375. To make it easier to win over the Pneumatomachoi, he wanted to avoid using words already controversial (like *homoousias*) to describe the Holy Spirit while also avoiding terminology not found in the New Testament: he never wrote "God, the Holy Spirit" or "the Holy Spirit is God." He wanted to prove the divinity of the Holy Spirit and demonstrate that the Spirit is uncreated, "without beginning," from the traditional practice of the Church and the Pneumatomachoi's own words.

Basil pointed out that all Christians, including the Pneumatomachoi, conclude the singing of the psalms with a doxology:

> Glory to the Father, through the Son, with [or "in"] the Holy Spirit:
> now and ever, and unto ages of ages. Amen.

The Pneumatomachoi argued that these prepositions, "through" and "with," imply that the Son and the Spirit are less than the Father. Basil said that "through" and "with" are used in connection with the Father in many places and that therefore the prepositions imply equality rather than diminishment or subordination. "For to say 'Paul and Silvanus and Timothy' (I Thess. 1:1) is the same as 'Paul with Timothy and Silvanus,' for the combination of the names is similarly preserved in each expression" (*On the Holy Spirit* 59).

Basil suggests that to avoid such confusion, though, it might be better to use "and" rather than "through" and "with": "if, in giving praise, a friend joins the names with the word 'and,' and gives glory to the Father and the Son and the Holy Spirit, as we have learned in the Gospels concerning baptism, let it be done in this way—no one would object. Please let us come to terms on these points" (*On the Holy Spirit* 60).

This means that the liturgical doxology would become

> Glory to the Father, **and** to the Son, **and** to the Holy Spirit:
> now and ever, and unto ages of ages. Amen.

It also means that during baptism, the clergy would declare, "The servant of God, N., is baptized in the name of the Father **and** of the Son **and** of the Holy Spirit." Very quickly, the Church did adopt Basil's suggestion, replacing "through" and "with" by "and." It is the form "and" that is still in use today.

In fact, the closing doxology of every liturgical prayer offered in Eastern or Byzantine churches has been shaped by the conflicts with the Arians and the Pneumatomachoi. Liturgical prayer is always offered to the Father but the concluding doxology is always addressed to "the Father and to the Son and to the Holy Spirit, now and ever, and unto ages of ages." The Son and the Spirit are clearly given the same glory and honor as the Father; all three are glorified as equal partners. And the people all respond, "Amen!" thus affirming their solidarity not only with the intention(s) of the prayer but with the understanding of the Trinity with which it concludes.

His most important argument, however, is that the Church has always prayed and acted in a way that implies that the Spirit is divine and uncreated in the same way that the Father is divine and uncreated. Why else would the Church baptize in the way she does?

> We know one cleansing, saving baptism, since there is one death for the sake of the world and one resurrection from the dead, of which baptism is a type (Ephesians 4:5). For the sake of this, the Lord, who directs our life, established with us the covenant of baptism, which contains a type of death and of life. The water fulfills the image of death, while the Spirit furnishes the pledge of life.
>
> And what was sought is now clear to us, namely, why water is associated with the Spirit. It is because there are two purposes laid down in baptism, first to abolish the body of sin so it no longer bears fruit unto death (Romans 6:6, 7:5), and second, to give life in the Spirit and so bear fruit in holiness (Galatians 5:25, Romans 6:22). The water furnishes the image of death, just as the body is received in burial, but the Spirit infuses life-giving power, renewing our souls from the death of sin to their original life. This, then, is what it means to be begotten again from water and the Spirit: as death is accomplished in the water, our life is worked through the Spirit. In three immersions and in the same number of invocations, the great mystery of baptism is accomplished, in order that the type of death may be fully formed and the baptized enlightened in their souls by the handing on of the knowledge of God. Thus, if there is some grace in the water, it is not from the nature of the water, but from the presence of the Spirit [*On the Holy Spirit* 35].

Basil asks the Pneumatomachoi: If the Spirit is not divine, how can he make mortals holy?

> Through the Holy Spirit comes the restoration to paradise, the ascent to the kingdom of heaven, the return to adopted sonship, the freedom to call God our Father and to become a companion of the grace of Christ, to be called a child of light, to participate

in eternal glory, and generally, to have all fullness of blessing in this age and the age to come. We see as in a mirror the grace, as already present, of the goods laid up in store for us in promises, and we enjoy these goods through faith. For, if such is the pledge, how great will the fullness be? If such is the first-fruits, what will be the fulfillment of the whole? [*On the Holy Spirit* 36].

It is not only what the Church believes about baptism that is based on unwritten tradition. Even the manner in which the Church baptizes is based on unwritten tradition:

We bless the water of baptism and the oil of the chrism, and besides this the catechumen who is being baptized. On what written authority do we do this? Is not silent and mystical tradition our authority? Nay, by what written word is the anointing of oil itself taught? And whence comes the custom of baptizing thrice? And as to the other customs of baptism: from what Scripture do we derive the renunciation of Satan and his angels? Does not this come from that unpublished and secret teaching which our fathers guarded in a silence out of the reach of curious meddling and inquisitive investigation? Well had they learned the lesson that the awesome dignity of the mysteries is best preserved in silence. What the uninitiated are not even allowed to look at was hardly likely to be publicly paraded about in written documents [*On the Holy Spirit* 66].

Basil points out that even proclaiming one's faith when being baptized is based on an unwritten tradition: "the very confession of our faith in Father, Son, and Holy Spirit: what is the written source?" (*On the Holy Spirit* 67).

These ancient practices, performed without explicit instruction, are among many such practices that shape Christian life. Basil repeatedly stresses that much of what the Church does is based on unwritten sources, believed to come from the apostles and other early fathers of the Church. This rule of unwritten tradition, he argues, cannot be set aside. He wonders why anyone would even want to do so.

Of the beliefs and practices whether generally accepted or publicly enjoined which are preserved in the Church, some we possess derived from written teaching; others we have received delivered to us "in a mystery" by the tradition of the apostles; and both of these in relation to true religion have the same force. No one would deny these points, at least no one, who has even a little experience of ecclesiastical institutions. For were we to attempt to reject such customs as have no written authority, on the ground that the importance they possess is small, we should unintentionally injure vital parts of the Gospel; or, rather, should make our public definition a mere phrase and nothing more. For instance, to take the first and most general example, who has taught us in writing to mark those who have trusted in the name of our Lord Jesus Christ with the sign of the cross? What writing has taught us to turn to the East for prayer? Which of the saints has left us in writing the words of the invocation at the displaying of the bread of the Eucharist and the cup of blessing?[1] For we are not, as is well known, content with what the apostle or the Gospel has recorded, but both in preface and conclusion we add other words as being of great importance to the validity of the ministry, and these we derive from unwritten teaching.

The Apostles and Fathers who laid down laws for the Church from the beginning thus guarded the awesome dignity of the mysteries in secrecy and silence, for what is talked about randomly outside by the common folk is no mystery at all. This is the reason for our tradition of unwritten precepts and practices, that the knowledge of our dogmas may not become neglected and condemned by the multitude through familiarity.... Thus we all look to the East at our prayers, but few of us know that we are seeking our ancient fatherland, the Paradise which God planted in Eden in the East. We pray standing, on the first day of the week, but we do not all know the reason. On the day of the resurrection (or "standing again" [in Greek, *Anastasis*]; see Col. 3:1) we remind ourselves of the grace given to us by standing at prayer, not only because we rose with Christ, and are bound to "seek those things which are above," but because the day seems to us to be in some sense an image of the age which is to come ... the day which knows no waning or evening, and no successor, that age which never ends or grows old. Of necessity, then, the church teaches her own foster children to pray standing on that day, so that we would not neglect the provisions for our journey to everlasting life by a constant reminder of it. Moreover all Pentecost [the 50 days between Pascha and the day of Pentecost itself] is a reminder of the resurrection expected in the age to come. For that one and first day, if seven times multiplied by seven, completes the seven weeks of the holy Pentecost. It begins on the first day [i.e., Sunday] and ends on the same day [i.e., Sunday, again], revolving fifty times through similar days in between. Eternity is like a circular movement, beginning from the same points where it ends. The ordinances of the Church well taught us to prefer to stand at prayer on this day, as if we were leading our minds from the present to the future. With each going down on the knee and rising up we indicate by our action that we have fallen through sin to the earth and are called up to heaven by the love of our creator.

Time will fail me if I attempt to recount the unwritten mysteries of the Church [*On the Holy Spirit* 66–67].

Basil is aware that some might accuse him of endorsing belief in three gods. He stresses that there is only one God and describes the Son as the perfect image (icon) of the Father which the Spirit, who is the light and knowledge of the Father, reveals.

Let them [the Pneumatomachoi] learn that "Christ is the power of God and wisdom of God" (I Cor. 1:24), that he is "the image of the invisible God" (Col. 1:15) and the "radiance of his glory" (Heb. 1:3) and that "God the Father sealed him" (John 6:27) and imprinted his whole self in Him [*On the Holy Spirit* 15].

There is one God and Father, one Only-begotten, and one Holy Spirit. We proclaim each of the persons singly; and, when we must count them together, we are not carried away to the concept of polytheism by uneducated counting [*On the Holy Spirit* 44].

How, then, if they are one and one, are there not two gods? Because we speak of a king, and of the king's image, and not of two kings. The majesty is not divided and the glory is not portioned out. The sovereignty and authority over us is one, and so the doxology ascribed by us is not plural but one; the honor paid to the image passes onto the prototype. Therefore, the image is the prototype by way of imitation [in the case of the king and his image]; the Son is this by nature. Just as in art there is a likeness according to form, so in the case of the divine and uncompounded nature the union consists in the communion of the Godhead.

Now, one is the Holy Spirit, and we speak of Him singly. He is joined to the one Father through the one Son, and through himself he completes the famed and blessed Trinity [*On the Holy Spirit* 45].

The Spirit of knowledge is somehow inseparably present, [and] supplies to those who love the vision of the truth and the power to see the image in himself ... it is written "in thy light shall we see light" (Psalm 36:9), that is, in the illumination of the Spirit, "the true light that enlightens every man that comes into the world" (John 1:9). So he shows in Himself the glory of the Only-begotten, and furnishes to true worshippers the knowledge of God in himself. The way, then, to knowledge of God is from the one Spirit through the one Son to the one Father, and conversely the natural goodness and inherent holiness and the royal dignity extend from the Father through the Only-begotten to the Spirit [*On the Holy Spirit* 47].

Basil remembers that the word "Spirit" is related to the word "breath" and tells his readers that the Son is begotten by the Father but the Spirit proceeds from the Father: "proceeding out of God, not begotten like the Son, but as Breath of his mouth. But in no way is the 'mouth' a member, nor is the Spirit breath that is dissolved; but the word 'mouth' is used so far as it can be appropriate to God [i.e., a metaphor], and the Spirit is ... life, gifted with supreme power of sanctification" (*On the Holy Spirit* 46).

Basil also preached a famous series of nine sermons called the "Hexameron," about the six days of creation described in Genesis 1. He apparently preached these during Lent, the usual time that Genesis would be read during the services, and without many notes. (People wrote down what he said as he was preaching and he then revised these transcripts to produce the written sermons we now have.) These sermons were very popular and inspired several other famous preachers to also preach their own series of sermons on the first six days of creation as well.

Basil began by reminding his listeners that Genesis was considered the work of Moses and that Moses, having been raised by Pharaoh's daughter, had received the best education possible. Although Moses was at least 80 years old when he first met God at the burning bush, he was able to respond to God's call and lead the people of Israel from bondage into freedom; he was also inspired to write down the history of Israel to that time, in order to share what he had learned directly from God.

One of the most important things Basil had to say about the creation of the world was that although science was constantly discovering new things and changing or developing new theories, the fundamental fact of God's creating the world remained unchanged. He affirmed the value of science and the need to understand the operations of the physical world even while underscoring God's oversight of these physical processes. In fact, Basil spent a great deal of time showing how the Genesis account could be understood in terms of the scientific knowledge of his day. Although we may disagree with many of the scientific facts that he was working with, his methodology remains the same today: there doesn't need to be any inherent disagreement between the record of Genesis and the scientific understanding of the world.

Basil described the physical world as a work of art that God has produced, although the exact means God used are beyond our understanding. Basil's own thoughts sound familiar to those who suggest a "big bang" began the physical world:

> Perhaps these words 'In the beginning God created' signify the rapid and imperceptible moment of creation. The beginning, in effect, is indivisible and instantaneous.... At the will of God the world arose in less than an instant and it is to convey this meaning more clearly that other interpreters have said: 'God made summarily,' that is to say all at once and in a moment [*Hexameron* 1.6].

Basil also discussed the meaning of time and the use of "days" in the creation account. He points out that the biblical text reads, "And the evening and the morning were one day." He commented, "Why does Scripture say 'one day, the first day'? Before speaking to us of the second, the third, and the fourth days, would it not have been more natural to call that one the first which began the series? If it therefore says 'one day,' it is from a wish to determine the measure of day and night, and to combine the time that they contain" (*Hexameron* 2.8).

A normal day not only clearly begins and ends with sunset but is also 24 hours long. However, the first day of creation is not a normal day. Neither is the first week a normal week. By saying that "one day" had elapsed rather than that the "first day" had concluded, Basil suggested that "it is because Scripture wishes to establish its relationship with eternity. It was, in reality, fit and natural to call 'one' the day whose character is to be one wholly separated and isolated from all the others.... It follows that we are hereby shown not so much limits, ends and succession of ages, as distinctions between various states and modes of action."

Day one is the first stage of creation. Basil wanted his congregation to understand that the word "day" here does not mean the usual 24-hour period but is better understood to mean an "age" or an "epoch," or even an "eon." He reminded them that Scripture uses the word "day" to mean "age" or even "eternity" in other places as well.

> "The day of the Lord," Scripture says, "is great and very terrible" [Joel 2:11], and elsewhere "Woe unto you that desire the day of the Lord: to what end is it for you? The day of the Lord is darkness and not light" [Amos 5:8]. A day of darkness for those who are worthy of darkness. No; this day without evening, without succession and without end is not unknown to Scripture.

"The day of the Lord" is another way to say "eternity." If you call it "the day of the Lord," that does not mean there is another one, Basil went on to say. It is unique. This eternal, everlasting day, being outside the regular cycle of seven-day weeks, is sometimes itself called the "eighth day." "This is the day that the Psalmist calls the eighth day, because it is outside this time of weeks. Thus whether you call it day, or whether you call it eternity, you express the same idea."

Basil suggested that this "day one" of creation is meant to suggest not only eternity but already anticipates the Resurrection of Christ. "Thus it is in order that you may carry your thoughts forward towards a future life, that Scripture marks by the word 'one' the day which is the type of eternity, the first fruits of days, the contemporary of light, the holy Lord's day honored by the Resurrection of our Lord. 'And the evening and the morning were one day'" (*Hexameron* 2.8). Basil was telling his congregation that every Sunday[2] is the "eighth day," the day of the Resurrection, and therefore every Sunday—the day on which the Eucharist is celebrated—can be their first experience of eternity.

Gregory of Nazianzus, "The Theologian"

Basil's best friend Gregory was born about the same time as Basil (AD 330) and was the son of the bishop of Nazianzus; Gregory's father and Basil's mother knew each other. The two families produced nearly a dozen saints over three generations, the relatives and friends supporting each other in their efforts to live as devout Christians.

Basil met Gregory when they were both students in Cappadocia (a region on the main road between Constantinople and Antioch); they also went to Athens to study together in AD 350. In Athens, they also became friends with a fellow student named Julian.

Gregory was baptized about the same time that his friend Basil was in AD 358–9 in either Athens or Cappadocia. Gregory went home to Nazianzus and wanted to became an ascetic but his father insisted that he become a priest there, probably with an eye to Gregory helping serve with his father. Gregory objected at first but eventually agreed to the ordination in AD 361. It was at this same time that Julian became the Roman emperor and began his efforts to re-establish the worship of the Greco-Roman gods. He ruled until AD 363 and became known as "the Apostate" because of these efforts.

Gregory was an excellent preacher and pastor who became popular with the congregation in Nazianzus. He was able to reconcile several factions in the congregation. He wrote against Julian's efforts to overthrow the Church and argued that the love and patience of God would overcome Julian's efforts in the end.

Basil was made archbishop of Caesarea in AD 370 and a year later the emperor Valens cut his diocese in half but Basil retaliated by making several new bishops for towns that had not previously had bishops. This included making his friend Gregory the bishop of a town called Sasima.

Gregory had originally thought that his friend Basil wanted to ordain him bishop so that they could serve together side-by-side in Caesarea. He was aghast when he realized that Basil wanted him to actually take up residence in Sasima and famously spent only one night in the town that he later described as "that utterly dreadful, pokey little hole; a paltry horse-stop on the main road ... devoid of water, vegetation, or the company of gentlemen." He was furious with Basil for having manipulated him for ecclesiastical politics. They were later reconciled but were never quite as close again as they had been before.

Gregory went back to Nazianzus to help his dying father serve the cathedral parish there. He was made an assistant bishop but refused to accept any other position there and after his father's death he entered a monastery. His friend Basil died while he was in the monastery. Unable to attend the funeral, Gregory wrote a letter of condolence to Basil's brother, Gregory of Nyssa, as well as several poems dedicated to Basil's memory. He said that "everyone, including non–Christians, mourned his death" because Basil had been so tireless in his work to aid the poor, the ill, and the needy.

The emperor Valens, who had opposed Gregory's and Basil's support of Nicea, was succeeded first by Gratian and then by Theodosius. The people of Constantinople had been much more supportive of the Arians and semi-Arians but supporters of Nicea began to come back to the city. Meletios, the archbishop of Antioch, asked Gregory to go lead the small congregation of Nicene supporters in the suburbs of the imperial capital.

Gregory eventually agreed to go to Constantinople and used his cousin's villa as a "house-church" for the Nicene parish. Theological arguments were popular and widespread throughout Constantinople. Basil's brother, Gregory of Nyssa, tells us that the theological disputes of the city during this period were so intense that

> the whole city is full of it, the squares, the market places, the cross-roads, the alley-ways; old-clothes men, money changers, food sellers: they are all busy arguing. If you ask someone to give you change, he philosophizes about the Begotten and the Unbegotten; if you inquire about the price of a loaf, you are told by way of reply that the Father is greater and the Son inferior; if you ask "Is my bath ready?" the attendant answers that the Son was made out of nothing [*On the Deity of the Son*]

Gregory's preaching became extremely popular, so much so that his Arian adversaries broke into the church during the celebration of Pascha in the spring of AD 379. Gregory was injured and a visiting bishop was killed. Gregory wanted to leave Constantinople but was persuaded to stay, even though many in the city laughed at him as a country bumpkin unable to deal with imperial politics.

Gregory Nazianzus	Basil the Great
AD 350: study together with Basil and Julian the Apostate	AD 350: study together with Gregory and Julian the Apostate
AD 358–9: baptized	AD 358–9: baptized
AD 361: ordained priest	Visited monasteries across Egypt and Middle East Opened monastery on home estate AD 360: gets involved with theological disputes
	AD 363: ordained priest
	AD 370: made bishop of Caesarea; preaches on the *Hexameron* (6 days of Creation)
AD 371–2: made bishop of Sasima by Basil	AD 371: Valens divides Caesarea; Basil makes more bishops
	AD 373: Athanasius dies and Basil becomes ringleader of the [Nicene] Orthodox
	AD 375: writes *On the Holy Spirit*
AD 378: Valens defeated; Gratian made emperor	
AD 379: Gregory preaches in suburbs of Constantinople	AD 379: Basil dies; "everyone, including non–Christians, mourned his death"
AD 380: Theodosius the Great is baptized	
AD 381: Council in Constantinople	

Emperor Theodosius the Great

The emperor Theodosius took ill in the autumn of AD 380 and was not expected to survive. He was baptized on his deathbed, as per the established custom. New, however, in Theodosius' case, was that he not only survived but fully recovered and then refused to step down from the imperial throne. There had never been an actual baptized Christian ruler before. Theodosius was the first. There were no role models for how to accommodate the demands of both statecraft and politics versus the ethical behavior demanded of baptized Christians. Theodosius was sailing in uncharted seas.

One of Theodosius' first acts as baptized emperor was to expel the Arian archbishop of Constantinople and appoint Gregory instead. He then ordered that all Arians—both clergy and layfolk—were to be expelled from the city.

Arian mobs, however, refused to surrender the cathedral of Hagia Sophia when ordered to do so and the most important churches in the city remained served by Arian clergy.

Later in his reign, Theodosius also allowed the destruction of the Greco-Roman temples, the closure of the philosophical academy in Athens, shut down pagan priesthoods and the Vestal Virgins in Rome, and closed the Olympic Games because of the non–Christian religious rites associated with them. He made membership in Nicene Christianity a requirement for holding public office. In AD 390, he ordered the massacre of the residents of Thessalonica in retaliation for riots against local soldiers; Ambrose of Milan refused to let the emperor enter the cathedral in Milan or receive Holy Communion until he had performed several months of penance; this would have been impossible to enforce if the emperor had not already been baptized.

Theodosius proclaimed that right-worshipping or right-believing ("Orthodox") Christianity consisted of (1) faith in the Trinity as defined at Nicea and (2) communion with the apostolic churches of Rome or Alexandria. He called a second imperial ("ecumenical") council to be held in Constantinople in May, AD 381. The council was to deal with the remaining Arian and semi-Arian theologians, including the Pneumatomachoi, as well as disciplinary measures to deal with the schisms that resulted from doctrinal divisions. Various methods to reconcile the non–Orthodox with the Orthodox were promulgated.

This second ecumenical council reiterated the Creed from Nicea but removed the anathemas from its conclusion and replaced them with a series of statements about the Holy Spirit and other related subjects:

> And [we believe] in the Holy Spirit, the Lord, the Giver of Life, who proceeds from the Father; who with the Father and the Son together is worshipped and glorified; who spoke through the prophets; and in one, holy, catholic, and apostolic Church.
> We acknowledge one baptism for the remission of sins.
> We look for [i.e., anticipate, eagerly await] the resurrection of the dead and the life of the world to come. Amen.

These statements, like the original creed at Nicea, were proclaimed by the council in the plural, "We believe" although most layfolk would only have heard or uttered the creed themselves during baptism or the ordination of a bishop, when the candidate for either baptism or ordination would recite the creed in the singular "I believe." (The creed did not become a regular part of the celebration of the Eucharist for several hundred years.)

The creedal statements about the church, baptism, and the resurrection were all considered aspects of the Holy Spirit's presence and activity and therefore related to the proclamation of the Spirit's divinity. The one Church was the place where the one Spirit of God could be found; there was only one baptism, that celebrated by the Orthodox rather than by the Arians or semi-Arians or other heretical groups, that could incorporate someone into the one Church of the one Spirit; the resurrection of the dead and the life of the world to come, the eternal "eighth day" that Basil preached about, awaited all mankind but was only eagerly awaited with anticipation by those already incorporated into the life of the Spirit in the Church.

In terms of reconciling and reintegrating the non–Orthodox into the Orthodox churches, there were two parties: one advocated strict rules, with no sympathy for the formerly Arian or semi-Arian, while the other was more willing to accept those who moved from Arian or semi-Arian positions to embrace Orthodoxy as understood by Theodosius and the council at Constantinople. In places where there were two bishops, one formerly Arian or semi-Arian, and one consistently Orthodox, one had to be either demoted or moved to another city.

Another important statement by the council about bishops and hierarchy was the declaration that New Rome (i.e., Constantinople) was to be considered the most important ranking archbishop in the empire, second only to "old Rome" on the Tiber. The council stated that Old Rome had always been given precedence because it was the capital of the empire and that it should still be accorded prominence as the former capital. This statement ignored the apostolic founding of the church in Rome by both Peter and Paul, which many people had considered just as important—or even more important—a reason to give precedence to Rome. This usurpation of second place in the ancient ranking of the archbishoprics also especially angered the pope of Alexandria as it demoted him from second- to third-ranking in the hierarchical schema.

In the midst of all the arguments about which bishops were entitled to serve where and which ranked higher than others, Timothy the pope of Alexandria denounced Gregory's occupation of the archbishopric of Constantinople as uncanonical since he was still the official bishop of Sasima. Rather than fight, Gregory retired to his family's country estate since he had never liked crowds in general or Constantinople in particular. He died in AD 389.

The "Theological Orations" of Gregory Nazianzus

Gregory is one of the few people officially designated "the theologian"; the other official theologians are the Apostle John the Theologian and Symeon, the "New" Theologian ("new" because he lived in the 10th–11th centuries, several hundred years after the Apostle John and Gregory Nazianzus). (In Elizabethan English, to call someone a "divine" was to say they were a "theologian"; thus, when English speakers refer to the apostle and evangelist as John the Divine, they are also referring to him as "the Theologian.") During Gregory's tenure as pastor of the house-church, not only were his sermons extremely popular but five in particular came to be considered his "Theological Orations" par excellence.

Gregory began this series of sermons by taunting his theological enemies—the Arians, semi-Arians, and Pneumatomachoi—who are "verbal tricksters, grotesque and preposterous word-gamesters" who delight in "profane knowledge and vain babblings and contradictions … in the strife of words which lead to no result." Gregory promises his congregation that he will provide them the true doctrine of proper theology.

Gregory asks his opponents if they can join him in meeting the requirements to be a true theologian. "Do we commend hospitality? Do we admire brotherly love, wifely affection, virginity, feeding the poor, singing psalms, nightlong vigils, penitence? Do we, through prayer, take up our abode with God? Do we make life a meditation on death? Do we establish our mastery over our passions, mindful of the nobility of our second birth [baptism]? Do we tame our swollen and inflamed tempers" (*Oration* 27.7)? As far as Gregory is concerned, good theology is the result of good people living good lives and bad theology is the result of bad people living lives of self-indulgence and sin. He reminds them that the true theologian is the truly sophisticated, the truly educated one which is a refutation of the heretics' claim that the Orthodox were only illiterate, rude, unsophisticated country bumpkins who could not understand the complexities of real theology.

Gregory goes on to ask if humans can know God and he answers himself with another question: if we cannot understand the world around us, how can the heretics claim to understand God so completely? God, Gregory preaches, is the Incomprehensible. The Arians and semi-Arians define God too much and claim to know Him too completely; they say that God's defining characteristic is that He is Unbegotten and that therefore the Son, who is begotten, cannot be God.

Gregory responds:

> All truth, all philosophy, to be sure, is obscure, hard to trace out. It is like employing a small tool on big constructions, if we use human wisdom in the hunt for knowledge of reality. We do not abandon the senses, they go with us, when we look at supra-sensible realities. But by these same senses we are perplexed and led astray. We cannot get nearer the truth by meeting things in their naked reality with naked intellect. Our minds cannot receive direct and sure impressions [*Oration* 28.21].

Gregory goes on to say that not even the great Solomon was able to grasp the full revelation that God offered, even though he was "the superior of his predecessors and contemporaries in education, gifted by God with breadth of heart and an expanse of vision ampler than the sand…. The more he entered into profundities, the more his mind reeled." Gregory also cites

King David's perplexity at trying to find words to describe the incomprehensibility of God.

> David at one point calls God's judgements a "great abyss" fathomless by sense; at another point he says that the knowledge even of his own make-up was "too wonderful" for him, "too excellent" for him "to be grasped."

> Why does the soul give life, yet have its share of pain? What makes the mind both confined and boundless, both at home in us and touring the universe in rapid, flowing course? How does it come about that the same living thing is both mortal and immortal? Changing its state, it dies; giving birth makes it immortal. Now it goes away, now it comes back again, channeled like a constant, flowing river.... There are many facts about rest in sleep, about our imagination at work in dreams, about memory and recollection, about calculation, anger and desire—to be brief, about all that runs the affairs of this little world called Man [*Oration* 28.21–22].

Gregory reminds his listeners that David sang in the psalms about his own unfathomable human nature; if the Arians and Pneumatomachoi think they can describe the nature of God, then surely they can describe human nature as well!

Rather than rely on intellectualism and cold rationalism, Gregory suggests that poetry is better suited to theology.

> Faith rather than reason shall lead us, if that is, you have learned the feebleness of reason to deal with matters quite close at hand and have acquired enough knowledge of reason to recognize things which surpass reason. If so, it follows that you will not be a wholly earthbound thinker, ignorant of your very ignorance.

> Poets speak reasoned truth, not metaphor [*Oration* 28.28, 30].

When Gregory turns his attention to the Holy Spirit and the dispute with the Pneumatomachoi in particular, he cites John 15:26 to argue that the Spirit proceeds from the Father while the Son is begotten, although the real distinction between "procession" and "begotten" is known to God alone.

> Insofar as he proceeds from the Father, he is no creature; inasmuch as he is not begotten, he is no Son; and to the extent that procession is the mean between being generator and being generated, he is God.... What then is "proceeding?" You explain how the Father is unbegotten and I will give you a biological account of how the Son is begotten and how the Spirit proceeds—and then let the both of us go crazy for prying into God's secrets [*Oration* 31.8].

He concedes that most of the Pneumatomachoi are Orthodox at least as regards the Son; i.e., they agree with Nicea that the Son is *homoousias* with the Father. But they insist that the Spirit is not *homoousias* with the Father and the Son. Instead, Gregory points out, the Pneumatomachoi teach that the Spirit is an energy—maybe not a person at all?—or if the spirit is a person, then he is a created entity.

If there was a "when" when the Father did not exist, there was a "when" when the Son did not exist. If there was a "when" when the Son did not exist, there was a "when" when the Holy Spirit did not exist. If one existed from the beginning, so did all three. If you cast one down, I make bold to tell you not to exalt the other two. What use is incomplete deity? Or rather, what is deity if it is incomplete? If he did not exist from the beginning, he has the same rank as I have, though with a slight priority—we are both separated from God by time. If he has the same rank as I have [see II Peter 1:4], how can he make me God, how can he link me with deity? [*Oration* 31.4].

Gregory also makes a comment that God is neither male nor female, although the nouns we use to describe the divine persons are masculine and that some of the attributes of the persons (such as "holy") are grammatically feminine (*Oration* 31.7). Gregory insists that how we listen to language is as important as the language itself is: both Orthodox and non–Orthodox could use the same terms, pray the same prayers, and hear them in radically different ways to mean completely different things. "The language gives no grounds for any deficiency or subordination" (*Oration* 31.9).

But how, asked the Pneumatomachoi, can two persons have a common source and one be a son but the other not? Gregory answers by using the example of Adam, Eve, and Seth.

What was Adam? Something molded by God. What was Eve? A portion of that molded creation. Seth? He was the offspring of the pair…. Were they consubstantial [i.e., *homoousias*]? Yes, of course they were. It is agreed, then, that things with a different individual being can be of the same substance.

Were not Eve and Seth of the same Adam? Whose else? Were they both offspring? Certainly not. Why?—because one was a portion of Adam, the other an offspring. Yet they had a mutual identity—they were both human beings, nobody can gainsay that [*Oration* 31.11].

Gregory proclaims that if there is no Trinity, then there is no salvation. But God sets out to persuade his creation of the truth rather than force them to submit. He reveals only what can be understood at the most opportune time. He recounts the gradual self-revelation of God in both the Old and New Testaments. "You see how light shines on us bit by bit, you see in the doctrine of God an order, which we had better observe, neither revealing it suddenly or concealing it to the last. To reveal it suddenly would be clumsy, would shock outsiders. Ultimately to conceal it would be a denial of God" (*Oration* 31.27).

Just as the Old Testament "made a clear proclamation of the Father, a less definite one of the Son" and the New Testament "made the Son manifest" while "giving us a glimpse of the Spirit's Godhead," so now it is in the life of the Church that the Holy Spirit is clearly revealed (*Oration* 31.26). "Were the Spirit not to be worshipped, how could he deify me through baptism? If he is to be worshipped, why not adored? And if to be adored, how can he fail to be God? One links with the other, a truly golden chain of salvation. From the Spirit comes our rebirth, from rebirth comes a new creating, from new creating a recognition of the worth of him who effected it" (*Oration* 31.28).

One of Gregory's insights came to be considered a bedrock of Orthodox theology; joined to Athanasius' teaching "that God became human so that humanity could become God," Gregory taught that the incarnation of the Son was so total that "whatever was not assumed was not saved" (*Epistle* 101.5). In Gregory's context, he was arguing against the idea that Christ had no human mind but only a divine one. Gregory insists that "Christ touched and made his own [assumed] all the human condition in all its aspects. To deny Christ a human mind is therefore to cut the human mind off from the redeeming power of God."[3] This succinct statement that whatever was not assumed was not saved became the yardstick by which much later theological speculation was measured.

Because of this all-encompassing radical incarnational vision, Gregory of Nazianzus did argue that "heaven is common to all" and that "although there is one Lord, one faith, one baptism, there is not one road to salvation" in his *Oration* 32 and *Oration* 33. Because of the incarnation, the body is saved as much as the soul is; in *Oration* 7, Gregory describes how—after death—the soul must wait for the body in order to enter into glory, united with God.

Even though heaven is open to all and there is no one road to salvation, Gregory was not blind to the fact that not everyone would accept God's offer of salvation. Gregory preached, in fact, that it was this human rejection of God, of goodness and truth, which had resulted in the crucifixion of Christ. In his *Oration* 45, Gregory mused, "To whom was Christ's sacrifice on the Cross offered?" and answered by pointing out that we had been held in bondage by the Evil One and that offering the blood of the God-man to the Evil One was immeasurably more than the Evil One deserved.

> We were detained in bondage by the Evil One, sold under sin, and receiving pleasure in exchange for wickedness. Now, since a ransom belongs only to him who holds in bondage, I ask to whom was this offered, and for what cause? If to the Evil One, fie upon the outrage! If the robber receives ransom, not only from God, but a ransom which consists of God Himself, and has such an illustrious payment for his tyranny.... [Impossible!] [*Oration* 45.22].

Gregory goes on to say that the Father was not the one oppressing us, so how could the sacrifice be offered to him? In fact, the Father had refused to accept Abraham's offering of his son Isaac and given Abraham a ram to offer instead; how then could the sacrifice of his own divine Son have pleased him?

Rather, Gregory said, the sacrifice was offered to us, to humanity, because we were the ones who demanded that God be killed in order to "overcome the tyrant and draw us to himself." Humanity demanded that the incarnate Son be put to death because humanity always turned its collective back on God and rejected the divine overture but when the incarnate Son died and embraced Death, then Death itself died and humanity was freed. (Throughout later Byzantine liturgical hymnography and saints' lives, the Devil or Evil One was generally a comic character; the real enemy, the true foe of humanity, was always Death.)

Gregory was also the first to refine the idea of *theosis* ["deification"] as a consistent concept to describe salvation. "Let us become like Christ, since Christ became like us," Gregory preached in his first sermon. He paraphrased Athanasius: "Let us become gods for his sake, since he became man for ours." *Theosis*, for Gregory, became a visual metaphor (we "reflect Gods brightness" [*Oration* 27.9]), as well as a spatial metaphor (we ascend to God, come close to God), as well as an ethical and social metaphor to describe the behavior of those engaged in being saved. Salvation, *theosis*, was never static but was a dynamic process in which the human person is always ascending/reflecting more brightly/behaving more like God. Whereas some preachers taught that salvation meant humanity could regain the Paradise that Adam and Eve were exiled from, Gregory taught that salvation brought humanity to a place better than Paradise: God himself was the destination of the saved.

Gregory's insights continue to live on and shape the vision of Orthodox people to this day. Several passages of *Oration* 31 have come to be paraphrased as the hymnography in the Vespers and Matins of Pentecost in the Orthodox liturgical tradition, just as Gregory's first and last sermons on Pascha have been paraphrased to become the primary hymns of the midnight Paschal service. Many of the most well-known Easter hymns sung by western Christians are themselves paraphrases of Gregory's sermons as well.

> It is now needful for us to sum up our discourse as follows: We were created that we might be made happy. We were made happy when we were created. We were entrusted with Paradise that we might enjoy life. We received a commandment ["Do not eat the fruit of that tree"] that we might obtain a good repute by keeping it; not that God did not know what would take place, but because he had laid down the law of free will. We were deceived because we were the objects of envy. We were cast out because we transgressed. We fasted because we refused to fast, being overpowered by the Tree of Knowledge. For the commandment was ancient, coeval with ourselves, and was a kind of education of our souls and curb of luxury, to which we were reasonably made subject, in order that we might recover by keeping it that which we had lost by not keeping it. We needed an incarnate God, a God put to death, that we might live. We were put to death together with him, that we might be cleansed; we rose again with him because we were put to death with him; we were glorified with him, because we rose again with him [*Oration* 45.28].

SUGGESTIONS FOR FURTHER READING

Basil the Great, *On the Holy Spirit*. (Trans. Stephen Hildebrand) St. Vladimir's Seminary Press, 2011.

Gregory of Nazianzus, *On God and Christ: The Five Theological Orations and Two Letters to Cledonius*. (Trans. Lionel Wickham and Frederick Williams) St. Vladimir's Seminary Press, 2002.

John McGuckin, *St. Gregory Nazianzus: An Intellectual Biography*. St. Vladimir's Seminary Press, 2001.

Donald Winslow, *The Dynamics of Salvation: A Study in Gregory of Nazianzus*. Philadelphia Patristic Foundation, 1979.

4

Constantinople, Alexandria and the Mother of God

When Gregory of Nazianzus left Constantinople, after the council which had proclaimed the divinity of the Holy Spirit and amended the Nicene Creed, the Emperor Theodosius appointed Nectarius to serve as archbishop of the imperial capital. Nectarius, only a catechumen, was baptized, ordained, and installed as archbishop. The Arians and Pneumatomachoi refused to accept the revised Nicene Creed and Nectarius presided over another council in AD 383 called by the emperor Theodosius to deal with the ongoing conflict. The emperor served himself as arbiter of the dispute and—after deliberating with Nectarius and the assembled theologians—rejected the teaching of the Arians and Pneumatomachoi. Theodosius ordered all bishops who refused to accept the councils of AD 325 and 381 to stop celebrating services, to stop teaching in public, and to stop ordaining new clergy. Any bishop caught continuing any of these practices faced stern civil penalties.

Theodosius died in AD 395 and named Arcadius, his 18-year-old son, as the next emperor. Arcadius shortly thereafter married the beautiful Eudoxia, the orphan daughter of a "barbarian" (i.e., a Frank) military officer. Nectarius served as archbishop until he died in AD 397. Arcadius and his advisors searched for someone to appoint as the next archbishop of Constantinople and chose a well-known preacher of Antioch, the presbyter (priest) known as John Chrysostom ("the golden-mouthed").

John Chrysostom

John had been born in a good family of Antioch, around AD 350. His father died when John was an infant and his mother, a baptized Christian, struggled to provide him the best classical education available. On completing his education, John briefly worked as a lawyer or rhetor but was himself baptized when he was 20 years old. John then spent several years living with a monastic brotherhood in the mountains outside Antioch; he left the monks because of his severe stomach problems that developed and which plagued him the rest of his life. (Contemporaries attributed John's stomach problems to his excessive fasting while in the mountains but other psychological or physical causes are more likely the root of his condition.)

When he returned to Antioch, Meletios, the archbishop of Antioch, took John under his wing; he both ordained John as a deacon and appointed John his secretary. He was ordained priest by the next archbishop and began preaching in Antioch's cathedral in AD 386. His sermons focused on biblical interpretation and applying the biblical texts to the daily lives of his congregation. He insisted that care for the sick, the poor, and the needy were essential if anyone wanted to consider themselves a true Christian.

> They [the rich and greedy] are a kind of robbers lying in wait on the roads, stealing from passers-by, and burying the goods of others in their own houses as if in caves and holes. Let us not therefore call them fortunate because of what they have, but miserable because of what will come, because of that dreadful courtroom, because of the inexorable judgement, because of the outer darkness which awaits them. Indeed, robbers have often escaped the hands of men.... [But] no one will escape [God's] judgement, but all who live by fraud and theft will certainly draw upon themselves that immortal and endless penalty, just like this rich man. Collecting all these thoughts in your minds, therefore, my beloved, let us call fortunate not the wealthy but the virtuous; let us call miserable not the poor but the wicked [*First Sermon on Lazarus and the Rich Man*].

Shortly after John's ordination, there were riots in Antioch against imperial taxes and tax-collectors. Statues of the Emperor Theodosius were defaced, which made the riots an act of treason. Theodosius ordered the public baths, theatres, and hippodrome closed. He sent judges to investigate. Ringleaders of the riots were identified and executed as were city officials who were judged to have failed in their duty to keep the peace. Further punishments of the city and its inhabitants were expected. Archbishop Flavian went to Constantinople to plead for the people and John preached a series of sermons in the cathedral while the archbishop was away. John preached these sermons, known as *On the Statues*, during Lent in the spring of AD 387. These sermons were extremely popular and cemented John's reputation and popularity. Throughout John's career as a preacher, stenographers in church would take notes as John preached. John would review these notes and he would then publish his sermons, based on the notes.

Not only were John's sermons popular but the way he offered liturgical prayer was also popular as well. As with Basil, clergy were still able at this point to offer the prayers of the Eucharist and other services in their own words so long as they followed the standard outline. John's versions of these prayers were also copied down and circulated, eventually displacing the prayers of Basil on most Sundays—primarily because John's prayer for the Anaphora, the "great thanksgiving" of the Eucharist, was considerably briefer than Basil's prayer was. John's prayers became the standard prayers the Orthodox use at the Eucharist to this day.

Flavian was able to convince the Emperor Theodosius to spare Antioch any further punishment. The people credited not only Flavian's diplomacy with winning the emperor's favor but John's prayers and the repentance that he had spurred them all on to embrace. His reputation spread and copies of his sermons circulated far and wide. He was made archbishop of Constantinople in October, AD 397.

One of the first things he did when he was enthroned as archbishop of Constantinople was abolish the popular banquets and dinner parties that his predecessor Nectarius had frequently hosted. He claimed that his stomach problems made it impossible for him to participate in such lavish dinners and that he preferred to spend the money on aiding the poor and hungry. But the aristocracy and social elites who had become accustomed to dining with the archbishop were furious at the slight.

John sold many of the church's chalices and other treasures, in fact, in order to raise money to fund hospitals, homes for lepers, hospices, shelters, and soup kitchens. He cut other expenses and set about reforming ill-behaved clergy, men who practiced "spiritual marriage" (living with a woman while claiming to be engaged in ascetic practice), widows who shirked their pastoral or liturgical responsibilities while still receiving support from the church, and monks who preferred to live in Constantinople rather than their monasteries. Large segments of the city were enraged at what they felt was John's cavalier and high-handed treatment of them.

But he was extremely popular with the lower classes in the city. His attempts to respond to their needs endeared him to the large underclass and prevented those angry with him from taking any overt action against him. Also, much of what he said about church rules and the responsibilities of the well-to-do was true and at least formally acknowledged by even the most dissolute of the nobility or misbehaving church workers.

Only two years after John came to Constantinople, in AD 399, he denounced the "anthropomorphists," a theological opinion popular among some of the desert monks in Egypt that attributed human emotions and other human attributes to God. Theophilus, the pope of Alexandria, was furious not because he agreed with these monks but because he interpreted John's actions as a plot to extend the power and influence of Constantinople in church matters at the expense of his own. Then, in AD 401, four monks known as the "Tall Brothers" came to Constantinople from Egypt seeking refuge from Theophilus. The Tall Brothers, with 50 other monks, had been the intellectual leaders of the anthropomorphist monks and had been accused of "Origenism" by Theophilus, i.e., of being too fond of allegorical interpretation of biblical texts and other questionable teachings of the great scholar who had died nearly 150 years before and which their fellow peasant monks were too unsophisticated to understand. The Tall Brothers and their followers had been driven from one of the great monastic centers of Egypt by Theophilus who had intended them to either be killed or simply disappear into the desert.

When they arrived in Constantinople, the Brothers filed a formal protest against Theophilus with John. They said that the real reason that the pope of Alexandria was so angry with them was that they had been outspoken opponents of his fundraising methods and their sheltering of others with whom Theophilus was already angry. John wrote to Theophilus, hoping to mediate a reconciliation between the Brothers and the pope of Alexandria.

In the meantime, John asked his friend the wealthy deaconess Olympia to shelter the Tall Brothers and their followers. As the Tall Brothers had been excommunicated by Theophilus, John honored that and refused to give them communion until the dispute had been settled. But the story quickly circulated among John's enemies that John had sheltered the Tall Brothers on church property and had given them communion in defiance of Theophilus.

Theophilus insisted that John had no authority in what was essential a local matter between himself and the monks of Egypt. The Brothers appealed to the Emperor Arcadius and the Empress Eudoxia who then appointed John to adjudicate the matter. Epiphanios of Cypress, a well-known scholar and bishop as well as a friend of Theophilus, went to Constantinople to intimidate John but went back to Cyprus chagrined as he found that the majority of the people supported John and might well riot against Epiphanios and his efforts to malign their popular pastor.

While he was waiting for Theophilus to respond to his letters, John went on a pastoral tour throughout the countryside east of Constantinople and got involved in an accusation that the archbishop of Ephesus was guilty of "simony" (selling church positions or sacraments). John investigated and presided at a church trial of the archbishop of Ephesus. John found the man guilty, deposed him, and appointed a new archbishop. He deposed other bishops who had been implicated in the scandal and ordained replacements for them as well. Although John seems to have been correct in his judgement and his actions were in the right morally, technically the archbishop of Constantinople had no jurisdiction to get involved in the affairs of the church in Ephesus. John's actions made Theophilus' accusations seem reasonable: John was acting in a high-handed manner, inserting himself in local disputes he had no business interfering with, and attempting to extend the power of Constantinople at everyone else's expense.

When John returned to Constantinople, John preached a sermon in defense of a widow whose small property had been seized by the empress. The possibilities for biblical allusion were too rich to be resisted: John reportedly compared the empress to Jezebel, King Ahab's wife, who had appropriated the vineyard of Naboth by having the man stoned to death on a false charge (I Kings 21:5–16). John also preached a sermon against the vanity of women which most people understood to be a thinly veiled criticism of the Empress Eudoxia. Whether John intended it that way or not, Eudoxia was stung by the common interpretation of John's words. She allied herself with Theophilus and other enemies of John.

"The Oak," a suburb of Constantinople in which resided a substantial number of people from Egypt, was the site of a synod called in AD 403 to deal with John's supposed interference in local Egyptian church affairs. The Synod of the Oak, as it is called, resulted in Theophilus—who had come from Alexandria to Constantinople—making peace with the Tall Brothers but John refused to attend because he refused to dignify most of the trumped-up charges against him with a response. (Among the 27 charges against him were accusations that he had opponents of the Tall Brothers thrown into jail, that he had called the much-esteemed scholar Epiphanios of Cyprus a crazy man, that he had sold church property that was not his to sell and pocketed the money, and that he ate alone so that he could indulge in gluttony without witnesses.) As a result, John was deposed and sentenced to exile. There were riots in Constantinople when people heard this news. The empress had a miscarriage and there was an earthquake as well. Eudoxia interpreted all these as signs of God's displeasure with the synod's decision to depose John and convinced her husband to recall and reinstate the popular archbishop.

John continued his policy of denouncing the oppression of the poor by the powerful. Also, a city official erected a statue of Eudoxia near the Hagia Sophia cathedral and dedicated it on a Sunday morning with a show of actors and dancers. The noise of the music and the applause of the audience was so loud that it could be heard inside the cathedral during the Eucharist. John was incensed. He lost his temper and complained in public that the statue and its dedication were an insult to the church.

Eudoxia took this as a personal insult and began planning another synod to depose John. John heard about these plans and soon, on the feast of St. John the Baptist, preached that now "another Herodias is enraged, again she dances, again she seeks to have [another] John's head on a platter!" Everyone understood who he has talking about and this time his words of criticism were taken as treason. He was exiled again only to be recalled, again.

The groups of his supporters and the groups of those who opposed him engaged in an uneasy truce. Bishops gathered, invited by the emperor and empress, to attend another synod to decide whether to endorse or reject the decision of the Synod of the Oak. Lobbyists from both John's supporters and his detractors assailed the bishops with petitions and gifts. John's sermons continued to draw crowds. The emperor and the empress waivered but finally decided to join John's opponents. The gathered bishops told John that he was not to preside at the upcoming celebration of Pascha in the cathedral and the emperor ordered that he be placed under house arrest, kept inside his residence and away from the church. News spread through the capital. Tensions ran high. Although John was forbidden to attend the cathedral or celebrate the services in public, the clergy that supported John did celebrate Pascha in the cathedral. In the midst of the baptisms of scores of adult catechumens, imperial soldiers burst into the baptistery and broke up the celebration with extreme brutality and sacrilege. Clergy were beaten with bats. Half-dressed women fled into the streets. (At this time, adults were baptized in the nude and the women had apparently either already undressed or were in the process of undressing when the soldiers interrupted.) The baptismal water turned red with the blood of the injured.

Barred from the churches of the city, John's supporters regrouped the next morning in the public baths to finish the celebration of the paschal baptisms. The cathedral stood empty, even though the imperial family was scheduled to attend a service there later in the day. Again soldiers were sent to break up the service in the baths and people again re-grouped in a horse-racing course northwest of Constantinople.

John remained under house arrest for two months and his supporters were forbidden to use the churches of the city for those two months as well. Finally the emperor grew tired of the disturbances and tension; he ordered John to leave the city, thinking the unrest would settle down if John were no longer present. The emperor was wrong.

In the resulting riots, the cathedral of Hagia Sophia was burned to the ground. John's supporters continued to meet in private homes and boycott the services in the city churches. John himself died in exile in AD 407 but many of his supporters—both clergy and layfolk—kept holding their own celebrations of the Eucharist in protest of the emperor and the new archbishop he appointed. These protest services continued until John's relics were brought back in honor to Constantinople in AD 438 by Theodosius II, the son of Arcadius and Eudoxia.

The Fall of Rome

In AD 410, shortly after John's death, the city of "Old" Rome—the original capital of the empire on the Tiber—fell to the invading barbarians led by Alaric. This catastrophe was unbelievable. Most people had thought that Rome would never fall, no matter how many of the barbarians overran other portions of the empire in Western Europe. Many traditional Romans thought the city was being punished for having abandoned the old gods for Christianity while Christians in the western empire thought the fall of Rome meant the end of the world was about to happen.

The remnants of the empire in the west collapsed as well. The various tribes of barbarians—the Vandals in North Africa, the Ostrogoths in Italy, the Visigoths in Toulose and Spain, the Franks in Gaul—became the dominant political powers for the next several centuries. Only the Franks were eventually Orthodox as the other tribes all embraced Arian or semi-Arian versions of Christianity even as they tried to adopt aspects of Roman culture; in fact, Clovis (AD 481–511) was hailed as a "new Constantine" because he accepted Orthodox baptism, rather than from an Arian, and united the Franks into a cohesive kingdom.

The fall of Old Rome left the popes of Rome as the only vestige of imperial presence in the city or the West, more generally. Its prominence—due both to its having been the capital and to the presence of both the apostles Peter and Paul as the founders of the Christian community there, making it one of the few directly "Apostolic" churches in the West—resulted in the popes taking on more and more responsibility for the civil welfare of the populace. The fall of Old Rome also led to a plummet in the literacy rates among people in the West; knowing Greek as well as Latin became exceedingly rare which resulted in increasing estrangement from the theological and political elites in Constantinople.

One reason the famous North African bishop, Augustine of Hippo, wrote his book known as *The City of God* was to explain how the fall of Old Rome was not the fault of the Christians. Augustine did have several suggestions for how Christians should think about the fall of Rome and the end of the world. The Apostle Paul remarked in a cryptic fashion: "For the mystery of lawlessness is already at work; only he who now restrains it will do so until he is out of the way" (II Thess. 2:7). The "mystery of lawlessness" was the Antichrist who was thought to be the personification of chaos and destruction. Who was it that restrains the Antichrist? Evidently St. Paul thought his audience knew that. Later readers had to surmise. Augustine admitted at first that he had no idea who or what St. Paul was talking about but then goes on to suggest that it was the imperial power of Rome that was meant (*City of God* 20.19).

It was the power of Rome, even in her pagan days, which kept anarchy and destruction at bay. By making universal peace a reality, Rome made the experience of beauty—in all its meanings—possible and beauty was considered one of the attributes of the Divine. The peace of the Roman empire also made the preaching of the Gospel possible. Although the fall of Old Rome in the west allowed the barbarians to inflict chaos on the territory they overran, the empire itself continued in the new capital of Constantinople, and therefore the empire continued to keep the Antichrist at bay. There would be many Antichrists, suggested both Augustine and John Chrysostom; each would be worse than the others until the final Antichrist who arrived immediately before the Second Coming of Christ. The barbarians in the West might be harbingers of the Antichrist but they were not that last, worst Antichrist.[1]

Imperial officials were able to hold Ravenna, on the northeast coast of Italy, as an imperial outpost until AD 476; Justinian was able to retake it in AD 540 during his wars expansion during which he reincorporated most of Western Europe into a single empire again but his efforts were for naught. The western empire unraveled again after his death. Although the people of Constantinople continued to think of themselves and call themselves "Romans," they had less and less to do with the city on the Tiber.

Nestorius and Cyril of Alexandria

After John went into exile, the Emperor Arcadius appointed a new archbishop of Constantinople that was ignored and boycotted by most of the city. Arcadius died in AD 408 and was succeeded by his seven-year-old son Theodosius II although it was his older sister Pulcheria who was the real ruler.

None of the various archbishops who were appointed by either Arcadius or Theodosius were able to win over the support of the people, even if they were themselves respected for their charity or piety. Finally, Theodosius decided to appoint an outsider altogether. He thought that someone who had no local ties would be able to unite both John's supporters and his detractors. A well-educated Syrian monk known for his sermons, Nestorius was enthroned as archbishop of Constantinople in April, AD 428. (Theodosius also thought that since Nestorius came from near Antioch, it would help convince John's supporters to accept him, since John himself had come to Constantinople from Antioch.)

Nestorius was friends with well-known Antiochene teachers of biblical studies and interpretation and was closely associated with the Syrian tradition of teacher-saints, especially Diodore of Tarsus and Theodore of Mopsuestia. (Theodore had the same status and venerability in Syria as Athanasius of Alexandria but was less known internationally.) It is important to remember that the Antiochene school of theology and interpretation tried to avoid philosophical speculation and allegory and were generally opposed to the Alexandrian style of doing theology which favored such abstraction.

Nestorius set out to reform church life in the capital. He ordered monks living on their own in the city to return to their monasteries. He enforced the laws against heretics and had the last Arian chapel in the city demolished.

Nestorius did himself no favors by insulting the emperor's sister Pulcheria since she was still the real ruler, even as her brother grew older. He refused to give her communion in the altar area as was customary for the imperial family: he doubted her virginity and said that if she were truly a virgin then she should be living in a monastery rather than the imperial palace! He removed an altar covering that Pulcheria had donated, made of one her costly, imperial robes; he said that "a virgin's robe would be a fitting gift for the Virgin's Son but a matron's dress is not worthy to be placed in the Holy of Holies."

A contingent of Egyptian monks resident in Constantinople had an argument with Nestorius' father confessor soon after the new archbishop arrived. The subject of the argument was whether the Virgin Mary should be called *Theotokos* ("birth-giver of God" or "Mother of God" are both acceptable translations) or *Anthropotokos* ("birth-giver of a man"). This title *Theotokos* for the Virgin was incredibly popular and had been used since before the council of Nicea in AD 325. The monks were adamant that Mary deserved the title *Theotokos* and demanded that Nestorius himself make a statement to repudiate his father confessor and proclaim Mary as *Theotokos*.

Nestorius was shocked at the controversy. The discussion of Mary as *Theotokos* vs. *Anthropotokos* had never aroused much passion back home in Antioch. "Strictly speaking," he said, "both are inaccurate because both titles can be misunderstood." He suggested *Christotokos* ("mother of Christ") as an alternative that would be acceptable to both sides of the debate.

"If Mary is not, strictly speaking, the *Theotokos*, then her Son is not, strictly speaking, *Theos*!" the monks retorted. The international monastic network spread the news of Nestorius' objection to this traditional title far and wide. The monks looked to Cyril, the pope of Alexandria, as the father of all monks throughout the world, for defense and guidance. Both Cyril and the church of Alexandria were powerful and wealthy. The Alexandrian agents in Constantinople were also happy to report this newest outrage of an archbishop of Constantinople against Alexandrian tradition to Cyril back home.

Cyril himself had been born in AD 378, the nephew of Theophilus; Cyril became pope of Alexandria when Theophilus died in AD 412. Prior to that, Cyril had studied theology and had been ordained reader when he was 25 years old by his uncle in AD 403. He was in Constantinople with his uncle for the Synod of the Oak which condemned John Chrysostom in AD 407. When Theophilus died, Cyril had been made pope unusually quickly—within a week!—and there were riots in support of the "opposition candidate" Timothy, who as the Archdeacon of Alexandria was responsible for managing the wealth of the Alexandrian church. (In many places, it was customary for the archdeacon of that place to succeed the bishop or archbishop.)

Nestorius is reported to have said that Cyril was stuffy and difficult to read; given Nestorius' own reputation for abstract and difficult-to-read texts, this is a case of the "pot calling the kettle black." Cyril was also a rigid and proud man who insisted on enforcing the imperial laws suppressing non–Orthodox Christian religious practice (including Jews and pagans, as well as the Arian or semi-Arian Christians). However, in this period Alexandria was considered the "capital" of the Jewish world and had a large Jewish population. Cyril provoked frequent clashes between the Orthodox and the Jewish or other non–Orthodox residents of the city; he even attempted to drive the Jewish residents from the city once, in defiance of imperial law. He often used the desert monks as storm troopers or "brown-shirts," his personal police force.

Orestes, the imperial governor of Egypt, often clashed with Cyril in his attempts to keep the peace in Alexandria. His refusal to accede to Cyril's wishes made him a target of the monks' violence. The populace of the city often backed Orestes in his efforts to resist Cyril and came to the prefect's aid on at least one occasion when his own bodyguard deserted him in the face of an attack by the monks. Hypatia, a well-known and influential mathematician and philosopher in Alexandria, also supported Orestes. (Hypatia taught many students from the wealthy and important families throughout the empire and many of her students later became leaders of the imperial government or the Church.) The mob, inflamed by the monks, famously murdered her in the cathedral during Lent and mutilated her body in retaliation for her opposition to Cyril as well.

In Constantinople, Nestorius organized a series of theology lectures in the cathedral of Hagia Sophia. He invited his father confessor to give the first lecture, which was titled "On the Error of Calling Mary *Theotokos*." In the cathedral, the father confessor said, "Let no man call Mary *Theotokos* for she was only a woman and it is impossible for God to be born of a woman." The next Sunday, which was the Sunday before Christmas, Maximian—a bishop who was known to still be a supporter of John Chrysostom (whose relics would not be brought back to the capital in honor for another decade) and antagonistic toward the emperor and the archbishops he had appointed, including Nestorius—preached in the cathedral that Mary most certainly ought to be honored with the title *Theotokos*. The congregation erupted in cheers and applause. Nestorius, who was there, stood up and gave an impromptu response. He repeated his opinion that *Theotokos* was an inappropriate title. People walked out on him.

The next year, AD 429, Nestorius preached a series of sermons against the use of the title *Theotokos* but these sermons were as much against all his enemies and detractors as about Mary's role in salvation. The monks in Constantinople were outraged. They said that this attitude made Jesus no more than a prophet rather than *homoousias* with the Father. Monks demonstrated in the cathedral during Nestorius' sermons; others carried placards around the city streets accusing Nestorius of heresy. Nestorius had the monks arrested and beaten but public support for the monks only increased. The emperor's sister Pulcheria also supported the monks and none of the nobility would publicly contradict her.

At Pascha, Cyril in Alexandria wrote a letter to the monks of Egypt warning them against Nestorius and his teaching.

> The Word of God, therefore, took descent of Abraham's line and participated in flesh and blood, making his own the body from a woman, so that through the union he might be understood as God who has also become a man like us. Most assuredly, the Emmanuel is from two realities, that is of Godhead and manhood. Indeed, the one Lord Jesus Christ who is the one true Son, is at once God and man. He is not God in the way that others are 'by grace'; rather, he is true God revealed for our sake in human form [*Letter to the Monks of Egypt* 18].

Of course, this letter was circulated in the monastic circles of Constantinople as well. Nestorius opened a commission to review Cyril's behavior and wrote his own letter to the monks, asking, "Why is the pope of Alexandria interfering in the business of the archbishop of Constantinople?" He also sent copies of his sermons to Celestine, the pope of Rome, expecting the pope of Old Rome to support the archbishop of New Rome.

The popes of Rome had never accepted the proclamation that Constantinople, the New Rome, should rank higher than Alexandria and Antioch in the world hierarchy. Celestine was also a friend of Cyril and wrote to Cyril, as the second ranking prelate in the empire, asking him for more information about what was going on. Celestine set up a commission—including the archdeacon Leo, later to be Pope St. Leo the Great, and the famous monk John Cassian—to investigate Nestorius' teaching.

Cyril responded to Nestorius by writing his first letter directly to Nestorius himself. He claimed that Nestorius had started the dispute and that he was only doing what the pope of Rome had asked him to do. Cyril sent his own selections of Nestorius' sermons to Celestine in Rome. A guest bishop, invited by Nestorius the next year to preach in the cathedral, said that "whoever dares to call Mary *Theotokos* is anathema!" Nestorius celebrated the Eucharist together with the visiting bishop and received communion together with him. Cyril wrote a second letter to Nestorius and warned the archbishop of the theological dangers of refusing to call Mary *Theotokos*; he also wrote a series of tracts known as *Five Books Against Nestorius*.

Nestorius responded by deposing the leading monastic agitators in Constantinople. The deposed monks appealed to the emperor for an ecumenical council to resolve the issue. Nestorius wrote a sarcastic letter back to Cyril hinting that the emperor was on Nestorius' side. Cyril wrote to both Theodosius and Pulcheria, explaining how important a proper understanding of Christ and his mother were to a proper understanding of the Eucharist as well. The emperor resented what he saw as Cyril's attempt to tell him what to do.

Nestorius asked Theodosius to appoint "select, educated bishops" to discuss the matter in Constantinople. Pulcheria, who supported the monks in opposition to her brother Theodosius, convinced him that such a meeting would be better held in Ephesus, however; she said there were better hotels in Ephesus and more food since it was located closer to the farms. But it was also the site of a major shrine church dedicated to Mary as *Theotokos*.

The clergy of Constantinople were themselves demanding that Nestorius be deposed. It was about now that the commission in Rome announced their decision in the basilica of St. Mary Major in Rome, the most important Marian church in the old capital. The commission found that Nestorius' teaching was at odds with Nicene orthodoxy. Pope Celestine issued a demand that Nestorius recant and profess the orthodox faith as held in Rome and Alexandria. He appointed Cyril, the pope of Alexandria, as his executive representative in the east to deal with Nestorius. If Nestorius did not repent, then Cyril was to appoint a new archbishop—ignoring the usual role of the emperor in naming the archbishop of the new capital!

Cyril called a council in Alexandria to announce and confirm the Roman proclamation. Theodosius furiously resented Old Rome's interference in New Rome's business and ordered his own council to meet. Following the council in Egypt, Cyril sent Nestorius a third letter.

> We would not be so concerned if you were only injuring yourself by thinking and teaching the things you do, but you have scandalized the entire Church and have cast among the people the yeast of a strange and alien heresy, and not only among the people [at Constantinople] but everywhere the books of your sermons have been circulated. So how could we justify our silence any longer? [*Third Letter to Nestorius* 1].

> In the crucified body he impassibly appropriated the suffering of his own flesh and 'by the grace of God he tasted death on behalf of all' (Hebrews 2:9). He surrendered his own body to death even though by nature he is life and is himself the Resurrection (John 11:25). He trampled upon death with unspeakable power so that he might, in his own flesh, become the 'first fruits of those who have fallen asleep' (I Cor. 15:20), and might lead the way for human nature to return to incorruptibility [*Third Letter to Nestorius* 6].

> Since the holy virgin gave birth in the flesh to God hypostatically united to flesh, for this reason she is *Theotokos*.... He had no natural need, or external necessity, of a temporal birth in these last times of this age, but he did this so that he might bless the very beginning of our own coming into being, and that since a woman had given birth to him as united to the flesh, from that point onwards the curse upon our whole race that drives our earthly bodies to death should cease. He did it to annul that sentence: 'In sorrow you shall bring forth children' (Genesis 3:16), and also to demonstrate the truth of the prophet's words: 'Death swallowed us up in its power, but God wiped every tear from every face' (Isaiah 25:8) [*Third Letter to Nestorius* 11].

Cyril concluded the letter with 12 statements of doctrine that are known as "The Twelve Anathemas." Unaware that Theodosius was planning to call a council, Cyril threatened Nestorius with deposition and excommunication if he did not agree with these 12 statements.

The Twelve Anathemas

What was it that Nestorius was teaching that Cyril found so objectionable? One important aspect of the dispute was that what people heard in Nestorius' words—i.e., the implications—was just as important as the explicit statements he actually made.

Diodore of Tarsus had been one of the leading theologians in Antioch. He had taught John Chrysostom. He had supported the Nicene *homoousias* and had been exiled by the Emperor Valens; during his exile he met the great Basil and Basil made him bishop of Tarsus at the same time that he made his friend Gregory Nazianzus the bishop of Sasima. As bishop of Tarsus, Diodore continued to support the Nicene theologians while developing his own theological system.

Diodore evidently suggested that in Christ there were two sons of God: one was divine, *homoousias* with the Father, but the other was a human being who was juxtaposed to the divine Son. In this way Mary was mother of the human being (*Anthropotokos*) and mother of Christ (*Christotokos*) but not the mother of the divine Son.

Nestorius seems to have continued to elaborate this idea of "the two sons." He said that there was a conjunction, indwelling, juxtaposition of the two—the Divine and the human—in Christ. The divine Son appropriated the human son, the Divine was in "habitual possession" of the human. These descriptions were always modified by the words "perfect," or "exact" and "continuous"; this was an "association" of the two that was rooted in the grace and good pleasure of the Father.

What Nestorius' enemies heard implicit in his words was that this made Jesus no more than a prophet-deluxe. Nestorius stressed that the union of Divine and human in Christ was not *hypostatic*, that it was not "personal." It was a moral union, based on the will and love of both the human and the Divine sons for each other. Nestorius insisted that there was no room for paradox, intuition, imagination, poetry, or mysticism when describing this union.

Nestorius used the image of a *prosopon*, the mask an actor wore on the stage to indicate what role he was playing in a show,[2] to describe the juxtaposition of human and Divine in Christ. He famously used the example of a glass filled with oil and water in which the oil and water were contained in one vessel but clearly remained two distinct substances that did not mix together; he said that this vessel was a *prosopon*, a mask, so that when people looked at Christ they saw only one face rather than both the Divine and human.

When Nestorius preached, he did not say that Jesus raised his friend Lazarus from the dead; rather, he insisted that it was the Divine son who raised the friend of the human son. He taught that in every episode of Christ's life that it was possible to identify what the Divine son did as opposed to what the human son did. He was emphatic that it was the human, not the Divine, son who died on the cross.

On the other hand, Cyril was helping to forge the modern notion of "person" as a dynamic spiritual subjectivity and consciousness. He agreed with Gregory Nazianzus that the proper understanding of Christ and the proper understanding of salvation were inextricably linked: "What was not assumed was not saved." Gregory had also said that there was only one Son, not two, and that this one Son had assumed human nature, becoming comprehensible and capable of suffering in his humanity while remaining incomprehensible and incapable of suffering in his divinity. Gregory wrote that

> if anyone does not believe that Holy Mary is *Theotokos*, he is severed from the Godhead. If anyone should assert that [the divine Son] only passed through the Virgin as through a channel ... he is equally godless. If anyone should assert that the manhood was formed and was afterwards clothed with the Godhead, then he too is to be condemned.... If anyone introduces the notion of two sons, one of God the Father, the other of the mother, and discredits the unity and identity, may he lose his part in the adoption promised to those who believe aright [*Letter* 101.4–5].

Cyril taught that Christ was present in the Eucharist the same way as he had been born of Mary, his mother: *mia physis tou theou logou sesarkomene*, "one nature of God the Word made flesh." He described this as a "hypostatic union," rooted in the personal coming together of Divine and human. There was one Divine *hypostasis* (person), the Son of the Father, who took human nature into himself and was born of Mary. This one *hypostasis* with two *ousias* was contrasted with the Trinity in which there were three *hypostasis* and only one *ousia*.

Because of this hypostatic (personal) union, it was possible for Cyril to indulge his love of paradox, poetry, intuition, and mystical or prayerful experience. He spoke of "the swaddling bands of God" (to achieve the same rhetorical effect, a modern preacher might refer to "the diapers of God"). He preached that Christ "suffered impassibly" on the cross, i.e., that he suffered without suffering which was a total paradox rooted in the impossibility of the Divine to suffer yet the impossibility that humanity could not avoid suffering in such circumstances. Cyril was emphatic that it was God the Word himself who died on the cross. It was the possibility to use such language to describe human and Divine experience in terms of each other that Cyril called "the communication of idioms." As far as Nestorius was concerned, the "communication of idioms" was only sloppy thinking.

Cyril was fond of citing both John 1:14 ("the Word was made flesh") and Philippians 2:6–11 (the description of the *kenosis*, the humiliation of the Word-made-flesh). Cyril taught that this union was a "wonderful transformation of human nature" and said the Transfiguration of Christ revealed his flesh as life-giving, replete with divine glory and majesty, worthy of adoration.

Cyril wrote that it is this flesh of Christ which is divine and life-giving that is shared in a material fashion in the Eucharist. The Eucharist communicates this blessing of transformation to material creatures. The bread and wine, commonly known as "the Gifts," are humble matter that becomes divine and adorable. Cyril taught that Christ acted as High Priest not for himself but for us and that this was only possible because he was one person who was simultaneously both Divine and human.

While Nestorius used the metaphor of oil and water to describe the juxtaposition of Divine and human in Christ, Cyril used the metaphor of wine and water to illustrate how both substances take on the appearance of each other and are inseparable and impossible to perceive distinctly apart from each other after they have been poured together. As far as Cyril was concerned, it was impossible to not call Mary *Theotokos* because the person born of her was simultaneously totally and completely both Divine and human.

He pointed out that the Ark of the Covenant had been made of both wood and gold, that a lily was both a flower and a fragrance, that a burning stick—in that instant when the blaze first catches—was both wood and fire, that burning charcoal (such as that touched to the lips of the prophet Isaiah by the seraph) was both coal and fire. The two realities are seen as the same thing. They are united in a natural way, engaging and acting together while also engaging or acting on each other. In each case, there is mutual engagement leading to radical transformation.

Cyril was able to summarize all this in the Twelve Anathemas he demanded Nestorius accept:

"If anyone will not confess that Emmanuel is truly God the Word and hence the Holy Virgin is *Theotokos*, (for she gave birth in the flesh to the Word of God made flesh), let him be anathema!"

"If anyone shall not confess that the Word of God the Father is personally (hypostatically) united to flesh so as to be one Christ with his own flesh, that is both God and man at the same time, let him be anathema!"

"If anyone says that Jesus as a man was only energized by the Word of God and that the glory of the Only-begotten is ... not properly his, let him be anathema!"

"Whosoever shall say that it is not the divine Word himself, when he was made flesh and had become man as we are … who is our great High Priest … let him be anathema!"

"If anyone does not confess that the Lord's flesh is life-giving … but shall pretend that he has served as only a dwelling place for the Divine … let him be anathema!"

"If anyone shall not recognize that the Word of God suffered in the flesh, was cruci-fied in the flesh, and tasted death in the flesh, becoming the first-born from the dead, although as God he is life and life-giving, let him be anathema!"

Part of Nestorius' difficulty was that he wanted to keep language from evolving and developing. Looking at his writings from our modern perspec-tive, we can see that he used terms and vocabulary as they had been used in prior generations, not as they were coming to be used in contemporary soci-ety. Nestorius understood *ousia* to mean essence or nature; he understood *physis* to mean the concrete reality of a thing, a synonym with *hypostasis*; he used *prosopon* to mean a thing's observable character or characteristics. As far as he was concerned, every *ousia* had to be present in its own *hypostasis*. He heard the words "hypostatic union" and imagined a union of Divine and human that was rooted in materiality of some kind; both he and Cyril abhorred the idea that there was any materiality in God himself.

Nestorius was a victim of his own arrogance and rigidity, his own inabil-ity to adapt to new language as much as he was a victim of Cyril's political machinations.

The Council at Ephesus

It was on Saturday, December 6, AD 430 that messengers from Alexandria arrived in Hagia Sophia during the Eucharist and confronted Nestorius and handed him Cyril's third letter as he sat on his archiepiscopal throne. He said that he would meet with them the next day and continued the celebration of the Eucharist. The next day, he refused to meet with the messengers.

The Syrian theologians back in Antioch, where Nestorius had come from, had originally urged him to comply with the decision of the pope of Rome and his commission but they were outraged by Cyril's third letter and the Twelve Anathemas.

The following Saturday Nestorius again celebrated the Eucharist in the cathedral and preached, "Egypt is the eternal enemy of Constantinople and Antioch!" He said Cyril was too proud and had too many political ambitions. The congregation applauded as he said that he would accept the use of the title *Theotokos* even though he still thought that *Christotokos* was more appropriate. He invited Cyril to come to Constantinople. When the monks heard that, they were sure that the emperor must have promised to arrest the pope of Alexandria. Why else would Nestorius invite his archenemy to the capital?

The imperial invitations to the emperor's council to be held in Ephesus were sent out that spring (AD 431). The council was scheduled to begin on Pentecost (June 7 that year). Count Candidianus of the palace guard was given a cohort of soldiers to escort Nestorius to Ephesus and to keep order during the council. Candidianus had the imperial letter which was necessary to read to officially open the council, which directed the bishops to settle the question concerning Mary's title *Theotokos* while also directing the soldiers to maintain the peace.

The emperor had invited each bishop to bring their "most eminent assistant bishops" to the council with them. This invitation was interpreted in various ways by various bishops. Nestorius brought 16 bishops who supported him. The archbishop of Palestine also brought 16 but these were aligned with Cyril. Memnon of Ephesus brought 52 and Cyril himself brought another 50 (half of all the bishops in Egypt). There was only one bishop from North Africa because the barbarian invasions had cut North Africa off from the empire.

The archbishop of Antioch was coming with 43 bishops, all of whom were supporters of Nestorius, but the Antiochenes were late setting out for the council. In addition, what should have been a month-long trip took much longer. Not only were the Antiochenes late to start travelling, they encountered bad weather and floods. Many of the bishops in the Antiochene entourage were elderly; these men traveled slowly and several became ill or died along the way.

When Nestorius arrived in Ephesus, the bishops already there refused to greet him and the churches remained closed to him. When Cyril arrived, he was greeted as an honored guest. Ephesus in June was very hot and the hotels were cramped. Food and water were in short supply, despite what Pulcheria had anticipated. Everyone was under a great deal of stress and strain.

Candidianus ordered all the monks and visiting laymen to leave Ephesus. While waiting for the Antiochenes to arrive, both Cyril and Nestorius began to lobby the undecided bishops. But Nestorius' often sarcastic remarks were frequently misunderstood, driving away the sympathy that some had originally felt for him and his position.

The local Ephesians who felt strongly about the title *Theotokos* daubed paint on the hotels where the undecided bishops were staying and many of them were sure they were being marked for violence. The scared ones announced their support for Cyril.

Cyril suspected the Antiochenes of being deliberately late. He decided that the council had to open as many of the bishops already in Ephesus were themselves sick or dying as well as suffering from the shortages of food and water. But Candidianus, who was thought to be a friend of Nestorius, had to read the imperial letter to open the meeting. How could Cyril manage that?

On June 21, bishops coming from further away than Antioch arrived in Ephesus. A letter from the Antiochenes also arrived, claiming that they were at least another week away. Mid-morning, Cyril sent an announcement to all the bishops that they should come to the opening session of the council the next day. He also sent an "arraignment" notice to Nestorius to appear the next day, as if to be put on trial.

Therefore, the bishops gathered on June 22. Candidianus entered the assembly, protesting its illegality.

"How? Why is it illegal?" Cyril wanted to know.

Candidianus said, "Because it says so right here!"

"It says so? Right where?" Cyril asked. "What does it say?"

"Right here! In this letter! This is what it says!" Candidianus announced. He read the imperial letter to prove his point and realized immediately what Cyril had tricked him into doing.

By that evening the bishops had affirmed Cyril's second and third letters to Nestorius as the proper teaching, including the Twelve Anathemas. Nestorius was condemned and deposed. Candidianus was furious and sealed the city, forbidding any one to leave. He tried to stop any letters being sent.

When the Antiochenes arrived a few days later, they were furious at having been left out of the discussion. They held their own council and deposed Cyril.

On June 26, news of Cyril's council arrived in Constantinople and general rejoicing broke out that the title *Theotokos* had been vindicated. When the representatives of the Roman commission arrived on July 11, they confirmed that Cyril's council had been legitimate.

Theodosius was so put out at the whole business that in August he decided to depose both Cyril and Nestorius but his sister persuaded him to listen to both arguments—those for and those against the use of the title *Theotokos*—himself. So the emperor ordered certain bishops to be brought from Ephesus to Chalcedon, a suburban town near the capital, and in September—after listening to them all—he confirmed the deposition of Nestorius. Maximian, the new archbishop of Constantinople—who was the supporter of John Chrysostom who had preached on the Sunday before Christmas in favor of the title *Theotokos*—was installed by Cyril's representatives.

Back in Ephesus, the Antiochene bishops waiting to be allowed to go home asked Cyril to expand his thoughts behind each of the Twelve Anathemas. They hoped that there might still be room to come to a common understanding. Cyril circulated an "explanation" of the Twelve Anathemas, going into more detail about what each statement was about and tried to avoid his more aggressive language. He underscored that the only begotten Word of the Father was born of the holy virgin according to the flesh but this birth was not the beginning of his existence. This birth was "intended to deliver us from death and corruption when he became like us." It was important that "he who endured the noble cross for our sake and tasted death was no ordinary man conceived of as separate and distinct from the Word of God the Father but it was the Lord of glory himself who suffered in the flesh, according to the scriptures (I Peter 4:1)" (*Explanation of the 12 Anathemas*, ch. 31). Because of this, Cyril points out to the bishops that

> we do not offer the holy life-giving and bloodless sacrifice in the churches as if we believed that what we offered was the body of an ordinary man like us, and the same is true with the precious blood. On the contrary, we receive it as something that has become the very own body and blood of the Word who gives life to all. For ordinary flesh cannot give life.... His body is ... life-giving in so far as it has become the very own [flesh and blood] of the Word [*Explanation of the 12 Anathemas*, ch. 29].

The Antiochene bishops found nothing in Cyril's explanation of the Twelve Anathemas that they could agree with.

At the end of October, Theodosius allowed the bishops to leave Ephesus. Cyril was welcomed back to Alexandria, where he died in AD 444 and was succeeded by Dioscorus (who was neither as politically astute nor as theologically sophisticated as Cyril).

Nestorius was sent back to his monastery near Antioch. Shortly thereafter, nearly 20 bishops who had supported him were deposed. Theodosius ordered in AD 435 that Nestorius was to be exiled in Egypt, held in what was essentially a desert monastic prison overseen by Cyril. This desert monastery was frequently attacked by bandits; Nestorius was injured during one of these attacks. He evidently survived until AD 450 but there is no evidence as to when he finally died or under what circumstances.

Many of Nestorius' supporters—bishops, clergy, layfolk—fled imperial retaliation and went further east and eventually settled in Persia, outside the control of the emperor. These Christians joined with Christians that were already there, whose teaching and practices were descended from the "East Syrian" style of Jewish Christianity and who still used one of the most ancient sets of prayers for the Eucharist (attributed to the apostles Addai and Mari, disciples of the Apostle Thomas). The churches in Persia became known as "the Church of the East" or the "Nestorian church" as they continued to teach and proclaim Nestorius' teachings.

The Church of the East continued to send missionaries further and further east and rapidly grew, stretching from the Mediterranean to India and even China. During the ninth to the 14th centuries, the Church of the East was probably the largest Christian church in terms of geography.

The Ming dynasty seized control of China in AD 1368 and expelled the Christians. The Christians in Persia were nearly all martyred at about the same time. The Church of the East, once so prosperous and successful, was reduced to the areas of northern Mesopotamia (the area known today as northwestern Iraq, northeastern Syria, and southeastern Turkey) and the coast of India.

SUGGESTIONS FOR FURTHER READING

Augustine, *The City of God*. (Trans. H. Bettenson) Pelican Books, 1972; reprinted by Penguin, 1984.

John Chrysostom, *On Virginity, Against Remarriage*. (Trans. Sally Rieger Shore) Edwin Mellen Press, 1983.

John Chrysostom, *On Wealth and Poverty*. (Trans. Catherine P. Roth) St. Vladimir's Seminary Press, 1984.

J.N.D. Kelly, *Golden Mouth: The Story of John Chrysostom—Ascetic, Preacher, Bishop*. Baker Books, 1995.

John Anthony McGuckin, *Saint Cyril of Alexandria and the Christological Controversy*. St. Vladimir's Seminary Press, 2004.

Norman Russell, *Cyril of Alexandria*. Routledge, 2000.

Susan Wessel, *Cyril of Alexandria and the Nestorian Controversy: The Making of a Saint and of a Heretic*. Oxford University Press, 2004.

5

Chalcedon

The council at Ephesus met in June, AD 431. Cyril went back to Egypt in October or November, after Theodosius lifted the order keeping the bishops all inside Ephesus. The Antiochene bishops were livid and felt that they had been cheated of the opportunity to defend Nestorius. They were determined to have Cyril and his teaching, especially the Twelve Anathemas, declared heretical.

The Antiochenes were refused the use of the churches as they traveled back home to Antioch after leaving Ephesus. They held a series of councils en route, continuing to condemn Cyril at each one.

Cyril was concerned to achieve reconciliation between Alexandria and Antioch but he insisted that any reconciliation had to agree on the deposition of Nestorius and the single subject, the one *hypostasis*, of Christ. Maximian, now archbishop of Constantinople, wrote the usual letter to all the bishops and archbishops of the empire, announcing his election. Cyril wrote a very calm letter to congratulate him and carefully restated his position, how he "rejected the mad teaching of Apollinaris." (Apollinaris had been a Syrian, i.e., the region governed by Antioch, who had taught that the Divine had been united to the human in Christ by replacing Jesus' human mind.) Maximian deposed the bishops around Constantinople that had supported Nestorius.

John of Antioch

The emperor himself wrote to John, the archbishop of Antioch, to press him for reconciliation and reunion with Alexandria. He asked John to acknowledge that Maximian was the lawful archbishop of Constantinople (i.e., to admit that Nestorius had been deposed) and to condemn Nestorius' teaching. Theodosius promised John that both Celestine, pope of Old Rome, and Cyril, pope of Alexandria, would welcome the Antiochenes back into

87

communion with open arms. Theodosius was even able to enroll a famous ascetic, Simeon the Stylite, as a diplomat to encourage reconciliation between the Antiochenes, the Alexandrians, and the Romans.

John and the other Antiochene bishops rejected this imperial offer and made their own counter-offer: they would agree to proclaim the Nicene creed and the letter of the great Athanasius against Apollinaris but they rejected Cyril's three letters to Nestorius (including the Twelve Anathemas). In effect, this would undo the work of the AD 431 council in Ephesus.

Cyril himself answered the Antiochene proposal, explaining that Apollinaris' teaching was nothing like his own. (Cyril used the charge of Apollinarianism to tar Nestorius and the Antiochenes used the same charge against Cyril.) Cyril was too clever to agree to renounce his own epistles and negate the whole Ephesian council.

His letter defending himself was such a display of statesman-like diplomacy that he won over the imperial official that Theodosius had appointed to act as mediator between Cyril and John. It also won over the leading Antiochene theologians and bishops. Theodoret of Cyrus, one of the leading supporters of Nestorius, even thought the letter was an indication that Cyril had done an "about face" and was ready to accept the Antiochene position.

The many Antiochenes who decided that Cyril must have come over to their point of view based that opinion on Cyril's use of a phrase that said the Word-made-flesh acted "in two natures after the union." This was distinctly more Antiochene than Cyril's famous phrase, "one nature of God the Word made flesh." John of Antioch decided to send a delegation to Egypt to confer with Cyril in order to come to an agreement that could be openly proclaimed but that avoided an outright repudiation of Nestorius.

The delegation, led by a Bishop Paul, arrived in Alexandria and was told that Cyril could not meet with them as he was sick in bed. Cyril refused to meet with them because he was furious, suspecting the Antiochenes of trying to embarrass him and trick him into reinstating Nestorius or accepting Nestorius' teaching. Paul wrote to Cyril, insisting that John of Antioch had not sent them all the way to Egypt only to be ignored once they arrived. "Everyone is ready to anathematize Nestorius," Paul promised Cyril, but were waiting for the resolution of the current dispute between Cyril and John.

"If everyone wants it done, then you do it," Cyril taunted. "Don't wait for John to do it." So Paul celebrated the Eucharist with Cyril and proclaimed that Nestorius was anathema. Paul even preached in the cathedral on Christmas Day (AD 432), calling Mary *Theotokos* in his sermon. There was wild applause. Paul and the delegation returned to Antioch that spring (AD 433), thinking they had resolved all the issues.

John of Antioch realized that he would never be able to have the Twelve Anathemas condemned or revoked. His back against the wall, he recognized

Maximian as Archbishop of Constantinople and condemned the "blasphemous teachings of Nestorius." Hearing this, Cyril wrote a letter to John that is known both by its opening line ("Let the Heavens Rejoice") and as the *Formula of Reunion* (AD 433). "'Let the heavens rejoice and the earth be glad' for the dividing wall of partition is broken down and sorrow has ended and the cause of all dissension has been removed (Psalm 95:11, Ephesians 2:14). Christ the Savior of us all has granted to his churches the prize of peace."

Cyril quoted back to John a declaration of faith that Paul had brought from Antioch to Alexandria:

> And so we confess [Cyril quotes from the declaration the Antiochene delegation brought] that our Lord Jesus Christ, the only begotten Son of God, is perfect God and perfect Man, of a rational soul and body. He is born of the Father before the ages according to the Godhead, and the same one in these last days for us and for our salvation was born of the virgin Mary according to the manhood. The same one is *homoousias* with the Father according to the Godhead and *homoousias* with us according to the manhood, for there was a union of the two natures, and this is why we confess one Christ, one Son, one Lord. According to this understanding of the unconfused union we confess that the holy virgin is *Theotokos*, because God was made flesh and became man, and from the very moment of conception he united to himself the temple that was taken from her.

This declaration both affirms that Mary is *Theotokos* and denies the idea of the two Sons—one divine, one human—that had been so important to Nestorius and the Antiochene theologians. A capitulation on these points by the Antiochenes meant that Cyril's position had been totally vindicated.

One of the accusations that some Antiochenes had charged Cyril with was that he had taught that the divinity and humanity in Christ had been mingled, that the two natures had been "confused" or "blended" in some way. In the usual Antiochene view, the hypostatic union that Cyril championed had to involve a blending or mixing of humanity and divinity, i.e., a change in the Word himself. The idea that the Word had suffered on the cross was also seen as the Word changing or altering. Cyril spends some time writing to deny that he ever taught such a thing.

> But I am so far from thinking anything of the kind that I consider anyone who thinks there could ever be the shadow of a change (James 1:17) in the divine nature of the Word must be completely mad. For he ever remains what he is and does not change or undergo alteration. Moreover, all of us confess that the divine Word is impassible, even if in his all-wise economy [dispensation] of the mystery he is seen to attribute to himself the sufferings that befall his own flesh.... He bears the suffering of his own flesh in an economic appropriation to himself, as I have said, so that we may believe him to be the Savior of all [*Cyril's Letter to John of Antioch* ch. 9].

Cyril reminded John that he has always followed the opinions of the holy fathers who have gone before them both, "especially our blessed and all-renowned father Athanasius," and attached a copy of Athanasius' letter to Epicte-tus which he claimed some Antiochenes had circulated in a corrupt version.

When John received Cyril's letter, he tried to explain to the other Anti-ochene bishops and theologians that had not gone to Egypt with Paul that Cyril had fulfilled all the demands that had been made for a "further expla-nation" of his teaching. "Please do not say or do anything to upset this fragile peace," he begged his fellow Antiochenes.

A minority of Antiochene clergy saw communion with Cyril—unless it involved a repudiation of the Twelve Anathemas—as a betrayal of their fun-damental theological principles. They kept agitating and demanding more from both Cyril and John. "John is more concerned with politics than the truth," they said. They turned to Theodoret of Cyrus as their spokesman; Theodoret was willing to accept communion with Cyril but refused to anath-ematize Nestorius for another 18 years.

Rumors and gossip spread everywhere about which theological party or bishop had or had not backed down, who sympathized with whom, who denounced what. These rumors did nothing to solve the problems; in fact, they only delayed the resolution.

Maximian, the archbishop of Constantinople, died in AD 434. Proclus, a man who had been a candidate—three times!—before for the position of archbishop, was appointed by the emperor Theodosius. (Proclus was one of the bishops who had provoked Nestorius by preaching that Mary is *Theotokos* in Hagia Sophia.) Proclus was not only a good theologian, he was also a friend of the emperor's sister Pulcheria and master of political maneuvering. He was able to convince John to condemn the idea of the two Sons and much of the rest of the theology that had been customarily taught in Antioch—by Theodore of Mopsuestia, Ibas of Edessa, and even Theodoret of Cyrus—but without actually naming any of these theologians' names. This tactic was greatly resented by the other clergy and layfolk of Antioch.

Cyril jumped at the opportunity to have not just Nestorius but the entire Antiochene-style of doing theology condemned. He fanned the flames of the dispute, attacking the personal reputation of Theodore of Mopsuestia, one of the most highly revered teachers in the Antiochene tradition.

Proclus, as the archbishop of Constantinople, begged Cyril to stop the attacks and to leave well enough alone. Cyril did back off from his aggressive stance; it is possible that Pulcheria also requested (instigated?) his calmer approach. Cyril began to distance himself from his famous *mia physis* state-ment, "one nature of God the Word incarnate" and turned his attention toward local pastoral issues in Egypt, such as a controversy about whether the eucharistic Gifts of bread and wine were permanently transformed into the Body and Blood of Christ or whether the transformation was simply for the duration of the Eucharistic celebration itself.

John of Antioch died in AD 441 and his nephew Domnus was chosen as the new archbishop of Antioch; Domnus was completely under the theological thumb of Theodoret of Cyrus. Cyril himself died in AD 444 and was succeeded by Dioscorus, who had served as his secretary and had attended the Council of Ephesus with him, as well as serving as the archdeacon of Alexandria. Dioscorus was what many scholars now call a "Cyril-ian fundamentalist" who thought any deviation from Cyril's own words was a betrayal of everything Cyril had taught and fought for and was adamantly opposed to backing off in any way from the *mia physis* statement.

Finally, the peacemaker Proclus of Constantinople himself died in AD 446 and was succeeded by Flavian, who up to that point had been responsible for the care of the sacred vessels (chalices, etc.) of the Hagia Sophia cathedral. When Flavian was enthroned as archbishop, he rebuked the imperial Grand Chamberlain who was a eunuch named Chrysaphius for attempting to extort a gift of gold from Flavian for the emperor. Flavian refused to pay the bribe and chastised Chrysaphius, earning the powerful chamberlain's enmity in the coming controversies.

Leo of Rome

In Rome, Pope Leo was overseeing the survival of the old imperial capital. After the capital had moved to Constantinople under Constantine the Great, the imperial officials remaining in Italy were all located in Ravenna; the popes became the administrators of the city simply because there was no one else to do it. The popes began to negotiate treaties involving Rome and the surrounding territories, ransoming prisoners of war and other captives, constructing and maintaining public buildings of all sorts—including, but not limited to, the churches—as well as providing for the poor.

Alaric the Goth besieged Rome three times. He was finally able to seize control and occupy it in AD 410. Many people, including Augustine in North Africa, thought the fall of Rome to the barbarian Gothic invaders was a signal that the world was about to end. Surviving Romans began to flee, reducing the city's population to less than half of what it had been in the first century AD.

Food from North Africa—the source of most food supplies imported into Italy and Europe—became erratic, beginning in AD 429 as barbarians began to seize Roman territories there as well. The city of Carthage fell in AD 439, sending waves of refugees across the Mediterranean to Rome. Food shortages became dire.

Leo had served as archdeacon under Pope Sixtus III; it was common practice for the archdeacon under one pope to be elected to succeed him as the archdeacon was familiar with supervising papal finances and property as well as the social welfare programs supported by the papacy. The archdeacons also had the opportunity to observe the pope's diplomatic efforts up close and gain the experience needed to serve as the only public figure remaining in Rome and able to look after the city's people.

Leo was elected pope in AD 440. He rode out beyond the city to negotiate with Attila the Hun in AD 452 and was able to convince the Huns to spare the city. Leo is credited with single-handedly saving not only Rome but the Italian peninsula and ransoming the captives being held by Attila. In order to do this, Leo raised huge sums and used both his own family money and the strained financial resources of the papacy.

But in AD 455 the Vandals—another barbarian tribe—attacked Rome. They did not burn the city or slaughter the inhabitants—both standard procedures when invaders seized an important city—but they did take all the cash and valuables they could find as well as a huge number of prisoners. Leo had to replace all the silver chalices, patens, and other utensils that had been taken from the churches.

Leo was a popular preacher. He told the wealthy, "Food for someone in need is the cost of purchasing the Kingdom of Heaven" (Homily 9.2). On the anniversary of Alaric's sack of Rome, Leo praised the martyr-saints whose relics were venerated in the churches for protecting the city from a worse fate than it had suffered. On the feast of the Maccabees, he preached (Homily 84b): "If you think persecution has relaxed ... look closely at the hidden center of your heart.... Do not make peace with avarice and despise the rewards of dishonesty. Refuse to make a treaty with pride. Restrain yourself from anger. Every time we die to sins, then sins die in us. We die to the world not by destruction of our senses but by the death of our vices" (referring to Galatians 5:24, 6:14).

Leo died on October 11, AD 461.

(Much later, in the dispute between Rome and Constantinople over the patriarch Photius, Pope Nicholas called Pope Leo "the Great" in a letter to the emperor Michael III in AD 865 and Leo has had the title ever since. Even Photius himself acknowledged Leo's personal piety and his skill as the bishop responsible for the old capital.)

Ephesus II, the Council of Robbers

Shortly after Flavian was made archbishop of the capital, Theodoret of Cyrus and Ibas of Edessa were in Antioch and still smarting over the condemnation that Proclus had convinced John to proclaim more than a decade earlier. Theodoret and Ibas began to argue with the Egyptians—again! In opposition to Theodoret and Ibas, the Archimandrite[1] Eutyches of Constantinople suggested that Cyril's famous *mia physis* slogan be amended from "one nature of God the Word incarnate" to stress that the one nature was a new synthesis of both humanity and divinity, "one nature *out* of two natures" and to use the phrase *mono physis* to stress this unity. The emperor Theodosius and his grand chamberlain Chrysaphius (the godson of Eutyches and a eunuch) also ordered that all Christians believe in the Faith of Nicea, Ephesus, and "Cyril of blessed memory."

Pulcheria was adamantly opposed to Eutyches' doctrinal suggestion because she was engaged in a tug-of-war for power with his godson, Chrysaphius the grand chamberlain; the rope in this tug-of-war was Theodosius himself. She supported Eusebius of Dorylaeum who accused Eutyches of asserting that Christ was not *homoousias* with mankind. Flavian, the archbishop, wanted to avoid a council that would force people into defensive or offensive positions but Eusebius insisted that only a council could resolve the issue. Flavian summoned such a council and Eutyches was condemned. Eutyches appealed to the Emperor Theodosius, claiming the minutes of the council had been falsified. He also appealed over Flavian's head to Leo, the pope of Rome, who—when he was the archdeacon of Rome—had served on the Roman commission that condemned Nestorius. Eutyches felt certain that he would be vindicated.

In response to Eutyches' appeal, Theodosius convoked a council at Ephesus in AD 449 to review the situation. Theodosius invited Dioscorus of Alexandria to preside. A replay of Cyril's denunciation of Nestorius at Ephesus was all but guaranteed.

Leo of Rome, however, wrote in response to Eutyches' appeal, objecting to both Eutyches' theology and to the council to be held at Ephesus. The pope of Rome thought his *Tome (Epistle) to Flavian* should be enough to settle the matter.

The council opened at Ephesus in August, AD 449. Theodosius, Dioscorus, and Chrysaphias all wanted to promote the Egyptian theology and humiliate the Antiochenes. Eutyches was rehabilitated; Flavian and Eusebius were deposed. The bishops at the council asked three times to hear Leo's *Tome* but the secretaries simply filed it away and never read it.

In Rome, Leo denounced the "council of robbers" who hijacked the proceedings in Ephesus; this nickname, the Robbers' Council, has been attached

Syria	Egypt
Antioch	Alexandria
...**in** two natures	...**out of** two natures
Christ IS *homoousias* with us	Christ is NOT *homoousias* with us

to this second meeting in Ephesus ever since. In the aftermath of the Robbers' Council, the entire project to reconcile the theological factions or positions of Antioch and Alexandria had been placed at risk.

On July 28, AD 450, the emperor Theodosius fell from his horse and broke his neck. Pulcheria took the throne. As she needed a general to win the support of the army, she married the popular military leader Marcian and elevated him to the rank of emperor. She announced her intention to maintain her vow of virginity and, in fact, the couple never lived together. Pulcheria supported Rome and the moderate Antiochene theologians; this position automatically rehabilitated the ecclesiastical importance of Constantinople as well. By her order, Chrysaphius was immediately beheaded.

Marcian, the new emperor, wrote to Leo in Rome and suggested a new council be held and that this new council be under Leo's presidency. Anatolius, the new archbishop of Constantinople, had Flavian, who had died from wounds he had received from Dioscorus and Eutyches at the Robber Council, reburied with full honors. (One contemporary wrote that the second funeral more resembled "a triumph ... than a funeral procession.") Leo, from Rome, instructed Anatolius to remove Dioscorus of Alexandria and the other leaders of the Robber Council from the diptychs.[2]

Leo also tried to dissuade Marcian and Pulcheria from calling another council. Leo told them that his word as pope of Rome should be enough to settle the question. But Marcian and Pulcheria were not persuaded. The word of the pope of Rome might be enough to settle disputes in the West but the bishops of the eastern empire would not be satisfied by such a *fiat* from such a distance. The imperial couple called for a council to be held in the coming autumn (AD 451) at Nicea, the location of the first such imperial or "ecumenical" council. But there were military problems near Nicea and after everyone arrived there they were instructed to move to Chalcedon, which was safer (and it was also closer to Constantinople and therefore easier for the imperial officials to keep abreast of what was happening).

Chalcedon

Roman legates (i.e., representatives of Leo, pope of Rome) presided when the council convened in Chalcedon. Five hundred bishops, mostly from the eastern empire, were present. This was the largest gathering of bishops from across the empire in one place. Ever. Dioscorus, the pope of Alexandria, was treated as if he were a bishop on trial: the Syrian bishops who supported the theologians of Antioch said that they had been forced at Ephesus to sign a sheaf of blank papers that had been later filled in by Dioscorus to reflect his own opinions and attitudes and that these had been circulated as the "decisions" of the council. (The Syrian bishops were doing everything they could to distance themselves from being seen as having taken a pro–Alexandrian stance at Ephesus.)

It should be no surprise that the bishops at Chalcedon condemned Eutyches and that both Flavian and Eusebius were rehabilitated.

Dioscorus of Alexandria, however, continued to refuse to endorse the *Tome* of Leo. In response, he was charged with a variety of offenses, including that he was leading a dissolute life, that he had treated Constantinople's leading pro–Roman officials badly, that he had in fact opposed Cyril himself, that he had challenged imperial authority, that he had excommunicated Leo of Rome on his own authority as pope of Alexandria, and that many citizens of Alexandria were opposed to him and his oppressive stance as pope of Alexandria.

Dioscorus was deposed.

However, the theological question still remained: was Christ's humanity *homoousias* with us or not? The council appointed a commission to examine Leo's *Tome* and compare it with a variety of Cyril's statements and writings. The commission was told to pay special attention to phrases that involved the ideas that Christ was known "*in* two natures" or "*out of* two natures." The commissioners spent five days examining the texts of the two popes, Leo of Rome and Cyril of Alexandria.

After their examination, the *Tome* was read aloud to the assembled bishops in Chalcedon.

> In agreement, therefore, with the holy fathers, we all unanimously teach that we should confess that Our Lord Jesus Christ in one and the same Son, the same perfect in Godhead, and the same perfect in manhood, truly God and truly man, the same of a rational soul and body, consubstantial with the Father before the ages as regards his Godhead, and in these last days, the same one begotten from the virgin Mary, the *Theotokos*, as regards his manhood, for our sake and for the sake of our salvation; one and the same Christ, Son, Lord, only begotten, who is made known in two natures, without confusion, without change, without division, without separation; the difference of natures by no means removed because of the union, but the property of each nature being preserved and concurring in one *prosopon* and one *hypostasis*, not parted or divided into two *prosopa*, but one and the same Son, only begotten, divine Word, the Lord Jesus Christ, as the prophets of old and Jesus Christ himself have taught us about him, and the creed of our fathers has handed down.

Records indicate that the bishops burst out in a variety of spontaneous acclamations.

"Peter has spoken through Leo!"

"This is the faith of Cyril!"

"Eternal memory to Cyril!"

"This is the faith of the fathers!"

As far as the bishops at Chalcedon were concerned, Cyril of Alexandria was the test of Orthodoxy and Leo of Rome had passed the test. The

Antiochene insistence that the two natures persisted and endured in Christ was accepted but only if using Cyril's negative adverbs[3] that became a hallmark of Orthodox theology: *a-treptos* (without change), *a-meristos* (without division), *a-synchytos* (without confusion). This is a distinct shift in what had been the Antiochene position on the two natures, however. Leo's brilliance in the *Tome* was using the term "made known in" and the lack of distinction he made between the terms *prosopon* and *hypostasis*, which had previously been considered to be clearly distinct and had therefore implied the necessity of two persons if the presence of two natures was to be acknowledged. By making *prosopon* and *hypostasis* truly synonymous, Leo made it possible to affirm both the one person AND the two natures simultaneously. Although the Egyptian delegation protested, Theodoret of Cyrus, Ibas of Edessa, and Theodore of Mopsuestia—the three Antiochene theologians whose condemnation as supporters of Nestorius had so enraged the people of Antioch and Syria—were upheld as Orthodox.

In addition to the dogmatic issue of Christology (i.e., theology specifically about Christ), the council of Chalcedon turned its attention to several practical matters as well. One was the organization of the Church inside and outside the boundaries of the empire. Clergy unhappy with decisions of their bishop were given the option of appealing to the archbishop of Constantinople. Just as the council of Nicea in AD 325 had called the Emperor Constantine the "bishop" ("overseer") of anyone in the empire that was not a member of the Church, the council of Chalcedon proclaimed that the archbishop of Constantinople was the bishop responsible for all those Christians who lived in "all the barbarian territories," i.e., outside the imperial boundaries (Canon 28). This was seen as a direct slap-in-the-face to the pope of Rome. The Roman legates who were presiding at the council as representatives of Leo resigned in protest just before this canon was passed by the assembly.

Through the rosy-hued glasses of hindsight, Chalcedon is often seen as the culmination and resolution of all the Christological debates of the first 450 years of Church history. At the time, however, it seemed to resolve nothing. In fact, it seemed to fan the flames of dogmatic dispute and pour oil on the fire of animosity.

Aftermath of Chalcedon

Leo, pope of Rome, refused to acknowledge the council which had so wholeheartedly endorsed his *Tome*, primarily because of Canon 28. Mobs in Syria and Egypt alike objected to the council's decisions because each felt betrayed by the council's proclamations. In Palestine, the mob expelled their bishop Juvenal (who had been pro–Dioscorus) because he had signed the

Chalcedonian decrees. Imperial troops were sent to reinstall Juvenal as bishop of Jerusalem but the many monks in the area still refused communion with him. The famous monastic leader Sabbas was one of the very few pro–Chalcedonian monastics; he worked very hard to convince the others to accept both Juvenal and the council's proclamation of the faith.

In Egypt, bishops who had refused to accept the council and who had therefore been deposed, went into hiding with monks in the deserts. Troops were sent. Monks were massacred in order to flush out the bishops.

The crowds in Alexandria still acclaimed the deposed Dioscorus even though Proterius, who supported Chalcedon and its decisions, was installed as the new pope of Alexandria. Pulcheria died in AD 453 and Dioscorus died the next year. Marcian, the emperor, died in AD 457. In the lull, the people of Alexandria elected Timothy, who was extremely popular although nicknamed *Aelurus* ("the cat" or "the weasel" both because of his small size and his catty or weasel-like personality) to succeed Dioscorus as the anti–Chalcedonian pope. Timothy went into hiding to avoid arrest yet was able to instigate a mob to murder Proterius, the pro–Chalcedonian, during the celebration of baptisms at Pascha (much as the mob had attacked Chrysostom's supporters in Constantinople during the baptisms at Pascha). Timothy was exiled in AD 459.

A monk from Rome, a pro–Chalcedonian named Studius, arrived in Constantinople during AD 463 and founded a monastery that became famous for its liturgical practice and doctrinal adherence.

An anti–Chalcedonian mob in Antioch was able to have Peter the Fuller made the anti–Chalcedonian bishop there in AD 468. It was under Peter's authority that a new phrase was added to the popular liturgical hymn, the Trisagion: "Holy God, Holy mighty, Holy immortal: have mercy on us!" The pro–Chalcedonian liturgical teachers interpreted the hymn as an acclamation of the Trinity; the anti–Chalcedonians added the phrase, "who was crucified for us" and interpreted the entire hymn as addressed to Christ.

The new emperor, Basiliscus, recalled all the anti–Chalcedonian bishops from exile in AD 475 amid various efforts to refute the council even as the famous Daniel the Stylite was leading support in favor of Chalcedon in the imperial capital.

It was the emperor Zeno who issued the *Henotikon* ("act of union") in AD 482. In it, he decried the tens-of-thousands who had died in the riots over the Chalcedonian proclamation and condemned both Nestorius and Eutyches and everyone who taught contrary to "the councils" but he did not specify which councils he was referring to. He proclaimed the unity of the Church on the basis of these unspecified councils and because the document was so vague, everyone was willing to sign it. But it did nothing to calm tempers or soothe popular reaction in Egypt, Syria, and Palestine.

The situation remained dangerous. Severus of Antioch, an anti–Chalcedon monk, fled to Constantinople in AD 508 for protection from pro–Chalcedon monks and became a leader of anti–Chalcedonian activity in the capital. He was able to convince the clergy and singers at Hagia Sophia to sing the expanded version of the Trisagion. Riots erupted and statues of the emperor were torn down. The emperor was able to restore order by offering to resign but his popularity and reputation for piety convinced the crowd that his resignation would only make matters worse. Nevertheless, great unrest continued to fill the streets of Constantinople. Severus felt safe to return home in AD 511 and he was made bishop of Antioch. Once installed as bishop, he declared his interpretation of the *Henotikon* as a cancellation of both the *Tome of Leo* and the decisions of Chalcedon.

Back in the capital, the Circus parties came to the fore, especially the Blues and the Greens. The Blues were able to acclaim Justin I as emperor in AD 518. He was pro–Chalcedon and refused to accept communion until the archbishop clearly affirmed the council. He forced most anti–Chalcedon bishops from their cities but left Egypt alone; the political situation there was too volatile and the province too important as the source of most wheat and flour in the empire.

Justin also bestowed the title "ecumenical patriarch" on the archbishop of Constantinople. It was an honorific title, not meant to imply any sort of juridical authority. In fact, the honorific "ecumenical" was used to indicate that an office or activity was part of the imperial bureaucracy (cf. the ecumenical councils were those sponsored by the emperor) and was meant to underscore the archbishop's role in the governing of the empire, a theory that would later be described as the "symphony" of imperial and religious authority.

It was during Justin's reign that Julian of Halicarnassus, an anti–Chalcedon bishop, made a brief remark that the body of Christ was incorruptible while it was in the tomb and cited Cyril of Alexandria to support his opinion. Severus of Antioch disagreed, insisting that the Lord's body—if it had remained in the tomb—would have undergone the same process of decomposition as all human bodies. The dispute tore apart the theologians who opposed Chalcedon. As a result, there were two anti–Chalcedon bishops in many places: one who agreed with Julian and another who agreed with Severus.

SUGGESTIONS FOR FURTHER READING

John Meyendorff, *Christ in Eastern Christian Thought*. St. Vladimir's Seminary Press, 1975.
John Meyendorff, *Imperial Unity and Christian Divisions*. St. Vladimir's Seminary Press, 1989.
St. Leo the Great, *Sermons* (Trans. J. P. Freeland and A. J. Conway). Catholic University of America Press, 1996.

6

Justinian and Theodora

Justinian was born in AD 482. His family was of peasant stock and when his uncle Justin was acclaimed emperor, Justinian acted as his uncle's spokesman. Justinian even wrote about "our empire" to the Pope of Rome in AD 521 and when Justin died in AD 527, Justinian was crowned co-ruler with his wife Theodora (who was 18 years younger than her husband). Justinian was resented by the old nobility who valued connections and imperial blood. Theodora was resented because her father had been a bear trainer, she had been an actress (i.e., a position often synonymous with prostitution), and was perceived to be jealous and petty with those who opposed her. Fawned over and flattered to their faces, the imperial couple was often reviled behind their backs. Although the emperor and empress were apparently frequently at odds with each other, supporting rival political or ecclesiastical factions, it is unclear that they were not actually working in coordination with each other as an exercise of imperial *Realpolitik*.

Much younger than her husband, Theodora was born in AD 500, the daughter of the bear trainer of the Green team at the Circus. (There were four Hippodrome teams, identified by color; the two most important teams were the Greens and the Blues; the Blues had been instrumental to the rise of Justinian's uncle, Justin, as emperor before him. These teams of circus entertainers were generally aligned with political factions in Constantinople as well. The entertainers performed between chariot races in the Hippodrome; the chariot drivers were also identified by which color team they were part of.) Theodora's mother remarried but the new husband was rejected as the new bear-keeper; luckily, he was hired by the Blue team, whose own bear-keeper had just died. If the Blues had not hired Theodora's stepfather, the family would have been homeless and destitute. Theodora never forgot how the Greens had nearly destroyed her family or how the Blues had saved them.

Theodora became famous as a circus entertainer herself. Women who performed with the circus were thought to be little more than glorified prostitutes—similar to the strippers of burlesque houses in American theater.

Theodora was well known for her nearly nude performances in the circus and was hired to "entertain" at banquets hosted by the nobility as well.

She was known to have had many lovers before becoming the lover of the Syrian man who was the imperial governor of Libya. She gave up her stage career but was soon dismissed by the governor. She went to Alexandria and became friends with Timothy III, the Monophysite patriarch there. He allowed her to receive Holy Communion, which was usually denied to actresses unless they were dying and in need of the Last Rites. So Theodora also had reason to support the Monophysites later.

From Alexandria, she made her way to Antioch and met the chief dancer of the Blues team there; the dancer introduced her to Justinian. She and Justinian quickly established themselves as a couple, over the loud objections of Justinian's aunt, the empress Euphemia. Because of the disreputable profession, it was illegal for an actress to marry nobility and Euphemia was certain that her favorite nephew could do better than a woman like Theodora. Justinian's uncle, the Emperor Justin, was willing to change the law but Euphemia insisted that he not; when she died in AD 523, Justin changed the law and Justinian married Theodora in the Hagia Sophia cathedral.

She was crowned joint-*imperator* with her husband in AD 527 and insisted on the proper observance of court ritual so that the snobs of the nobility were forced to make *proskynesis* (prostrations) to her. She and Justinian closely monitored civil officials and magistrates together to wipe out bureaucratic corruption; because of this, and Theodora's own association with the lower classes, they became extremely popular with the masses. But this campaign also allowed Theodora to avenge herself against the Syrian governor of Libya, who had bought his office and recouped the purchase price by bribery and corruption.

Following the coronation, Justinian banned pagans from all government positions. He ordered that any Christian caught making a pagan sacrifice was to be executed. He denied stipends to pagan teachers and closed the great philosophical academy in Athens.

Judaism continued to be a religion which was legal to practice. There was even a building boom of synagogues in Palestine. But in North Africa, there were orders that synagogues and non–Chalcedonian churches were to be made into Orthodox churches; the same orders were given in Italy and Spain as Constantinople's political power was reasserted across Western Europe by military victory over the non–Roman kingdoms. Although the enforcement of these orders was lax, they provoked a rising sense of insecurity among Jewish communities which grew into open antagonism toward the emperor; in Palestine, this antagonism was exploited by the Persians who conquered Jerusalem in AD 614 (nearly 50 years after Justinian) and who were assisted in massacring the Christians by the Jewish residents.

Less than five years after the imperial couple was crowned, the Nika Rebellion, a week-long series of riots against Justinian and Theodora, erupted. The fighting was along the circus faction colors: the Blues supported the imperial couple while the Greens opposed them. Nobility who opposed Justinian and Theodora took advantage of the riots in an attempt to install a new emperor who was more to their liking. The riots were the most violent and bloodiest in the thousand-year history of the imperial city. Nearly half the city was burned or otherwise destroyed; tens of thousands were killed.

Justinian was willing to let the ringleaders of the rebellion go but Theodora insisted that they be executed in the Hippodrome; another 30,000–40,000—mostly Greens—were slaughtered as a result.

One of the buildings burned during the riots was the wooden cathedral of Hagia Sophia. The first (wooden) version of the imperial cathedral was burned to the ground during the riots surrounding the exile of John Chrysostom. It was replaced by another wooden cathedral by Theodosius II; it was this second wooden cathedral that burned to the ground during the Nika Rebellion against Justinian in AD 532. Justinian immediately began construction of the great stone edifice of Hagia Sophia to replace the charred wooden ruins. The new cathedral was completed by AD 537—amazingly quickly— and subsequently adorned with mosaics by succeeding emperors.

The new Hagia Sophia was modeled after the church of SS. Sergius and Bacchus, a pair of military saints, which Justinian had built as one of his first acts as emperor to atone for an attempted coup he had led against his uncle, Justin I. After the completion of the cathedral, the empress Theodora gave the church of SS. Sergius and Bacchus to the local Monophysites for their use.

The stone cathedral was damaged in AD 556 by an earthquake, which caused the great dome to collapse. It was rebuilt and this is the great church and dome that we see still standing today. But in the aftermath of the earthquake there were severe shortages of food and water in Constantinople. The plague broke out in the city as well. Public morale plummeted despite reports of military victories and success in several major campaigns because there were also reports of military failures in other campaigns. There was a failed assassination attempt against Justinian in AD 562 which drove the emperor to further paranoia and mistrust of nearly everyone until he died in his sleep on November 14, AD 565.

Theodora as Empress

Theodora, advertising herself as engaged in "constant toil and unsparing efforts to nourish the destitute," was also involved in a drive to shut down the brothels of the capital. She opened a women's monastery, known as "Repentance," for the ex-prostitutes.

The empress also forbade the exposure of unwanted infants and began a program to reward those who found children left outdoors to die. She worked to ease the punishments associated with adultery, making it illegal for a husband to kill an allegedly adulterous wife. Women prisoners were not to be jailed with male guards, as a step to prevent rape; rather, women prisoners were to be housed in female monasteries.

Theodora championed the right of women to own property in their own name and secured the right of a bride to receive a cash gift from her husband that was at least equal to the dowry he had been paid by her father.

When the southern regions of Egypt were opened for Christian missionary efforts, Justinian planned to send Chalcedonian missionaries in AD 540 but Theodora arranged for Monophysite missionaries to arrive first; her support of the Monophysites a result of the welcome she had received from the patriarch Timothy in Alexandria so many years before. A sheikh from southern Syria wrote to the empress in AD 541, asking for bishops to be sent to Syria to regularize the Church life of new converts there. The pope of Alexandria, Theodosius, was living in Constantinople at that time and had been very reluctant to create parallel episcopates of Chalcedonian and non–Chalcedonian bishops; he had been telling the Syrians to accept the local [pro-Chalcedon] bishops that were already there. But under pressure from the empress, he ordained two bishops—a man named Jacob and another named Theodore—and sent them to Syria with permission to ordain as many as 100,000 clergy for the Monophysite churches there. (The non–Chalcedonian churches in Syria have been known as "Jacobite" ever since.)

The empress also hid a number of Monophysite bishops, monks, and other clergy in her wing of the palace and when she died—apparently of throat or breast cancer—in AD 548, she made Justinian promise to keep protecting the Monophysites in the palace; many—including Justinian himself—were shocked that a Monophysite bishop who had been thought dead for nearly a decade appeared at Theodora's funeral!

As part of Justinian's justification for the continuation of imperial involvement in Church affairs, he developed the idea of the "symphony" of the imperial authority and the priesthood of the Church.

There are two great gifts which God, in his love for man, has granted from on high: the priesthood and the imperial dignity. The first serves divine things, while the latter directs and administers human affairs; both, however, proceed from the same origin and adorn the life of mankind. Hence, nothing should be such a source of care to the emperors as the dignity of the priests, since it is for their [imperial] welfare that they constantly implore God. For, if the priesthood is in every way free from blame and possesses access to God, and if the emperors administer equitably and judiciously the state entrusted to their care, general harmony will result and whatever is beneficial will be bestowed upon the human race.[1]

The idea of the symphony of Church and State shaped political theory throughout the Byzantine—and later Slavic—Orthodox world.

Theopaschite Controversy and the Three Chapters

Part of the ongoing theological discussion after the acclamation of Chalcedon was, "Can God suffer?" This discussion, known as the Theopaschite (*Theo*=God; *paskein*=to suffer) controversy, was a continuation of the dispute over Cyril's 12th Anathema and demonstrated the continuing need for language to evolve if the dispute were to be resolved.

At Nicea, the term *ousia* had been declared to be distinct from *hypostasis,* but Ephesus and Chalcedon had left unresolved if *physis* was or was not the equivalent of *hypostasis*. Nestorius and his supporters said, "Yes, *physis* is the equivalent of *hypostasis*; therefore there are TWO distinct persons within Jesus." Cyril and his supporters said, "Yes, *physis* is the equivalent of *hypostasis*; therefore there is ONE distinct person within Jesus." Everyone agreed that "the Word suffered in the flesh," but disagreed on how that was possible. Gregory Nazianzus had said, "We needed a God made flesh and put to death in order that we could live again." He had also spoken of "the blood of God" and of the "crucified God." But were these simply pious paraphrases or statements of truth and reality?

John the Grammarian, a pro–Chalcedon theologian, wrote an *Apologia* in AD 514–518 that asserted that as Christ was both *homoousias* with the Father and *homoousias* with us, then His humanity never existed apart from His divinity. John equated *physis* with *ousia*, understanding *ousia* to be "substance in common" or "shared existence." Cyril had understood *physis* to mean "concrete existence." John understood *hypostasis* to mean "existence separate from that which is experienced in common." John agreed with Cyril that there was one *physis*, i.e., one concrete existence, of God-the-Word-made-flesh after the incarnation.

But theologians in Antioch (going back to before John Chrysostom) had all taught that it was flesh that suffered and died on the Cross, not the Word of God Himself. Leontius of Jerusalem wrote in AD 532–536 that

the Word in these latter times, having himself clothed his hypostasis and his nature— which existed before his human nature—with flesh, and which, before the worlds, were without flesh hypostatized human nature in his own hypostasis.[2]

Christ does not possess a human hypostasis which is like ours, particularized and distinct in relationship to all beings of the same species.[3]

Leontius taught that humanity in Christ has no human *hypostasis*, no separate existence distinct from other humans; Christ's was not a particular humanity but a common, generic humanity. "Flesh," in the case of Christ, was shorthand for saying that Christ sums up all humanity, that He is the archetype of humanity, but that he is independent of the limitations of any one particular human person. What Leontius is saying is similar to Gregory of Nyssa's teaching that the "image of God" described in Genesis does not belong to every human individual but describes the human race as a whole.

According to Leontius, Christ's manhood, filled with divine energy, is the leaven in the dough of mankind. Leontius and his teaching became fundamental to the Byzantine understanding of salvation as deification, "becoming like God," each human person penetrated and permeated by these divine energies as Christ's humanity was.

In short, Leontius insisted that there was only one Person, one hypostasis, in Christ and that Person was divine although that divine person took a generic humanity into himself as well; for Leontius, *hypostasis* was not the equivalent of *physis* and that Cyril's term "*mia physis*" ("one nature") was to be understood as a gloss on Chalcedon's assertion of one *hypostasis* known in two *ousias*.

Chalcedon had declared Theodoret of Cyrus and Ibas of Edessa, both friends of Nestorius, as Orthodox theologians; therefore, Cyril's friends and supporters did not trust Chalcedon's teaching and repudiated the council. Justinian wanted to reunite the supporters of Nestorius and Cyril. So in AD 543–544, he condemned Theodore of Mopsuestia (the authority Theodoret and Ibas had referred to). Justinian also condemned Theodoret's attacks on Cyril's "Twelve Anathemas," especially the last anathema that denounces anyone who denies that God suffered and died in the flesh. Lastly, Justinian also condemned Ibas of Edessa who had described the reunion of Nestorius and Cyril in AD 433 as a surrender to Cyril's position. These three condemnations were known collectively as "the three chapters," i.e., three paragraphs.

When news of Justinian's three chapters reached Pope Vigilius in Rome, the reaction was swift. Rome violently objected to any act that condemned someone already dead or that impugned the teaching of Chalcedon (that had relied so heavily on Pope Leo's *Tome*).

In response to Rome's objections, Justinian composed a "Confession of Faith" in AD 551 that

- asserted the Orthodoxy of Cyril's theopaschite formulas;
- endorsed Leontius' distinction of *physis* and *hypostasis*;
- agreed that Christ's two natures can be distinguished by speech and thought, not as two distinct entities; and
- said that when Cyril said *mia physis* he meant *mia hypostasis*.

Justinian was certain that he had arrived at the long-sought solution to all the disputes but additional questions began to arise: Does ignorance equal sin? If so, how can Christ be ignorant, as in Luke 2:52? Can nature be corruptible or ignorant? Or can only a person be ignorant or corruptible?

The Fifth Ecumenical Council (Constantinople II)

The tug-of-war between the pro–Westerners (who rejected the Three Chapters) and the pro–Byzantines (who accepted the Three Chapters) fueled the dispute rather than resolve it. The new patriarch of Constantinople, installed in AD 553, invited Pope Vigilius to call a council in Italy to resolve the issue. The patriarch expected that the pope would preside over such a council. But Justinian refused to hold a council in Italy and opened a council in Constantinople which the Roman pope refused to attend. An overwhelming number of Syrians, however, did come to the royal city for the council and the pope was afraid of mob violence in the streets. The council upheld the Three Chapters.

Even so, the churches and bishops that rejected Chalcedon were not satisfied with Justinian's council and continued to agitate the people.

In response, Pope Vigilius and 16 Western bishops sent Justinian a list of Theodore of Mopsuestia's teachings that they were willing to condemn but not Theodore himself. Justinian rejected this offer and exiled the pope to Egypt. Although communion with Rome was upheld, the pope's name was removed from the diptychs (the list of bishops commemorated at the Divine Liturgy). The people of Rome petitioned Justinian to let the pope return to Rome; the emperor agreed, if the pope would accept the council that upheld his declaration of the Three Chapters. Vigilius condemned the Three Chapters and said nothing about the council itself.

Justinian's council, commonly counted as the fifth of the "ecumenical councils," was only gradually accepted in the West.

Liturgical Developments

As the dogmatic disputes were an ongoing backdrop to life in the imperial city, other aspects of church life were also continuing to develop with Justinian's input.

One of the most obvious liturgical developments was the construction and decoration of the great cathedral of Hagia Sophia. The grandeur of Hagia Sophia demanded an equal grandeur of music and celebration within it. There came a point when Justinian had to limit the number of cathedral staff—who were allowed to participate in the Great Entrance—to the following:

- 60 priests;
- 100 deacons;
- 40 deaconesses;
- 90 subdeacons;
- 110 readers;
- 25 psalmists/singers; and
- 100 ostiarii (lit., "doorkeepers" but who might also maintain the building and liturgical supplies).

(During the Great Entrance, the Holy Gifts of bread and wine, which had been prepared in the *skeophylakion*—a small building or chapel on the north side of the cathedral grounds—were brought into the cathedral and taken to the altar table in an elaborate procession. Psalm 23 was sung with a refrain of "Alleluia" during this procession. The well-known "Cherubic Hymn" which is now sung during this procession was introduced during the reign of Justin II, who followed Justinian on the imperial throne.)

Because many churches were becoming larger and larger buildings, it became common for priests to recite many of the prayers quietly as there were no technology available to enhance their voices; it was even the practice in some especially large churches to have a second deacon, further down in the congregation, act as a human loudspeaker to repeat the sermon or Gospel lesson phrase-by-phrase so that people could hear. But Justinian attempted to legislate that priests ought to still sing the full text of the prayers aloud.

Justinian is said to have composed the famous *Monogenes* ("Only-begotten") hymn—just before the promulgation of the Three Chapters—to be sung as the entrance hymn of the Divine Liturgy. Considering himself both a theologian and a poet, the emperor wanted to compose a brief hymn (*troparion*) that would encapsulate the theology he was sponsoring to unite those who rejected and those who accepted Chalcedon.

> **Only-begotten Son** and immortal **Word** of God.
> > Who for our salvation willed to be incarnate
> > > Of the holy **Theotokos** and ever-virgin Mary,
> > Who **without change** was made man and **crucified for us**,
> > > Trampling down death by death;
> O Christ our God,
> > Who is **one of the Holy Trinity**,
> > > Glorified with the Father and the Holy Spirit:
> Save us!

The hymn he composed relied heavily on the slogans and phrases popular among the followers of Cyril; the emperor's hymn stressed all key points important to those who rejected Chalcedon in an effort to move them to accept the imperial theological program. Justinian's hymn, with the Cyrillian phrases here in **boldface**, is still sung during the opening antiphons at every celebration of the Divine Liturgy. The hymn-text, like Justinian's support for the Aphthartodocetae who taught that Christ's body in the tomb would not have decomposed, reveal his personal pro–Cyrillian theological leanings even though he could not openly support the Monophysites.

The popularity of non–Chalcedonian theology is also reflected in the writings of Pseudo-Dionysius, an Egyptian or Syrian ascetic whose works were first attributed to the Dionysius mentioned in the New Testament, a disciple of St. Paul himself in Athens (Acts 17). It was during St. Paul's sermon in the Areopagus or public square of Athens that he pointed out the altar "to the Unknown God," which he identified with Christ. According to the New Testament, Dionysius converted to Christianity as a result of this sermon about the Unknown God and the later writing of Pseudo-Dionysius stress this "unknown" quality of the Divine. The works of Pseudo-Dionysius, most notably *On the Divine Names* and *Celestial Hierarchy*, stress the importance of negative or "apophatic" theology: it is always safest and best to say what God is NOT rather than what God IS.

It was the apophatic style of theology to proclaim that God is in-visible, un-knowable, in-comprehensible, un-created, and im-mortal.

Pseudo-Dionysius was fond of complicated ideas and word games. He invented the terms "hierarch" and "hierarchy" by taking the words for arch-priest (*arch-hierus*) and inverting them. He taught that the higher ecclesiastical rank a person held indicated that they were closer to God. Therefore, in the system described by Pseudo-Dionysius, only the Seraphim—the highest of the angelic ranks—had any direct experience of God. Seraphim would share what they had experienced with the Cherubim but the Cherubim, one step below them in the hierarchy, were—by nature—unable to comprehend everything the Seraphim had experienced. The Cherubim would share their experience with the Thrones, the next of the angelic ranks, and so on. Those lower down the hierarchy could only expect to learn of God from those above them, especially those immediately above them and they, in turn, would instruct those directly beneath them. In general, angels would reveal God to humans; among humans, clergy would reveal God to layfolk and among layfolk, males would instruct females although there were distinct ranks even within these general categories.

GOD

1. Seraphim
2. Cherubim
3. Thrones

4. Dominions
5. Virtues
6. Powers
7. Principalities
8. Archangels
9. Angels
   1. Bishops
   2. Priests
   3. Deacons
      1. Monks
      2. Laymen
      3. Penitents (male)
         1. Nuns
         2. Laywomen
         3. Penitents (female)

In the theological system of Pseudo-Dionysius, the celestial hierarchy and the earthly hierarchy are meant to reflect or mirror each other as the nine descending ranks of each hierarchy each initiate the lower ranks into the experience of the Divine. It is these roles of initiator and initiated that are most important in this theological system. The distinctions between initiator and initiated were, in fact, seen as so important that in the 11th century some Orthodox claimed that real bishops were not those ordained by the Church but those who were capable of initiating others into the mystery of God (i.e., mystical experience) which was seen as something apart from the sacraments and services of the Church.

Justinian and Theodora also funded the construction of the fortress-monastery of St. Catherine in the wilderness of Mount Sinai which was so isolated that many icons and manuscripts survived there when all others were destroyed throughout the empire during the iconoclastic period. It was in the monastic community on Mount Sinai that one abbot, John, wrote a spiritual handbook which he titled *The Ladder of Divine Ascent*. John led his monks in the struggle to bring order to the chaos of their own passions if not to the political or other forms of chaos in the world outside their doors. John did not preside at the long hours of the liturgical prayer of the community but he was present there with his brethren, day by day by day. As they stood there in the church, built 50 years earlier by the great imperial benefactors Justinian and Theodora (John, having entered the community at age 16, would have been living in the midst of the construction site during his most formative years), John would have seen Theodora's name prominently displayed in the carved work of the central beam before the altar-screen. He would have been very aware of her role in providing both for his community and for the larger Church throughout the empire. Prayer for both Justinian and Theodora would be offered on a regular basis in their role as departed benefactors (if not "second founders") of the monastery.

The Ladder of Divine Ascent was a very popular guide to the spiritual life. It had 30 chapters, rungs on the ladder each person is called to climb from earth to heaven in order to reach God; these chapters describe virtues to be embraced or vices to be rejected and is still often read during Great Lent in Orthodox monasteries or by layfolk in parishes. (This description of the spiritual life in terms of a *Ladder* has given rise to an iconographic genre, the *Ladder* itself. Monks are shown struggling to climb to its pinnacle, where Christ awaits. Devils are attempting to distract the monks and succeed in pulling some from the *Ladder*, causing them to plunge headlong to their doom in Hell. Some of these *Ladder*-icons show St. John at the top of the *Ladder*, leading the way. Others show him at the foot of the *Ladder*, pointing out to his monks the way they must begin the rough ascent.)

Theodora died in AD 548, apparently of cancer. Justinian died in AD 565 and was entombed in the Church of the Holy Apostles. The teaching of the council at Chalcedon remained as divisive as ever.

SUGGESTIONS FOR FURTHER READING

Procopius, *The Secret History* (Trans. R. Atwater). University of Michigan Press, 1961.

Pseudo-Dionysius the Areopagite, *The Divine Names and Mystical Theology* (Trans. J. D. Jones). Marquette University Press, 1980.

St. John Climacus, *The Ladder of Divine Ascent* (Trans. C. Luibheid and N. Russell). Paulist Press, 1982.

Hugh Wybrew, *The Orthodox Liturgy: The Development of the Eucharistic Liturgy in the Byzantine Rite.* SPCK, 1989.

7

Maximus the Confessor and the "One-Will" (Monothelite) Controversy

Justinian died in AD 565. Tensions between the pro–Chalcedon and anti–Chalcedon factions throughout the empire remained high. Maximus, who would become a leading figure in the ongoing dispute, was born (approx. AD 580).

The Persian empire had been expanding onto Byzantine territory since shortly after Justinian's death. The Persians were able to conquer Jerusalem in AD 614 and took the relics of the True Cross back to Persia as a trophy. To further complicate Byzantine politics, the Persian shah also agreed to financially support the Nestorian Christians in Persia at the same time that he was supporting the Monophysite Christians inside Byzantine territory; thanks to the shah's influence, a man known as Athanasius the Camel Driver was installed as Monophysite—also known as Jacobite, from the Bishop Jacob sent by Theodora to oversee the Monophysites in Syria—patriarch of Antioch.

The patriarch of Constantinople, Sergius, was from a prominent Syrian Jacobite family. He presided at the coronation of the emperor Heraclius in AD 610. Heraclius inherited an empire that was bankrupt and demoralized. He was able to rally support and raise both funds and morale; he was able to lead an assault on the Persians in AD 627 and recovered the True Cross, which he brought back to Jerusalem; the anniversary of the return of the Cross is still one aspect of the Orthodox celebration of the Exaltation of the Holy Cross in September. Heraclius was often styled as a King David–like hero; silver platters from AD 629–630 in the Metropolitan Museum of Art depict Heraclius taunting the Persians to single combat between himself and a Persian hero with the subjection of the loser's empire to the other, Heraclius then wrestling the Persian hero, and Heraclius winning the wrestling match just as David won his fight with Goliath.

While Heraclius was on campaign against the Persians, an army of Slavs and Avars—with Persian support—besieged Constantinople in AD 626. Patriarch Sergius, who had been left as regent by Heraclius, led the people in resisting the enemies outside the walls—including a series of processions with icons of the Mother of God and singing a new composition in her honor, the *Akathist* (the "not-sitting," i.e., standing) Hymn, which included the now-famous Kontakion of the Annunciation:

> O victorious Leader of triumphant hosts,
> We your people sing your praises, O Theotokos!
> As you possess invincible might
> Set us free from every calamity
> So that we may cry to you, "Rejoice, O unwedded Bride!"

The attackers dispersed and the populace acclaimed the Mother of God as their chief protector. (Later mosaics in Hagia Sophia would depict the emperors offering models of the imperial city to the Mother of God to watch over and protect and the parallelism between the emperor and the Theotokos—both charged with the safety of the city—is also made clear in the tenth-century writing of the Emperor Constantine VII.)[1]

In addition to organizing the defense of the imperial capital, Patriarch Sergius also had plans for reunion between the theological factions of the Church. He agreed that there was one divine person (*hypostasis*) in Christ, who had two natures but Sergius added that this two-natured Person expressed himself with a single energy; this became known as *monoenergia* (Greek, *mono-energia,* "one energy"). Sergius supported his teaching by citing both Cyril's use of *mia physis* (one nature of God the Word incarnate) and Aristotle's association of nature (*physis)* and activity (*energia*). Sergius was certain that everyone on both sides of the theological dispute would agree with the idea that Christ had acted with a single energy.

Sergius was not wrong, at first. He consulted with the monastic bishops of Egypt and Sinai who rejected Chalcedon; they approved this new formulation of the "one energy" that Sergius proposed. The non–Chalcedonian bishops of Armenia were less enthusiastic about the "one energy" but the bishops in the Black Sea region approved it and then the Armenians did so as well, together with the bishops in some areas of Syria and Mesopotamia.

It was during the early AD 620s, while these discussions with the non–Chalcedonians were going on, that Maximus was serving as the "first secretary" of the emperor Heraclius, one of the most powerful positions in the empire; Maximus was bright and had been well-educated and had come to the notice of the imperial bureaucracy. But after serving in this powerful position for three years, Maximus turned his back on politics and became a monk in a monastery in the suburbs of Constantinople. He was soon promoted to abbot of the monastery but when the Persians got too close for comfort, he fled to a monastery in Carthage (North Africa) founded for refugee monks.

At the monastery in Carthage, the famous abbot Sophronius took Maximus under his wing. Under the direction of Sophronius, Maximus studied the writings of both Gregory Nazianzus and Pseudo-Dionysius. The local people soon thought Maximus was an especially holy monk and the local imperial officials were impressed with him as well. He became a very influential spiritual guide and—unofficial—political advisor.

It was in AD 631 that a man from the region of the Black Sea named Cyrus who supported the teaching of Chalcedon became the pope of Alexandria. He was extremely popular in Egypt, largely because he announced that Egypt "was not accommodating to Chalcedon but Chalcedon is accommodating to us!" (It was during this period, in AD 632 that Mohammed died in Arabia.) In AD 633, at the Alexandria cathedral, Cyrus was able to proclaim reunion with the Jacobites-Monophysites and the Chalcedonians by describing Christ as having one "*theandric* activity," meaning divine-human (from *theos*=divine and *andros*=male but also human, in general). This phrase was taken from Pseudo-Dionysius' writings and was probably suggested to him by Sergius in Constantinople.

The aged Sophronius, visiting Alexandria when this reunion was proclaimed, protested the heretical nature of Cyrus' teaching. Sophronius went so far as to travel to Constantinople to lodge his complaint with the patriarch Sergius and the emperor Heraclius. Sergius, out of respect for Sophronius but unwilling to admit that the teaching of "one theandric activity" was improper, issued a decree that simply forbid anyone discussing whether Christ had one activity or two, or whether His one hypostasis was to be considered the equivalent of having one will. Sergius was convinced that the ecclesiastical reunion achieved in Egypt was too important and wanted to salvage his and Cyrus' accomplishment at all costs.

Sergius wrote to Honorius, the pope of Rome, to report both the proclamation of the reunion in Alexandria and Sophronius' complaint against it. Sergius told Honorius that it was his [Sergius] idea that the accepted teaching that Christ was one, divine person meant that he therefore had only one will—*mono thelos*—and that no one needed to count whether Christ had one energy or two.

Sophronius went home to Palestine in disgust and was elected patriarch of Jerusalem.

But Honorius wrote from Rome to congratulate Sergius on the reunion and the use of *mono thelos* to achieve it. A few years later, Sergius wrote a proclamation known as *Ecthesis* ("Exposition") in AD 636, but Sophronius and other Chalcedonians argued against it; the Emperor Heraclius signed it and made the *monothelite* ("one will") teaching imperial policy in AD 638.

Sergius died only a few months later. Honorius in Rome had died just before Heraclius signed the *Ecthesis*. The new patriarch of Constantinople, Pyrrhus, supported the Monothelite teaching but the new pope of Rome, Severinus, did not. He refused to agree with the *Ecthesis* and the emperor refused to allow Severinus to be enthroned as pope for at least a year. Even after he was enthroned, Severinus was held in a brutal imprisonment and died after a few months.

Someone asked Maximus in Carthage what he thought of the controversy and he openly condemned the Monothelite teaching.

Pope John IV (AD 640–642) totally rejected the Monothelite teaching that Heraclius was trying to impose by the proclamation of the *Ecthesis* and refused to commemorate the emperor or the patriarch during the liturgical services in Rome. Heraclius was heartbroken that his efforts to reunite the theological factions had only led to further divisions.

Heraclius himself died in AD 641, apparently blaming Sergius with his dying breath for all the problems and controversy and claiming that Sergius had pressured him into signing the *Ecthesis*.

It was during the conflict over the writing, signing, and proclamation of the *Ecthesis* that the Arabs, adherents of the new religion that Mohammed had taught, came sweeping across the Middle East. They took control of Damascus in AD 635 and Jerusalem in AD 638; Sophronius surrendered the city to them to save the people from a massacre and the churches from destruction. The Arabs overcame the Persian Empire as well in the AD 640s and took Alexandria in Egypt in AD 642. Thus most of the territory where the Jacobite/Monophysite/non–Chalcedonians lived was removed from imperial Byzantine control. The Arabs were happy to let the Monophysites continue teaching their understanding of theology without having to be united with the supporters of Chalcedon; most of the areas still under Byzantine imperial control supported the teaching of Chalcedon and had no more reason to try and unite with the Monophysites living under Arab control.

When Heraclius died, a power struggle erupted. Pyrrhus, the patriarch of Constantinople who had been handpicked by Sergius as his successor, got involved but his choice for emperor lost so he was exiled and eventually arrived at the same monastery in Carthage where Maximus lived. The new emperor accepted the request of Pope John and rescinded the *Ecthesis*. Pope John restored the commemorations of the emperor and patriarch.

A debate between Pyrrhus and Maximus was arranged in AD 645, each man defending his support or opposition for the Monothelite teaching; to everyone's surprise, in the end Pyrrhus accepted Maximus' arguments and accepted Orthodoxy, rejecting the Monothelite teaching he had so loudly supported before.

The Theology of St. Maximus

Maximus derived his idea of the "theandric" activity of Christ from *Letter 4* of Pseudo-Dionysius, in which Pseudo-Dionysius refers to the divine-human activity of Jesus expressed throughout Christ's earthly ministry and miracle-working. Christ is a single hypostasis, one person who is divine but who has taken on human nature—but not a human person—who expresses himself in this theandric manner. Because Christ has taken on human nature, he possess the common "natural" will of all humanity which is a yearning to be with God. But a human person has two wills: the "natural" will which is common to all humans and the personal ("gnomic will," from *gnome* meaning "inclination" or "intention") will which is particular to each human person and distinct from every other human person. It is the gnomic will which chooses to sin and distance itself from God. Because Christ was not a human person, he did not possess a gnomic will in rebellion against the natural will. By subjecting our personal (gnomic) will to our natural will, we too can act in a theandric fashion.

This theandric action that each human is called to embody is manifest in sharing God's *philanthropia*, his love for mankind; Maximus praises various imperial officials who embody God's *philanthropia* by building hospitals, monasteries, soup kitchens, hospices and hostels for travelers as well as the homeless and the aged, and provide burial for the needy (*Epistle* 44). True theology is expressed not only by intellectual agreement with the teaching of the Church but with the love for the neighbor and always involves a social dimension, "unselfish love and service to the needy and oppressed—including the wicked" (*Epistle* 12, *Centuries on Love* IV.90).

Maximus taught what is often called a "realized eschatology," i.e., that it is possible to experience the Divine here and now before the End of Days. He equates the Kingdom of God with the presence of the Holy Spirit, teaching that when Christians say "Thy kingdom come" in the Lord's Prayer, they are really asking for the coming of the Holy Spirit. When in the Spirit's presence, a Christian can experience the Kingdom of God now which is otherwise still to come. When the Spirit is present, the Eighth Day of creation has dawned and the Kingdom—the reign of God—inaugurated. "God's kingdom is not only a future event, but a daily, on-going experience."[2]

This tension between the now/not-yet aspects of Christian life and experience is seen in the experience of the apostles on Mount Tabor when they witnessed Christ's Transfiguration (Matthew 17:1–8, Mark 9:2–8, Luke 9:28–36). Maximus described the Transfiguration as the betrothal of humanity to divinity, the beginning of the deification of mankind which he also described as the Eighth Day of creation. Much as St. Basil the Great used the idea of the Eighth Day of creation to describe the experience of the Resurrection and communion between humanity and divinity, Maximus described the ongoing seventh day of creation as the fallen, sinful world we currently experience. In the world as it currently exists, it is "natural" for us to want to become divine but it is not inevitable. This deification, our salvation, depends on our gnomic will, our personal choices to move closer to God. (Here Maximus picks up on the ideas of Origen that spiritual movement is natural and constant; we are always moving either closer to God or further away. Origen said that moving away from God, losing our share in the divine glory, was its own punishment since it meant becoming mired in pain and isolation and cold; Origen's idea of Hell was not a place of burning, crackling flames but of frozen inertia, ice so bitter that it could be described as burning cold.)

Maximus liked to describe each human person, as well as humanity as a whole, as a microcosm of the entire world and the world as a macrocosm representing human experience. God's saving one implies saving the other: when we each make the right choices with our gnomic will, the entire world draws closer to God and when God acts to save the world around us—such as at the Baptism of Christ in the River Jordan—each human person is inevitably caught up in the backwash or the expanding ripples of that salvific action.

Maximus expands his ideas that Christ's theandric activity reveals Christ performing five mediations, overcoming five obstacles to communion between people, the world, and with God. Christ brings himself, as human, to his Father. Although he is the Word of God who can never be separated from the Father, by obedience he accomplishes everything that was necessary for our salvation, even though we had squandered and surrendered our potential for such obedience which had naturally been ours. First of all, he united the human race in himself by removing the hostility between male and female and revealed us to be simply human persons capable of living in conformity to him and the image of God we had been created in. With us and for us he embraced the whole creation and united everything so that it can never be parted again: Paradise and this world which we inhabit, heaven and earth, the things we can touch and the things we cannot. He recapitulated and summarized and united everything in himself, showing that the whole creation is one as if it were a single person and that all human persons can be so united as to be called one Man just as the three divine persons are so united that they can be called one God.[3]

The first, most basic mediation Christ performs is between male and female, overcoming the hostility between men and women by virtue of his having been born of a virgin. Christ experiences birth but without the pain of either sexual desire or traumatic childbirth. Because he is born without suffering, he is free to take on suffering later: his voluntary death was therefore not a judgement of fallen humanity but a judgement on sin itself.[4] Maximus' wrote that the hostility between men and women is rooted in lust which is not simply sexual desire; rather, sexual desire is the tip of an iceberg called "desire" that is an attachment to and enjoyment of this world as a fallen place. Maximus thinks the Fall itself is the result of desire (for the forbidden fruit) and anger (Adam and Eve blaming each other, as well as the serpent, rather than each of them admitting their own responsibility for their actions). This desire drives people to see each other as things rather than as persons, means to achieve particular self-serving ends. Frustrated desire becomes anger and this anger fuels both hostility and increased desire which in turn spills over into increasing anger because fallen desire can never be satisfied. Using each other rather than seeking communion with each other—mutual support and service to each other—both expresses and reinforces a hostile duality between all people in general but between men and women in particular.

Maximus cites the passage in Galatians, that "there is neither male nor female in Christ Jesus" (Gal. 3:28), interpreting "male" as anger and "female" as desire and lust; thus, "there is neither anger nor lust in Christ or in a perfect Christian." A Christian is not called to renounce sex but to renounce using another person as simply a means to an end and the anger that results from frustrated desire. All human passion—fallen drives, sinful compulsions, wicked obsessions—is meant to become virtue, using the energy behind passion to fuel righteousness rather than sin: anger should be directed at injustice rather than a neighbor, desire should be for caring for the needy rather than a sexual partner who is used instead of loved.

In his *Commentary on the Lord's Prayer*, Maximus also stresses that it is the proper use of anger and desire—rather than their elimination—that is the heart of the petition, "Hallowed be thy Name."

> We sanctify the name of the Father in grace who is in heaven by mortifying earthly lust, of course, and by purifying ourselves from corrupting passions, since sanctification is the total immobility and mortification of sensual lust. Arrived at that point, we quiet the indecent howling of anger which no longer has, to excite it and persuade it to be carried over to familiar pleasures, the lust which is already mortified by a holiness conformed to reason. Indeed, anger as a natural ally of lust, ceases to rage once it sees that lust is mortified.[5]

A person thus becomes "pregnant" with contemplation of God present in the neighbor which fuels a "desirous love" (*eros*) for God. This first mediation "may be said to restore this male-female aspect of human life to its proper place and use. Its transformation means its realization."[6]

The second mediation is that between Paradise and "this world," the hostility between the two having been overcome when Christ announced on the Cross that he and the repentant thief would be together in Paradise that same day. The conflict between Paradise and "this world" is not necessarily a conflict between Paradise and the earth; it is the conflict between virtue and vice. Maximus understood "this world" to be the situation of unbridled self-indulgence and pleasure while Paradise was the place of virtue. Paradise meant the repudiation of self-indulgence and pleasure, the embrace of mortification and the pain of self-denial. Virtue now is the anticipation of Paradise later. The good thief is promised Paradise because he takes responsibility for his wrongdoing and understands that he is the cause of his own suffering. Paradise is possible on earth when Christians embrace "a divine way of living," i.e., theandric lifestyle in anticipation of the resurrection.

"But the paradise of virtues is not a substitute for the visible Paradise."[7] The third mediation is between heaven and earth and is accomplished when Christ ascends on the 40th day after his Resurrection. Humans are called to a lifestyle that reflects that of the angels; Maximus takes the ancient description of monastic life as "the angelic life" and applies it to all Christians. Maximus taught that Christ descended so that humanity could ascend; in his *Commentary of the Lord's Prayer,* Maximus points out that the petition "thy will be done on earth as it is in heaven" underlines the common life of humanity and the angels. While people participate in the first two mediations by conscious choices and activities, we can participate in this third mediation by prayer and contemplation as well.

This leads directly to the fourth mediation, that of the intelligible or spiritual world with the sensible or physical world that we experience. Christ unites these worlds by his continued ascension through the nine ranks of the angels, with his humanity intact, until he takes his seat again at the right hand of the Father. The natural inclination of the world toward unity with God is manifest here; this natural inclination has been thwarted by the personal choices we humans make but can be reasserted by human activity in cooperation with Christ to be obedient to the Father.

The fifth and final mediation, between God and the world, unites the Uncreated with the created—even the immaterial angels are created beings, just as humans are. Both are called to live a divine life of charity best described as *philanthropia* (literally, "man-loving" or "lover of mankind"), which is the single most frequent description of God in the liturgical prayers. This loving union between Creator and created, as well as between each of the created beings—human and angelic—is accomplished in the liturgical act of offering the Eucharist and allowing that love to then spill out into our behavior between liturgical celebrations. It is Christ's intercession before the Father, his presentation of himself as sacrifice—as described in the Epistle to the Hebrews— that we are called to share in. The Eucharist is the betrothal and foretaste of the eternal and perfect Kingdom of God (*Centuries on Love,* IV.77). Echoing the earlier words of Gregory the Theologian, Maximus re-asserts that we are called to become by grace—love—everything that God is naturally: "'They [the Faithful who come forward to receive Holy Communion] also are and can be called gods by adoption through grace because all of God entirely fills them and leaves no part of them empty of his presence…. By this means God himself will be all in all equally in [all] of the saved: as a pattern of beauty resplendent as a cause in those who are resplendent along with him in grace by virtue and knowledge.'"[8] We are to see and understand the entire visible creation in a spiritual manner and act accordingly. "In this way God and man are united without confusion according to the model of the hypostatic union in Christ, as it is conceived within the theological tradition of Chalcedon."[9]

The crucial components of putting Maximus' ideas into practice were personal prayer, ascetic effort, and participation in the liturgical life of the Church—including receiving Holy Communion. His *Mystagogy* (his discussion of the services and sacraments of the Church) and his *Commentary on the Lord's Prayer* are the most succinct statements of his theology.

The Confession of Maximus

Pyrrhus and Maximus traveled to Rome together, bringing news not only of Pyrrhus' concession but that several local councils across northern Africa had condemned the *Ecthesis* as well. Rome again suspended communion with Constantinople as the *Ecthesis* had been reinstated as imperial policy. But Pyrrhus doesn't stay in Rome. He goes on to Ravenna, the imperial Byzantine headquarters in Italy, and reaffirmed his support of the *Ecthesis*, hoping to be reinstated as patriarch of Constantinople.

When the pope of Rome heard what Pyrrhus had done, he was so furious that he not only excommunicated and condemned Pyrrhus but he used a pen dipped in the consecrated wine of the chalice at the Eucharist!

In Constantinople, the emperor Constans II tried to restore some semblance of order to the conflict and issued the *Typos*, which made it illegal for any discussion at all of the number of Christ's wills and energies.

After the *Typos* was issued, the pope in Rome died. A new pope, Martin, was elected and Martin was not interested at all in cooperating with imperial policy. He instigated open rebellion against Constans' policy by refusing to seek the usual imperial confirmation of his election and convened a council in Rome's cathedral during AD 649 that refused to abide by the *Typos*. The council condemned the Monothelite position.

Maximus was still in Rome when the council was held and he acted as the official advisor to the bishops at the council. He made sure that the emperor himself was not condemned—and that none of the previous emperors were condemned either—but that the *Ecthesis* and *Typos* were both condemned as well as the leading theologians of both the "one will" and the "one energy" factions—including the deceased patriarch of Constantinople, Sergius.

The emperor was furious when news of the council and its decisions reached Constantinople. The emperor ordered the exarch (the imperial official representing the emperor) to go from Ravenna to Rome and arrest Pope Martin. When the exarch arrived in Rome, there were so many riots in support of the pope that the exarch gave up any attempt to arrest the pope; the exarch was so half-hearted in his support of the emperor that he was even persuaded to join a plot with the Arabs in Sicily to overthrow the emperor but the exarch died while he was still in Rome, in AD 652.

The new exarch had no qualms about facing down the Roman mob. He did arrest the pope, who was ill, and sent the pope to Constantinople. The pope was charged with treason in association with the previous exarch; as a result, he was deposed, defrocked, severely ill-treated in prison, and sent to the Crimea in exile. Pope Martin died in AD 655 because of his mistreatment.

The next two popes in Rome refused to acknowledge the *Typos* but remained in communion with the Monothelite patriarch of Constantinople, Peter, who had presided at Martin's trial. Only Maximus was left to oppose the Monothelite position. Maximus—with two disciples—was arrested in Rome when Martin died in the Crimea. Maximus was taken to Constantinople with his two followers and tried for treason with the exarch, as the pope had been. He was tortured and convicted, threatened with exile to Bulgaria, but refused to give in.

In AD 661 he was tried a second time in Constantinople. This time he was tortured and his right hand was amputated as his tongue was cut out of his mouth because of his writing and speaking against the imperial theological position. He was exiled to Georgia where he died, over 80 years old, on August 13, AD 662. Because he suffered and was tortured for the Faith confessed by the councils of Nicea and Chalcedon, confessing his adherence to the truth in the face of imperial persecution, he became known as "the Confessor," just those who suffered torture but were not martyred under the pagan Roman persecution of the Christians were known as "confessors."

No one—not even the then-current pope of Rome—protested the imperial mistreatment of Maximus.

But the pope of Rome and patriarch of Constantinople still refused to agree: Constantinople proclaimed that Christ had only one will, while Rome—following the teaching of St. Maximus—proclaimed that Christ had two distinct wills, divine and human. A new emperor was determined to heal this breach and after a series of delays, called a council in Constantinople on November 7, AD 680. The monothelite patriarch of Antioch cited the support of Pope Honorius of Rome in AD 638 for the monothelite position. But the tide had turned. The representatives of the current pope supported the two-will teaching as did the majority of the bishops present. The council, proclaiming itself the sixth ecumenical council, condemned both the *Ecthesis* and the *Typos* and all who taught that Christ had only one will—including the deceased pope, Honorius (citing the precedent of Justinian's fifth ecumenical council to condemn theologians who were dead and had used theological terms that had passed out of fashion).[10]

The next emperor called another council in AD 692 which met in the same domed hall (a *trullus*) of the imperial palace that the council of 680 had met in. This new council, known as the Council in Trullo because of its meeting place, was summoned to draw up disciplinary canons to bring order and consistency to a variety of church practices throughout the empire as well as deal with differences between Byzantine and Latin practice. The council condemned the practice of forcing priests to give up their wives, which many in the Latin-speaking West advocated. Because the one-will doctrine was still so popular in some places, Honorius was condemned again. Canons of the second and fourth ecumenical councils were cited, giving the patriarch of Constantinople precedence in issues of ecclesiastical jurisdiction.

Many of the monothelite bishops and theologians refused to acknowledge the council of 680, however. In AD 711, an emperor deposed the patriarch of Constantinople who taught the two-will doctrine and exiled others who refused to reject the council of 680. A new emperor seized the throne in June AD 713 and restored the bishops who taught the two-will doctrine. The one-will theologians finally admitted defeat.

SUGGESTIONS FOR FURTHER READING:

St. Maximus the Confessor, *Maximus Confessor, Selected Writings*. (Trans. G. C. Berthold). Paulist Press, 1985.

St. Maximus the Confessor, *On the Cosmic Mystery of Jesus Christ* (Trans. P. M. Blowers). St. Vladimir's Seminary Press, 2003.

Lars Thunberg, *Man and the Cosmos: The Vision of St. Maximus the Confessor*. St. Vladimir's Seminary Press, 2012.

Lars Thunberg, *Microcosm and Mediator: The Theological Anthropology of Maximus the Confessor*, 2nd edition. Open Court, 1995.

8

Icons and Iconoclasm

Iconoclasm was the furnace in which much of what we now think of as standard Byzantine Orthodox Christian practice was forged. Understanding the iconoclastic controversy and its resolution reveals the Orthodox sensibilities, the "sacramental consciousness" of the Byzantine Christians, in a way that no other event does. Iconoclasts intended to centralize both the Church and imperial bureaucracies in Constantinople. They wanted to "purify" the Church of practices they considered corrupt. They wanted to establish the right of the emperor to appoint bishops and decide church teaching. In many ways, the iconoclastic controversy in the Byzantine empire was a conflict between Church and State, the equivalent of the "investiture controversy" during the 11th–12th centuries in the West. The growing iconoclastic antagonism towards the veneration of relics, intercession by/for the dead and the communion of saints, together with the governmental animus towards monks and the resulting government seizure of church property as well as precious liturgical objects, all sound like aspects of the 16th century Reformation as well. The iconoclasts were also similar to the later Reformers in the West in their preference for the written Scriptures over the traditional, unwritten practice of the Church. Yet the Byzantine conflict was resolved without any ongoing permanent breach of church unity, unlike the Western European Reformation.

Muslim Influence?

Mohammad had taught that Jews and Christians, as "People of the Book," were to be subject to a special tax but allowed to continue the practice of their religions. Other religious faiths, known simply as "the idolators," were to be converted to Islam. The caliphs Yezid I (AD 680–683) followed by Omar II (AD 717–720) and Yezid II (AD 720–724) unleashed persecution of the Christians on the grounds that the reverence they paid to icons was identical with practicing idolatry. (This was also the period that the Byzantines were involved in the one-will controversy; the councils of AD 680, 692, and 711 were all held as the emperor was involved in military struggles with the Muslim enemies of the Byzantine empire.) Caliph Omar II wrote a letter to the Byzantine emperor, asking him to defend the Christian practices. Emperor Leo III replied.

Leo's letter to Omar is significant because Leo would soon be the first iconoclast ("icon-breaker") emperor; his letter gives us evidence of how icons were regarded just prior to the imposition of iconoclasm and reveals an early stage of his own views. His letter is also the first Byzantine text to refute Islam.

Leo's reply to Omar shows an extensive knowledge of both the Bible and the Koran. Leo describes the Muslim veneration of the Ka'ba, the small stone building in Mecca that all Muslims face when they perform their prayers, and then Leo writes about the Christian veneration of the Cross and the icons.

> We honor the Cross because of the sufferings of God the Word incarnate.... As for pictures, we do not give them a respect like that, because Holy Scripture does not give us any commandment about this [just as there is no commandment about facing the Ka'ba during prayers]. Nevertheless, the Old Testament does record the divine command which authorized Moses to make the Tabernacle with the figures of the cherubim and, moved by a sincere attachment for the disciples of the Lord who burned with love for the Savior himself, we have always felt a desire to conserve their images, which have come down to us from their times as their living representations. Their presence charms us and as we glorify God who has saved us ... we glorify the saints. But as for the wood and the colors, we do not give them any reverence.[1]

Leo was trying to make Omar see the Christian practices as similar to Muslim attitudes toward the Ka'ba. Leo also cites the Old Testament direction to adorn the Tabernacle with images of the cherubim, which he knows the Muslims accept as inspired by God. He reminds Omar of the Muslim veneration of the Ka'ba, a physical sign of God's interaction with the world in the past, and compares this veneration with the Christian veneration of the Cross, which is also a sign of God's interaction with the world. Just as Moses adorned the Tabernacle with the images of the cherubim, Leo says the churches have always been adorned with the images of the saints which show us not only what they looked like but enable us to glorify them since God has appeared in them: "God is wonderful in his saints" (Psalm 67/68:36). But the icons are preserved and appreciated for the saints they portray, not because the wood or colors and paints are special in some way.

Leo clearly knew and appreciated Muslim teaching and practice when he wrote his letter (sometime between AD 717–720), including the Muslim insistence on using only geometric figures in art and refusing to portray human figures. When he issued his iconoclastic edict in AD 726, he was taking another step in his appreciation for Muslim practice. A discussion about the propriety of icon-veneration was growing louder in the empire. Several leading churchmen wrote in favor of the veneration of icons even as townspeople in the provinces insisted that icons be removed from their churches.

Leo ordered that the image of Christ above the Chalke gate (the main entrance to the imperial palace in Constantinople) be whitewashed in AD 726. There were riots. Sources describe them as either "riots of women" or riots "led by women." In either case, there was public outrage at the soldiers whitewashing the icon above the gate. The extremely popular patriarch, Germanus (whose commentary on the Divine Liturgy remained the semi-official explanation of the Eucharist for several hundred years), condemned Leo and Leo had him deposed; the iconoclast Anastasius was installed as patriarch instead.

John of Damascus and the Icons

"I do not worship matter. I worship the creator of matter, who became matter for my sake and accepted to dwell in matter and through matter worked my salvation and I will not cease from reverencing matter through which my salvation was worked."[2] Theologians and writers inside the imperial borders were persecuted by the iconoclasts, their writings unable to circulate. Outside the boundaries of the empire, these restrictions did not apply.

In AD 675, John was born in Damascus, the capital of the expanding Muslim empire. His grandfather had been the governor of Damascus who had surrendered the city to the Arabs in AD 635 and remained in the administration of the city and his father served the caliph as treasurer. John served in the Arab imperial administration as well until he left to become a monk near Jerusalem, still in Arab-controlled territory. It was in the monastery that he took the name "John." He spent the rest of his life in the monastery there and died around AD 750. (There is a story that John was accused of theft and his hand cut off in punishment but—after his prayer to the Mother of God—his hand was restored to prove his innocence and that he added the extra hand to the icon of the Mother of God "of the three hands" in thanksgiving.)

John is said to have organized the vast collection of liturgical hymnography into the cycle of eight tones which repeats every two months and is still in use among Orthodox Christians. John is given credit for writing many of the texts still in use but his primary work was in organizing the hymns and poetry to be sung that had been composed by others. In this, he is similar to Pope Gregory the Great who is given credit for organizing the vast collection of western hymnography into what is now known as "Gregorian chant."

Another of his works is titled *On the Orthodox Faith* and served as the more-or-less official summary of Orthodox Christian theology for several hundred years. This, together with his *Concerning Heresy* (which includes one of the first Christian refutations of Islam and notably considers Islam to simply be another Christological error), were also extremely influential in translations among Latin and other non–Greek speaking Christians.

One of John's most memorable remarks in *On the Orthodox Faith* concerns the angels. In Book 2, chapter 3, he considers how angels are immaterial in comparison to humanity but quite substantial when compared to God for only God, as uncreated, is entirely spirit and totally immaterial. But Christians can nevertheless call angels "bodiless" because humans are so solid and material ourselves. This materiality is also how humans are superior to angels, John writes.

Because the angels are pure spirit and mind, rational thought unencumbered by a body, they cannot change their minds once they make a decision. Hence, once the devil and his angels chose to rebel against God, they cannot repent or admit their mistake. Because of this incapability of changing their minds, none of the angels who chose to remain faithful will ever rebel later and humans can therefore always trust their guardian angels to never "change sides," as it were, and betray their charges into the hands of the devil.

For the angels, a decision made once is a decision made forever. But humans, having bodies, can change their minds. Having sinned or fallen, they can get up again. Humans can repent. This capability of repentance is exemplified in the act of *proskynesis* or prostration, in which a person stands, drops to their knees and touches their palms and forehead to the floor and then immediately stands again. Because they have bodies and can repent, humans are superior to the angels who are frozen in their once-and-for-all decisions.

In John's writings against Islam, he considers the Muslim idea that God's sovereignty requires that God is responsible for all human action and that by forming a baby in a woman's womb as a result of adultery or fornication, God is cooperating with and complicit in the sinful act. John answers that God finished forming the world on the seventh day of Creation and that the world continues to operate according to principles set in motion during that initial creation. It is the responsibility of men and women to live righteously but if they do not, then the natural result of sexual intercourse is the birth of illegitimate children. (Muslim theology at that time was still grappling with the idea of human choice and free will and did not finally endorse human freedom to act until after the assassination of the caliph Walid II in AD 744 because if the murder "had been God's will rather than the free will of the assassin, then it would mean that the caliph had been murdered at God's command. It was more politically convenient to believe that the assassin acted on his own volition."[3])

But John is best known for his three treatises *On the Divine Images* in which he defends the practice of icon-veneration. Because the Emperor Leo and the iconoclasts primarily cited Scripture—such as the second commandment, "Thou shalt make no graven image ... nor bow down to them" (Exodus 20:4)—it was to the Scriptures that John turned to refute the iconoclasts.

John agreed that God taught the people to make no graven images nor to bow down before idols but he went on to say:

> Fleshly nature was not lost when it became part of the Godhead, but just as the Word made flesh remained the Word, so also flesh became the Word, yet remained flesh, being united to the person of the Word. Therefore I boldly draw an image of the invisible God, not as invisible, but as having become visible for our sakes by partaking of flesh and blood. I do not draw an image of the immortal Godhead, but I paint the image of God who became visible in the flesh ... [*On the Divine Images* 1.6].

> How does one paint the bodiless? How can you describe what is a mystery? It is obvious that when you contemplate God becoming man, that you may depict Him clothed in human form. When the invisible One becomes visible to flesh, you may then draw His likeness [*On the Divine Images* 1.8].

The incarnation of the Word in Jesus radically changed the relationship between people and images. Before the incarnation, no images were appropriate because God could not be seen. But after the incarnation, the Word had been seen and touched and so could be depicted.

John also pointed out that in the Old Testament, God had commanded images to be used to adorn the Tent of Meeting, the Ark of the Covenant, and the vestments of the priests. Cherubim were shown atop the Ark, on either side of the mercy-seat where God's glory appeared. The Tent of Meeting was itself an image of the heavenly sanctuary. God had inspired Bezalel to fashion the liturgical objects used in the worship of God and to adorn the Tent of Meeting and priestly vestments with embroidery and jewels. None of these were adored for their own sake but through them the people were "led to remember the wonders of old and to worship God, the worker of wonders. They were images serving as memorials; they were not divine, but led to the remembrance of divine power" (*On the Divine Images* 1.17).

John distinguished between adoration, due to God alone, and honor given to "something of great excellence" (*On the Divine Images*, 1.8), such as angels or the Tent of Meeting in the wilderness or Jacob bowing over his staff. He also pointed out that some iconoclasts were willing to make images of Christ or the Mother of God but not the saints.

> What foolishness! Your own impious words prove that you utterly despise the saints. If you make an image of Christ and not of the saints, it is evident that you do not forbid images but refuse to honor the saints.... The saints during their earthly lives were filled with the Holy Spirit and when they fulfill their course, the grace of the Holy Spirit does not depart from their souls or their bodies in the tombs or from their

likenesses and holy images, not by the nature of these things but by grace and power [*On the Divine Images* 1.19].

Reverence God and his friends; follow the inspiration of the Holy Spirit [*On the Divine Images* 1.16].

Iconoclasts also condemned the Orthodox reliance on unwritten Tradition and practice, preferring to hold people accountable to written texts, such as the Ten Commandments and canon law. But one icon-venerating patriarch of Constantinople retorted that "iconoclasts reproach us for leaning on unwritten Tradition but unwritten Tradition is the strongest argument of all. It is the basis of all customs that have become habit which, over time, take on a value more solid than nature."[4]

John of Damascus had pointed out that the ink of the words in the Gospel book was itself matter and that nevertheless God manifests himself through that matter so that the iconoclasts were inconsistent in refusing to acknowledge God's presence in other material images. "The images are to the eye what words are to the ear," John wrote. The Orthodox saw the traditional practices of the Church as the authoritative interpretation of the Scriptures, which themselves had been established in a process of gradual selection and traditional practice over the early centuries of the Church's life. Rather than cite a particular text or verse in a vacuum, out of the context of the Church's life, the Orthodox saw written and unwritten authorities supporting each other—with perhaps the unwritten authority even taking precedence over written texts—much as St. Basil the Great did in his defense of the divinity of the Holy Spirit in the fourth century. John went on to say that many of the liturgical practices which the iconoclasts accepted–such as the triple immersion at baptism or the practice of standing to pray toward the east— had been handed down as unwritten Tradition and quoted the Apostle Paul: "Stand firm and hold to the traditions which you were taught by us, either by word of mouth or by letter" (2 Thess. 2:15).

John also asked, "What right have emperors to style themselves lawgivers in the Church?" He answers that only apostles, prophets, teachers, and shepherds are called to build up the body of Christ and that the Apostle Paul nowhere mentions emperors. "Political prosperity is the business of emperors; the condition of the Church is the concern of shepherds and teachers" (*On the Divine Images* 2.12).

The First Wave of Iconoclasm

The monks quickly became the ringleaders of the popular resistance to Leo's reform project. Although the iconoclasts stressed that living people were the "living images of God," they began to attack and persecute monks and monasteries: monks were arrested, tortured, and then executed or banished or forced to marry and live as laymen. Iconoclasts seized reliquaries and liturgical valuables, melting them down and burning the relics inside. Because many monasteries depended on donations for their prayers and services for the departed for financial support, these prayers and services were outlawed.

Leo the emperor also ordered Pope Gregory II in Rome to ratify his imperial edict with a church council and to destroy the religious images in the West. The pope refused to call the council. He refused to destroy any images. He also refused to forward any tax collections to the emperor.

A revolt broke out in Greece against Leo and his iconoclastic policy during the next year, which he brutally suppressed; this added fire to the iconophile ("icon lover") or iconodule ("icon venerator") resistance.

Leo issued an even sterner edict against icons in AD 730. Persecution of the Orthodox defenders of the icons increased. Churches were seized and either torn down or whitewashed inside to cover the images on the walls. Smaller icons, painted on wood, were burned. Only the icons in the monastery of St. Catherine, on Mount Sinai, were spared because the monastery was beyond the reach of Leo's imperial enforcers. Because the Orthodox were denied use of the churches, the priests began to use a special cloth called the *antimension* ("instead of the table") that was consecrated by the bishop and which had relics sewn into it, instead of the consecrated altar-tables—which had contained relics—to celebrate the Eucharist in private homes or chapels. (The use of these *anitmensia* became not just expected but required; modern Byzantine Christian practice still requires the use of the *antimension* even though consecrated altar-tables are available in Orthodox churches.)

The pope did call a council in Rome in the next year, in AD 731; the council condemned iconoclasm and excommunicated Leo. Leo sent a fleet to punish his subjects on the Italian peninsula but a storm wrecked the fleet before it could get to Italy and the Italians were never subject to the Byzantine emperor in Constantinople again.

Leo died in AD 741 with open rebellion and iconophile resistance to his policies everywhere. His son, Constantine V (nicknamed *Copronymus*, a vulgar reference meaning "dung-named" because he defecated in the font when he was baptized as a baby, and *Cabillinus*, which means "horsey" because he was said to look like a horse's face), ruled from AD 741 to 775. Constantine continued to enforce iconoclasm and refused to ever use the words "saint" or "holy," insisting that the Church of the Holy Apostles be referred to simply as the Church of the Apostles.

Leo's son-in-law Artabasdus led a revolt against Constantine, making the defense of the icons his rallying cry. Even though he was crowned by an iconoclastic patriarch in Hagia Sophia in AD 742, Artabasdus restored the icons and stopped the persecution of the Orthodox. But Constantine was able to seize Constantinople back in AD 743 and had Artabasdus blinded, beginning an onslaught of furious revenge against the iconophile Orthodox. He had the patriarch flogged, blinded, and driven through the streets.

In Rome, the pope wrote to Constantine asking for military support against the Lombards but the emperor had no military forces to spare so the pope turned to the Franks for aid, beginning the process that would eventually lead to the official breaking of the Church into Greek-speaking Orthodoxy and Latin-speaking Catholicism.

Constantine insisted that Jesus could not be depicted because if he could be depicted, it would mean depicting—and therefore imposing a limit on—Christ's divinity which is limitless and cannot be depicted. Constantine called a council to proclaim iconoclastic teaching and condemn the veneration of the icons. He wrote that only the Gifts of bread and wine in the Eucharist were the adequate image of Christ. He claimed that the iconophiles were guilty of either Nestorianism (because they were dividing the humanity and divinity of Christ when they depicted him) or were Monophysites (because they were confusing the humanity and divinity of Christ). He wanted Germanus, John of Damascus, and George of Cyprus (not to be confused with a Byzantine geographer of the same name)—the three leading theologians defending the icons—to be condemned as the "unholy trinity."

The council he called in AD 754 was attended only by iconoclastic bishops. They approved Constantine's policies but condemned the ongoing desecration, burning, and looting of churches. Moreover, the council disagreed with Constantine by insisting that the titles "holy" and "saint" were appropriate to use in some cases and confirmed the status of Mary as *Theotokos*.

After the council, Constantine began a campaign to purge Orthodox iconophiles from the imperial bureaucratic service and continued removing images from the walls of churches. Monasteries were turned into barracks and corrals; it was illegal to be seen wearing a monastic habit.

Constantine himself died in the next year, in AD 755, and his son Leo IV became emperor. Leo kept the iconoclastic laws but stopped enforcing them. He allowed the exiles to come home. His wife Irene was a devout Orthodox iconophile but despite her efforts, Leo became angrier and angrier at the iconophile resistance to official imperial policy and—at the end of his reign—unleashed a fierce wave of iconoclastic persecution against the Orthodox defenders and venerators of the icons. He punished the nobility who had icons in their homes and was about to banish his wife Irene when he died in AD 780. Irene became the regent for her son, Constantine VI.

Together, Irene and her son restored images and relics in the churches.

Monasteries were reopened. Sons of nobility entered the monasteries and became novices. Irene wanted to restore communion with Rome, which had been broken throughout the iconoclastic period, but the imperial soldiers were themselves still very much in favor of iconoclasm. She could not afford to antagonize the army.

She and Constantine opened a council in Constantinople in AD 786 to condemn iconoclasm. The soldiers began to break up the meetings of the bishops so Irene sent the troops out on a series of missions and brought in new troops that she could trust.

The bishops were able to regroup and regather in Nicea, a suburb of Constantinople, just as the first ecumenical council had met there in AD 325. The bishops proclaimed that images were to receive *proskynesis* (lit. "prostration," i.e., the same veneration given to the emperor and other important people) but not *latreia* (the worship appropriate only for God). The honor paid to the images is relative and passes from the image to the prototype, just as honor paid to the imperial images is actually paid to the emperor. This council praised Germanus, John of Damascus, and George of Cyprus as the "glorious trinity." The bishops condemned the imperial (state) appointment of bishops and declared that only bishops should be involved in the selection of new bishops. They condemned simony, the practice of paying for sacraments—such as a man paying to become a bishop. They ordered that any bishop who consecrated a church without placing relics in the altar-table should be deposed.

The acts (records) of the council were translated into Latin and sent to Rome. But there were problems. The pope had wanted church property that had been confiscated by the iconoclastic emperors to be restored and there was no mention of this at the council. The version of the acts sent to Charlemagne and the Franks mistranslated key terms and reversed the terms *proskynesis* and *latreia*. Western theologians preferred to think of images as "books for the illiterate" rather than as the sacramental consequences of the Incarnation.

Although Irene's council eased the relationship between the pope and the imperial church in Constantinople, the relationship with Charlemagne (son of the Frankish ruler that the popes turned to for assistance against the Lombards) continued to deteriorate. The empire of the Franks continued to expand and Charlemagne began to act like a Roman emperor rather than a barbarian king: he standardized weights and measures, supported the arts, engaged in massive building projects, and issued laws in the classical style of Rome. He proposed marriage to Irene, who declined his offer; he was then crowned as "Holy Roman Emperor" by the pope on Christmas Day, AD 800. One justification for this was the Frankish claim that the throne in Constantinople was technically empty since—according to Frankish law—a woman could not own property or rule. The Byzantine authorities saw both the coronation and its justification as a profound affront.

SUGGESTIONS FOR FURTHER READING:

Daniel J. Sahas, *John of Damascus on Islam: The "Heresy of the Ishmaelites."* Brill, 1972.

St. John of Damascus, *Three Treatises on the Divine Images* (Trans. A. Louth). St. Vladimir's Seminary Press, 2003.

St. John of Damascus, *Writings* (Trans. F. H. Chase, Jr). Catholic University Press, 1958.

9

Iconoclasm, Part 2

Constantine VI had his own problems with marriage, as well. Irene had arranged his betrothal to Charlemagne's daughter but then broke off the promised marriage and forced Constantine to marry a woman named Maria instead. He later decided that he wanted to divorce his wife Maria and marry her lady-in-waiting Theodote, who happened to be a cousin of Theodore the Studite, a leading iconophile theologian and monastic. The patriarch refused to allow the divorce as a wife's infidelity was the primary legal justification for divorce at that time and there was no evidence that Maria had committed adultery. Constantine insisted that Maria had attempted to kill him—which was another legitimate reason for divorce—but the patriarch laughed in his face and refused to believe the accusation. Because Constantine kept threatening to renew iconoclasm or have Maria executed, the patriarch eventually allowed the emperor to divorce Maria and marry Theodote in AD 795. But the marriage was not celebrated by the patriarch, as would have been the normal practice; instead, a simple parish priest named Joseph was called in to perform the wedding.

Theodore the Studite, the new bride's cousin, was infuriated at this breach of church law regarding the sanctity of marriage. He insisted that the priest Joseph be deposed and excommunicated as well as everyone who had received communion from him, i.e., the emperor and his new bride and most of the imperial court.

Constantine attempted to meet with Theodore to discuss the issue of his marriage but Theodore refused. So the emperor sent troops to the monastery where Theodore lived and the community was broken up. Theodore himself was flogged and then sent into exile at Thessaloniki, with the other monks, but they were all able to return to Constantinople in August, AD 797 when Constantine was blinded and overthrown by his mother Irene who became the sole ruler of the empire.

There were long-term revolutionary consequences to what seemed a rather brief dispute about the imperial divorce and remarriage. Theologians and bishops and priests began to break off communion with each other based on whether they did or did not accept the legitimacy of the emperor's divorce and remarriage. Called the Moechian schism or Moechian controversy (from *moichos*, "adulterer"), the dispute focused on whether Constantine should have performed the penance for adultery because his second marriage was—technically speaking—illegitimate and illegal. The typical penance for adultery would have involved several years of fasting and abstaining from communion, as well as giving up his sexual relationship with his new wife. It seems that the emperor was allowed to do the expected penance but without breaking off his sexual relationship with his new wife. This established a revolutionary precedent that penances could be performed simply as the price to be paid for a relationship that the church disapproved of. Enormous consequences of this would develop in the tenth century.

Irene had the priest Joseph deposed.

Everyone thought that was the end of the business. But the emperor Nicephorus, who followed Irene on the throne, asked the new patriarch of Constantinople to reinstate the priest Joseph because he had been successful on a diplomatic mission that Nicephorus had sent him on. Joseph was reinstated and, at the time, Theodore the Studite did not object. Shortly after that, however, Theodore did object to associating with the Priest Joseph or with anyone else who did associate with him because Theodore said that Joseph's reinstatement had been uncanonical. Theodore's objections to associating with anyone who accepted Joseph again as a priest implicitly included the emperor Nicephorus.

In AD 808, Theodore offered to meet Nicephorus, perform the usual *proskynesis* ("prostration") before him, and explain his reasoning. Nicephorus did not accept Theodore's offer. Theodore's brother Joseph, the archbishop of Thessalonica, came to the capital to visit Theodore at Christmas but the Archbishop Joseph refused to attend the Eucharist at Hagia Sophia on Christmas Day because the Priest Joseph and his supporters—including the emperor—would be there. Nicephorus was furious and had Theodore, his brother the archbishop, and several of their supporters arrested and exiled.

But when another new emperor was enthroned, Theodore and his brother and the others were recalled from exile and the Priest Joseph was defrocked, again. Although this aspect of the dispute looked settled, uneasy feelings and mistrust remained on all sides. The intransigence of the Orthodox iconophiles and their rigid insistence on what seemed to many as arbitrary rule-keeping and subservience to the monastic rigorists left them considerably weaker in the eyes of the public, who were more likely to agree with the bishops that pastoral accommodation and cooperation with the emperor was better.

The Second Wave of Iconoclasm

In addition to the disputes about the legitimacy of Constantine VI's second marriage and the status of the Priest Joseph, iconoclasm was also still popular in some regions, especially with the troops who remembered Constantine V as a great general who led successful campaigns against the Muslim enemies of the empire. After Irene herself was deposed by a coup in AD 802 by Nicephorus, a short series of emperors were too busy with military affairs to care much about church controversies. But the military disasters of Michael III in AD 811–813 moved the troops to force him to resign and they acclaimed one of their generals, Leo V, as emperor.

Leo was convinced that all the imperial troubles were due to God's anger at Irene's repudiation of iconoclasm and the subsequent idolatry of the iconophile Orthodox. So in AD 814 he ordered the destruction of icons to begin again. Theodore the Studite took up his pen once more, this time to defend the iconophile theology.

Leo called an iconoclast council in AD 815 which denounced the council in Nicea that had affirmed icon veneration in AD 787. Leo continued his campaign against the icons, ordering Theodore the Studite into exile again three times; from exile, Theodore wrote his treatises *On the Holy Icons* as well as many letters to support iconophile Orthodox. Many people fled from the imperial persecution—monks and layfolk and large numbers of artists—and went where the iconoclastic emperor could not reach them.

Many of these refugees arrived in Rome. Between AD 817–824, Pope Paschal I employed many of these artists; several churches in Rome were built or rebuilt in Byzantine iconophile style for the refugees. The basilicas of St. Prassede and of St. Mary in Cosmedin are among the churches that date from this period and are still stunning examples of Byzantine iconography.

Leo was murdered on Christmas Day in AD 820 and another general, Michael II, was acclaimed emperor by the troops. Michael asked Louis "the Pious" (the son of Charlemagne) to extradite all the iconophile refugee monks and bishops who had fled west to escape persecution back to Constantinople to face imperial justice.

Michael's son Theophilus became emperor in AD 829 and was an extremely fierce iconoclast. His wife Theodora was a secret Orthodox iconophile, who had been taught to venerate icons by her mother; Theodora was caught in the act of veneration of her icons and we know that some of these icons were actually small statues because she defended herself by claiming that she was simply playing with her dolls when she was caught kissing them.

Many of the more famous iconophile martyrs and confessors suffered under this second wave of iconoclastic persecution, including the monk

Lazarus the iconographer (who had restored the image of Christ above the Chalke gate), Joseph the hymnographer (who is credited with an outstanding amount of liturgical poetry and hymnography which is still used), Theophanes and Theodore the *Graptoi* (the "written upon," monks from Palestine who had lines of their own poetry cut into their skin by the iconoclasts).

Theophilus died of dysentery in AD 842 at the age of 29. His widow Theodora was appointed regent for their son Michael III, who was three years old. Theodora opened the prisons and released the Orthodox iconophile prisoners. She called the exiles back home. But she hesitated to revoke the iconoclastic laws until the iconoclastic patriarch of Constantinople retired. Methodius, who had been a famous "confessor" in prison being tortured as an Orthodox iconophile, became the patriarch of the city.

Theodore the Studite and the Icons

Theodore grew up in an aristocratic family in Constantinople. He was taught by a tutor and prepared for a career in the imperial administration. But his uncle Plato gave up his imperial position and became a monk, and eventually an important abbot, in Bithynia (on the south coast of the Black Sea). Theodore followed his uncle to Bithynia and eventually became abbot of the same monastery after Plato retired to become a hermit. After his role in the Moechian Schism, Theodore was back in Constantinople and appointed abbot of the monastery in the Studite neighborhood there. He organized processions—parades? riots?—in protest of the iconoclastic policies of the emperor and was exiled. He died in AD 826, still in exile.

Theodore's defense of the icons was more philosophical than John of Damascus because the iconoclasts had become more philosophical in their rejection of images. Most iconoclasts said that the only legitimate images of Christ were the Holy Gifts of bread and wine shared in Holy Communion at the Divine Liturgy. Christ said, "Do this in memory of me" and therefore, all other means of representing him were illegitimate. Theodore responded that the Holy Gifts are not images but true Mysteries/Sacraments. He also pointed out that if the Eucharist is the only legitimate representation of Christ, then the written representations of Him in the Gospels should also be rejected. All the verbal or visual forms of "remembering" Christ—in addition to the Eucharist—were legitimate or none of them were.

Theodore wrote that if Christ cannot be portrayed it is either because he lacks human nature or that his humanity is swallowed up by his divinity. In either case, the iconoclasts are embracing a version of the Monophysite heresy. If Chalcedon is correct about Christ's humanity and divinity being united without change or confusion or division or separation then, Theodore wrote, Christ can be portrayed like any human person. It is a person that is depicted, Theodore insisted, not a nature which is portrayed. Therefore, the icons portray a divine person who took on human nature and the divinity is usually indicated by the use of the cross-in-the-halo behind Christ's head which is inscribed with the Greek words for "I AM" (the name God gave to Moses at the Burning Bush: "Tell the people that I AM has sent you").

Some iconoclasts taught that Christ could be depicted before the Passion and Resurrection but not afterwards. Theodore pointed out that Christ was seen as a man by the apostles after the Resurrection. Not only was he seen, but he ate fish and was touched by Thomas as well. If Christ cannot be portrayed both before and after his Resurrection, then humanity was not truly united to God and no humans can become "partakers of the divine nature" (2 Peter 1:4).

Partaking of the divine nature, commonly called *theosis*, is—for Theodore and for Byzantine Christianity as a whole—simply another way to describe "salvation." Humans become by grace all that God is by nature, referring to the theology hammered out in earlier disputes. Defending icons was defending the possibility of salvation.

Iconoclasts also complained that icons were not formally blessed in church, which means there was no prayer for the priest to read to bless them; later, the Orthodox did develop a prayer to bless images before they could be venerated. But Theodore argues that images reveal their prototypes simply by being authentic images, just as each human person is an image of God simply by virtue of being an authentic human. The greater the person's authenticity, the greater the likeness to God, the more clear the image. Furthermore, if iconoclasts were willing to venerate the Cross, they should be willing to venerate the image of Him who sanctified the Cross by dying on it.

The iconoclasts wanted to limit God's self-revelation to the spoken word and the Eucharistic Gifts but Theodore had a "sacramental consciousness" that saw all material as having the potential to reveal God.[1] Theodore saw the incarnation and the veneration of images as two sides of the same coin: "That which was from the beginning, which we have heard, which we have seen with our eyes, which we have looked at and our hands have touched— this we proclaim concerning the Word of life" (I John 1:1).

The Triumph of Orthodoxy

Methodius was willing to allow iconoclastic bishops retain their positions so long as they renounced iconoclasm. A council in October that same year— AD 842—reaffirmed Nicea II which was acclaimed as the seventh ecumenical council and condemned iconoclasm without naming any of its imperial sup-porters or sponsors. Methodius' willingness to be lenient with all the icono-clasts helped ease the way for the general acceptance of the Orthodox iconophile position. The next spring, March 11, AD 843, Methodius with Theodora and Michael led a procession with icons into Hagia Sophia to celebrate the "restoration of the icons." The anniversary of that day, which happened to be the first Sunday during Great Lent that year, became the annual celebration of "the Triumph of Orthodoxy" and is still celebrated every year on the first Sunday of Great Lent in the Byzantine Orthodox liturgical practice.

More About Icons Later

But there was more to discuss about icons later. The *Stoglav* ("Hundred Chapters") Council was called in Moscow by Ivan the Terrible in AD 1551 to answer questions the czar had about theological and disciplinary matters. The Great Council of Moscow was called in AD 1666. Each of these Russian councils discussed icons and iconography as well.

The Stoglav Council addressed the relationship of iconography and the developing technology that was changing the availability of icons. The cus-tomary, traditional way of painting icons by hand had always been expensive and made private ownership of icons unlikely for the poor; a poor family might have one hand-painted icon which was passed down from one gener-ation to another. But in the 1550s, printing and other methods of mechanical reproduction were making inexpensive copies of icons available. Were these mechanical reproductions still "icons" in the same way that hand-painted icons were? The council said, "No."

Iconography was a holy profession, undertaken with frequent consul-tations of the artist's spiritual father. Icons were to be painted by hand with humility and piety, the Stoglav Council said, with scrupulous attention to the spiritual and physical purity of the iconographer. "Cursed is the one who is lax or slothful about doing the Lord's work," the council warned (Jeremiah 48:10). Iconographers were directed to paint icons according to ancient mod-els, not modern fancy. The work of Andrei Rublev, whose most famous icon was that of the Old Testament Trinity (the three angels who came to visit Abraham in Genesis 18), was endorsed as the standard all iconographers should aspire to.

What about damaged icons? They were to be repaired or burnt, just as damaged service books and Bibles were.

Prints or etchings of icons were to be used for educational purposes only, not displayed in churches for veneration. (Iconographers circulated pattern-books and models for each other to follow, often including visual examples as well as written instructions.) Although no explicit reasons are given, several can be surmised given what the council says about hand-painted icons. For one thing, prints were too easily damaged and unlikely to be disposed of properly. Printing quality was also more difficult to control and church authorities less able to hold printers to the physical and spiritual standards expected. Printers might not even be Orthodox, which all iconographers were presumed to be. It was the personal touch of the iconographer's spiritual practice that was just as important as his artistic ability. Printed icons lacked that personal quality.

The council could also have been concerned to keep iconographers in business. If the much cheaper prints were acceptable for use in church, how long could the hand-painted icons continue to be produced? Who would be willing to keep paying the price of hand-painted icons?

Later, the Great Council reiterated and upheld the teaching of the Council in Trullo that Christ was only to be depicted as a human, not as a lamb (canon 82); the use of the lamb to depict Christ was based on John the Baptist's declaration that Jesus was "the Lamb of God." They allowed wings to be painted on John the Baptist to illustrate his role as messenger but frowned on using a lamb to illustrate the Lamb of God metaphor. They insisted that "grace and truth themselves" were preferable over "ancient figures and shadows as symbols of the truth."

Another question that both the Stoglav Council and the Great Council addressed was the propriety of depicting God the Father as an old man or the making of any images of God the Father at all. Such imagery was becoming more popular in western Christian images and was being circulated in the eastern Christian world as well. But these images were highly suspect because there was no Byzantine precedent for them. Was such imagery legitimate or not?

The two councils said, "No." Even though the Old Testament said that Adam saw God walking in the garden of Eden and that Isaiah saw God on his heavenly throne and that Daniel saw the Ancient of Days, the councils cited John of Damascus who taught these were appearances of the Word of God in anticipation of the incarnation. The Father himself had never been seen and was never incarnate and so was impossible to depict. The voice of the Father had been heard at times, such as at Jesus' baptism or Transfiguration ("This is my beloved son, in whom I am well-pleased" and "Behold my son; listen to him," in Matthew 3 and 17, Mark 1 and 9, Luke 3 and 9) but there was no way to depict sound. Iconographers, the councils taught, were to depict the Father as an old man with white hair and a beard only in iconographic style illustrations of the Book of Revelation or as the personification of the idea of "Paternity" or "Fatherhood," although these personifications were suspect as well.

Neither was the Holy Spirit to be depicted as a dove. The Spirit was seen as a dove at Christ's baptism and as a cloud on Mt. Tabor at the Transfiguration and as fire on Pentecost but was never truly incarnate as any of these. The Spirit could be depicted as a dove in icons of Christ's baptism because that is what St. John the Baptist saw but the dove could not be used otherwise in images of the Holy Trinity; images of God the Father as an old man, Christ, and the dove between them—although increasingly common in areas exposed to western art—were forbidden.

SUGGESTIONS FOR FURTHER READING

St. Theodore the Studite, *On the Holy Icons* (Trans. C. Roth). St. Vladimir's Seminary Press, 1981.

Kenneth Parry, *Depicting the Word: Byzantine Iconophile Thought of the Eighth and Ninth Centuries*. Brill, 1996.

Oleg Tarasov, *Icons and Devotion: Sacred Spaces in Imperial Russia*. Reaktion Books, 2002.

10

Constantinople, Rome and Leo VI

Methodius, a moderate liberal who was disliked by the Studite monks and their supporters, was enthroned as patriarch of Constantinople in AD 842. He and the empress Theodora were able to celebrate the "Triumph of Orthodoxy" in AD 843. In an attempt to placate the remaining iconoclasts and avoid new riots or an attempted iconoclastic coup, Methodius excommunicated the Studite "rigorists" and those who insisted that previous iconoclasts—emperors—be named and excommunicated posthumously as well as those who were still willing to pray with the Priest Joseph or his supporters.

Methodius died in AD 847 and the empress Theodora appointed Ignatius to replace him. She did not call a synod or a meeting of bishops to rubber stamp her decision; she simply announced her appointment and had Ignatius installed. Ignatius was more inclined to be somewhat more strict than Methodius had been since he was the son of the iconophile emperor Michael who had been overthrown by the iconoclast Leo V; Leo had Ignatius castrated so as to remove him as a possible future political threat since a maimed or "incomplete" man could not be crowned as emperor. Theodora herself was overthrown in AD 858 and Ignatius resigned. Photius, a layman and scholar who had been the private tutor of Theodora's children and the chief of the imperial secretaries, was elected as the new patriarch of Constantinople.

Photius was seen as a "compromise candidate" between the new government (liberals) and the old government (conservatives) but Photius himself was reluctant to accept the position of patriarch. Only after both the bishops and the new emperor repeatedly urged him to accept the results of the election did he consent to be enthroned as patriarch. Nevertheless, the Studite conservative party in the Church and government wanted to stir up trouble by insisting that Photius was technically ineligible for election as he was still a layman at the time of the election. In an attempt to placate the conservative party, Photius was deposed and Ignatius reinstated as patriarch.

But the next year, AD 859, those conservative agitators were themselves deposed and Ignatius removed from office by a council overseen by Photius.

Photius sent the customary letter to Nicolas I, the pope in Rome, announcing his election and enthronement as patriarch. Nicholas was then involved in an effort to consolidate the political power of the papacy against the Franks in Western Europe; part of this effort was Nicholas' aim to have Illyricum (the east coast of the Adriatic Sea) and Sicily returned to papal jurisdiction. So, as part of his larger plan and to bolster the prestige and ecclesiastical influence of the papacy, Nicholas announced he would hold a council to review the dispute between Photius and Ignatius.

The council opened in Constantinople in AD 861 with the papal legates representing Nicholas. The council affirmed the right of appealing to Rome, at least when doctrinal matters were involved. The council confirmed the deposition of Ignatius, in part because he had deposed the archbishop of Syracuse several years earlier, in AD 854, which was cited as an illegitimate abuse of power. (The archbishop had been a moderate who called Ignatius a "parricide" for abandoning the moderate policies of Methodius.) The council re-condemned iconoclasm and ordered that no more laymen were to be chosen for the episcopacy; in the future, all candidates had to at least be priests, if not already bishops somewhere else. But Photius' reinstatement as patriarch was declared legitimate.

Nevertheless, an agitator—unhappy with the results of the council— went to Rome to protest the actions of the legates and the decisions of the council. He wanted Ignatius reinstated as patriarch even though Ignatius himself had been unwilling to appeal to Rome. As a result of the agitator's efforts, in AD 863 Pope Nicholas declared that Photius was deposed. There seems to have been no response from Constantinople to this announcement.

At the same time the agitator had left for Rome, the missionaries Cyril and Methodius had been sent to Moravia (equivalent to modern Moravia, Slovakia, and half of Hungary) in AD 862 in response to the request of Prince Rastislav who had asked for Byzantine missionaries to come and teach Christianity to his Slavic-speaking people. As part of these missionary efforts, Cyril and Methodius—who were brothers—began to translate the Bible and service books from Greek into Church Slavonic. As part of the Byzantine missionary expansion, missionaries were also sent to the Bulgarians in AD 864 and began to baptize there, using the translated service books of Cyril and Methodius.

Cyril (Constantine) and Methodius

Prince Rastislav had sent envoys to Constantinople asking for an alliance against the Franks and Bulgarians. As part of these negotiations, the prince also asked for missionaries familiar with the Slavic language(s) be sent to educate his people. (Earlier, during the AD 800s, German missionaries—and maybe also some Irish monks—had come and taught in Moravia but the prince had only recently asserted a precarious independence from Louis the German and needed a non–German form of Christianity.)

Photius—and the Byzantine churchmen as a whole—were very missionary minded and saw the advantages of such an alliance with the Moravians. The brothers Constantine and Methodius who came from Thessalonica, a Greek city with a large number of Slavic-speaking residents, were selected for this mission. Constantine was a professor—who had studied under Photius—in Constantinople, as well as a priest and a missionary and a diplomat. (He had gone on a mission trip to the Arabs in AD 855.) Methodius had served a governor near Thessalonica and was a diplomat, priest, and missionary as well. (He had gone on a mission together with his brother in AD 860 to the Khazars.)

In preparation for their trip to Moravia, Constantine invented an alphabet for the Slav language, based on the letters of the Greek alphabet and practiced it with a dialect of Slav from southern Macedonia, near Thessalonica. This original alphabet is known as Glagolitic and came to also include letters based on modified letters from Hebrew and Middle Eastern languages. (The "Cyrillic" alphabet was invented in the next generation by disciples of Constantine's, who adapted a more modern style of writing Greek to use with Slavonic.) The missionaries arrived in Moravia in AD 863.

They had two immediate tasks: train local clergy and translate the liturgical texts. (The emperor had promised Rastislav that the Slavs would "be numbered among the great nations who praise God in their own language.") Up until that point, the Slavs had used the Latin services the Germans had taught them but now Constantine and Methodius translated the daily services and the Divine Liturgy into Slavic, using their Glagolitic alphabet.

But the next year, in AD 864, Louis the German forced Rastislav to submit and also accept Frankish (pro–Roman) clergy into Moravia who were hostile and suspicious of Constantine and Methodius (who nevertheless continued their work). It was at this point that the Bulgarians were baptized.

The Bulgarians had several questions about their new faith and wrote to Constantinople for answers. The answers they got—including the order to give up robes or caftans and wear pants, like men in all the "civilized nations" of the world!—infuriated the Bulgarians and in AD 866 they defected from the Byzantine jurisdiction of Constantinople in favor of placing themselves under the jurisdiction of Rome (which had promised to give them a patriarch of their own). In AD 867, Photius held a council in Constantinople that condemned the Frankish missionaries working among the Bulgarians. (The missionaries were condemned for heresy and Nicholas in Rome was condemned personally for supporting them. This was a carefully worded condemnation of Nicholas and not a condemnation of the papacy itself.) That same year, the imperial throne was taken by Basil I who murdered the imperial supporters of Photius. Ignatius was reinstated as patriarch and began efforts to curry favor with Rome.

Photius and Ignatius each sent representatives to Rome to explain the situation and ask the pope to resolve their dispute. A council in Rome condemned the 867 council of Photius (that had condemned the Frankish missionaries), deposed all the clergy ordained by Photius—which the emperor had NOT wanted to happen—and allowed the clergy who supported Ignatius to continue in office only if they condemned Photius "and all heresies," and acknowledged the authority of Rome as supreme arbiter of church disputes.

Pope Nicholas also summoned Constantine and Methodius to Rome in AD 868 to answer questions about their missionary work as he also wanted to establish Roman jurisdiction over the Slavs. On their way to Rome, the two brothers stopped in Venice to debate the "tri-linguists," who insisted that their missionary and translation work was illegitimate because only three languages—Latin, Greek, and Hebrew—were appropriate to use when worshipping God.

The problem of language was emotionally charged. Even though John Chrysostom himself had supported the presence of a Gothic-speaking chapel for the Goths who were then living in Constantinople, certain clergy among the Byzantine intelligentsia were against the invention of Slavonic and Constantine had been afraid he would be charged with heresy for his linguistic work. Byzantines were notorious snobs about the "barbarian" tongues, including Latin. (Georgian monks on Mt. Athos at this same time were ill-treated by the Greek-speaking monks until the Mother of God appeared in a vision to rebuke them: "Do you think Greek is the only language pleasing to God?!" Nevertheless, a metropolitan of Athens in the early 1200s was still known for saying, "Asses will more readily perceive the melodious sound of the lyre and beetles that live in shit will more readily perceive perfume than Latin-speakers will comprehend the harmony and elegance of Greek.")

During the debate in Venice, Constantine pointed out that many nations—Armenians, Persians, Georgians, Goths, Khazars, Arabs, Egyptians—had traditionally used their own languages to worship God. He also pointed out that the recently converted nations were like the servants hired at the 11th hour in the parable (Matthew 20) who received the same salary as those who were hired to work from the beginning of the day. Methodius said, "All tongues are equal in God's sight. It is through a man's most intimate language—his mother tongue—that God can come into closest contact with the human soul." Anytime a person heard the services in their own, most intimate language and understood the Word of God was "a second Pentecost," Constantine argued.

By the time the brothers arrived in Rome, Pope Nicholas had died and Pope Hadrian II was pontiff. The brothers reported to him about their highly successful mission work. Their own personal piety and learning were widely admired and they were strongly backed by Rastislav in Moravia and Prince Kostel in Pannonia (modern Hungary). But the pope's problem was the use of Slavonic language and Byzantine liturgical texts versus the use of Latin and Roman services. Which was worse: to accept the brothers' work and set a precedent breaking the Latin uniformity of Western European Christianity or lose papal jurisdiction and influence in Moravia, Pannonia, and the Balkans?

Hadrian made his decision. He gave absolute support and approval to the Slavonic missionary work. He provided service books in Slavonic to the four principal churches in Rome. He denounced the tri-linguists.

While in Rome, Constantine became ill and was tonsured as a monk, taking the name Cyril (by which he is still most commonly known). He died on February 14, AD 869 and begged Methodius to never give up on their Slavonic mission work:

> Behold, my brother, we were both harnessed to the same yoke, plowing the same furrow. I am falling down by the gate, my day's work finished, but you have a great love for the [monastic life on Mt. Olympus]. Do not abandon your teaching for the sake of the life on the mountain. For how better can you be saved?[1]

Methodius was made archbishop of Pannonia (Hungary) and papal legate to the Slavonic nations. But the Frankish and German clergy whose authority was annulled when Methodius was installed as archbishop convinced Louis the German to arrest Methodius for usurping the rights of the archbishop of Salzburg. Methodius was held in jail for two-and-a-half years. He was only released because Pope John VIII forced Louis the German to release him. Methodius was invited by the emperor to visit Constantinople in AD 882; when he arrived, he set up a Slavonic-speaking chapel.

Methodius died in Moravia in AD 885. His enemies were able to exile his disciples—who fled to Bulgaria—or sell them into slavery; the Byzantine imperial representative in Venice saw some of them in the slave market there, bought them, and sent them to work as missionaries in Bulgaria. The next pope, Stephen V, refused to recognize the Slavonic services as legitimate. The entire experiment of Slavic-speaking Christianity seemed doomed.

But it took another 200 years to really stamp out Slavic-speaking Christianity in Central Europe, a sign of its strength and popularity. The Slavic-speaking Christianity that the Bulgarians finally embraced—because they wanted their own style of Christianity, neither Greek nor Latin—flourished. And in AD 988, Vladimir the prince of Kiev invited Constantinople to send Slavic-speaking missionaries to Rus to baptize and teach.

The news of the council, which had been held in Rome in June 869 and had condemned Photius, reached Constantinople that autumn. The conservative party of Byzantine rigorists held their own council that condemned Photius as well as condemning "excessive" lay—that is to say, imperial—participation or interference in the election of bishops. (This council was later cited by Pope Gregory VII in his efforts against the German emperor Henry IV at Canossa in January, AD 1077.) The council also affirmed Rome's primacy "of honor." Photius was exiled to a monastery.

About this same time, the Bulgarians—disappointed by Roman failure to fulfil their promise of a patriarch or archbishop—returned to the jurisdiction of the Byzantines in Constantinople. Ignatius then sent clergy who supported Photius to minister among the Bulgarians, which meant that there were hardly any pro–Photius clergy left in Constantinople. But Photius himself was recalled from exile to serve as tutor of the emperor's children.

Now that Photius was back in Constantinople, he and Ignatius were reconciled in AD 876. Ignatius died in AD 877 and Photius was installed again as patriarch. Legates from Rome arrived in AD 877 to argue against the Byzantines accepting the Bulgarians back into their jurisdiction and to ask for imperial aid against Saracens in Italy but they had no instructions about what to do regarding Photius and Ignatius.

So another council was held in Constantinople in AD 879–880. The council reaffirmed Nicea II and the condemnation of iconoclasm. This time, the council affirmed that it was acceptable for laymen to be elevated directly to the episcopacy without having to have been clergy beforehand. The council condemned the use of the Filioque. Both the Roman council of AD 869 (which had condemned Photius) and the Constantinople council of AD 869 (which had also condemned Photius) were annulled. The council agreed to maintain Roman jurisdiction over the Bulgarians, pending imperial approval. (The emperor, in fact, never let the Roman clergy back into Bulgarian territory.)

Each time Photius had been condemned by the pope or his representatives, it had meant that Photius was excommunicated in Roman eyes. Now there was no hindrance to proclaiming full communion between Photius and Rome. Thanks to this most recent council, the unity of the Greek- and Latin-speaking churches was openly manifest again. Everyone breathed a sigh of relief.

Until the Emperor Leo VI decided that he wanted his younger brother Stephen installed as patriarch in AD 886. So Photius was deposed and exiled once more and Stephen installed. Photius was exiled to a monastery and died there—but this time he was in full communion with Rome.

Leo VI was crowned emperor in 886, which is when he replaced Photius—who had been his tutor—with his brother Stephen as patriarch. Leo came to be nicknamed "the Wise" due to his financial skill at helping the imperial economy grow and the Byzantine monetary system became the standard against which all medieval currency was measured. He promoted reading and literacy and oversaw the construction of the church of St. Lazarus when the saint's relics were brought from Crete to Constantinople. He was also said to go out walking in disguise to find injustices or political corruption that needed reform. He was popular.

The Four Marriages of Leo VI

But his personal difficulties and multiple marriages nearly overwhelmed everything else he did. The *tetragamia*, the "affair of the four marriages" of Leo VI, has been called the most dangerous political crisis of the Middle Byzantine period.[2] Shifting allegiances, changes in civil law, early or unexpected deaths, clergy both willing and unwilling to comply with imperial designs, secret negotiations, pious public sentiment, loud-spoken monastics, differing interpretations of how to apply *oikonomia* (the principle of applying the spirit, rather than the letter, of the law for the benefit of the sinner) in the case—all these contributed to the chaos.

Church practice would never have had to deal with the question of remarriage if it were not a legally available option. Allowed by Roman law before Constantine's conversion, remarriage continued to be practiced in the Roman Empire until Constantine's new marital legislation, portions of which appeared in the year AD 320. Additional provisions were issued in AD 331. Profoundly altering the relationship between a man, his wife, and their children, the new law included a provision restricting divorce to only a few acceptable causes.

Leo's brother Stephen served as patriarch until his death at age 23 in AD 893, followed by Anthony II (AD 893–901). While Anthony was patriarch, Leo married the saintly but physically unattractive Theophano in AD 888. Disliked by Leo, she died childless in AD 897 and Leo married his African mistress Zoe Zaoutzaina shortly after Theophano's death. Zoe gave birth to a daughter but both mother and daughter died in AD 899. Leo sought a dispensation for a third marriage in the year AD 900 from the patriarch Anthony, as the law stipulated, and then wed the raving beauty Eudokia who died a year later in AD 901 during childbirth (as did the baby boy she was in labor with). That same year, the patriarch Anthony died and was succeeded by Nicholas I 'Mystikos' ['the secretary,' an imperial post], who had been a friend and supporter of Photius and champion of *oikonomia* against the monastic rigorists. He was also the *thetos adelphos*, the "adopted brother" of the emperor Leo and so Leo expected his unqualified support.

It was Arethas, archbishop of Caesarea in Cappadocia, a monastic rigorist and rival of Nicholas' for the patriarchal throne who set out to embarrass Nicholas in AD 902 or 903 by proclaiming that God thought it necessary to create only one wife for Adam![3] Leo responded by taking another Zoe, this time Zoe *Carbonopsina* ('of the coal black eyes'), as his mistress.

Zoe and Leo lived together in the imperial palace and when Zoe became pregnant, Leo insisted that she give birth in the imperial birthing chamber (a privilege reserved for legally-wed and crowned empresses) in order to underscore the imperial rank and legitimacy of the child to be born. Zoe gave birth to the bastard boy Constantine *Porphyrogenitus* ('the purple-born,' the imperial color of the hangings in the imperial birthing room) on September 2, AD 905.

There was strong opposition from much of the church hierarchy to both Zoe giving birth to the boy in the imperial setting and the insistence that the boy be called *Porphyrogenitus*, a statement of the baby's imperial status; there was opposition to any official recognition of the boy or his mother. Leo insisted that the boy be recognized as his son and so Patriarch Nicholas finally agreed to a "state baptism" for the baby Constantine so long as Zoe was sent away. Leo agreed, Zoe moved out of the imperial palace, and baby Constantine was baptized on January 6 (the feast of Christ's baptism), AD 906 in Hagia Sophia (the 'Great Church' and imperial cathedral of Byzantium). As part of the negotiated settlement involving the baptism, the elderly Studite monk Euthymius (Leo's own spiritual father) was to be the boy's godfather, even though Euthymius was too old and weak to hold the baby as the godfather normally would. However, it was only three days later that Zoe was officially escorted back into the palace and in April, AD 906 a parish priest known as Thomas performed the (fourth!) wedding for Leo and his new bride, thus legitimatizing the boy Constantine. Leo then crowned Zoe empress.

Outrage broke out in response. Public outcry, organized by Arethas and Studite monastic leaders, was intense. (The Studite monks had led the protests a century earlier against the second marriage of Constantine VI as well.) Nicholas, as the student of Photius, was furious both at the monastic interference in church policy and at Leo for breaking the terms of their agreement and attempting to justify his actions by marrying a fourth time. Monastic interference or not, the public sentiment demanded a response from the patriarch and so on Christmas Day, AD 906, Nicholas had the central doors of Hagia Sophia closed in Leo's face as the emperor arrived to attend the Divine Liturgy for the feast and then Nicholas refused to have Zoe commemorated in the Liturgy as empress.

In the days following Christmas, Leo was able to negotiate with Nicholas and was allowed to enter Hagia Sophia through a side door to attend a celebration of the Liturgy but not receive Holy Communion inside the altar area (which, like entering the cathedral through the main, central doors, was a jealously guarded imperial prerogative); it is unclear if this meant Leo approached the chalice as a simple layman or if he was not allowed to receive Communion at all. Leo also sent messages to Rome and the other Eastern patriarchs to ask for their opinions concerning his marriage(s). He knew in advance that Rome would have no opposition to his marriages—because Roman theology clearly stated that a marriage dissolved when one of the couple died and all Leo's previous wives were dead—and that the eastern patriarchs might be divided: some, like Alexandria, were generally eager to oppose anything Constantinople wanted but others would be eager to curry favor with the capital, especially in exchange for financial or other support.

In AD 907 Leo heard that the messengers with the answer were en route from Rome to Constantinople and he ordered that Nicholas be arrested, even before the Roman decision was received in Constantinople; Nicholas was forced to abdicate "without even a shirt or a book" to take with him.[4] These mutual recriminations and arguments between the emperor and patriarch were exactly what the adopted brother relationship between them ought to have avoided. To share the bond of *adelphopoiia* would normally obligate each man to publicly support and defend the other against public calumny. Nicholas, caught between the rock of the emperor's will and the hard place of traditional ecclesiastical canons, did the best he could to negotiate and compromise; Leo, refusing to abide by the agreements he had made with Nicholas undercut the patriarch at every turn. Leo then consulted with the elderly Euthymius, who had led the Studite opposition to the emperor's marriage to Zoe, and Euthymius—always in favor of consulting Rome, as the monastic party had been throughout the controversies over the position of Photius—urged his imperial spiritual son to heed the response of the Roman pontiff. Euthymius was persuaded to accept the role of patriarch and, in obedience to the Roman letter, condoned and granted retroactive permission for the emperor's fourth marriage. But in loyalty to his fellow monastics, Euthymius deposed the Priest Thomas who had performed the illicit wedding and still refused to commemorate the "empress" at the Divine Liturgy.

Chaos broke out in Byzantine church life now as the old party alignments were turned topsy-turvy. The Studite monks now backed the deposed Nicholas, who had refused to recognize Leo's marriage to Zoe, and Arethas led the court clergy in support of Euthymius and the recognition of the fourth marriage. To solidify baby Constantine's claim to the imperial throne, Leo had the two-year-old boy crowned as co-emperor in AD 908; it was only four years later, in AD 912, that Leo VI (then only aged 45 years old himself) became ill and died.

In the days leading up to Leo's death, his half-brother Alexander seized control of the government (as Constantine was only seven years old at that point) and—before Leo himself was even dead—deposed Euthymius from the patriarchate and reinstated Nicholas. (It was by Alexander's order that the elderly Euthymius was insulted and treated so roughly by the soldiers that they knocked out two teeth and beat him unconscious when sent to remove him from the patriarchal residence.) Nicholas, now out for revenge, deposed all the bishops ordained by Euthymius or his supporters and even ordered Euthymius' horse to be drowned! Arethas led the bishops who refused to leave their posts and Nicholas broke off communion with Rome to underscore Leo's illegal marriage and Constantine's illegitimate status. This only gave Arethas and his party further ammunition in their arguments that it was Nicholas who was upsetting good church practice and refusing to follow canonical order.

Alexander died in May, AD 913 and Patriarch Nicholas becomes the president of the Regency Council to rule on young Constantine's behalf. Nicholas made a series of decisions that proved extremely unpopular, however, and was deposed in February, AD 914.

Zoe herself became Regent on behalf of her son and offered the patriarchate back to Euthymius—who declined her offer! He urged her to reinstate Nicholas with the proviso that he restrict himself to church business. She did so.

Zoe was herself deposed in AD 919 and the Grand Admiral Romanus Lecapenus was crowned emperor; he made Constantine marry his daughter to unite the families and secure his hold of the throne. Therefore, in AD 920 Nicholas was able to preside at a church council which published a *Tome of Union* to settle the ecclesiastical confusion and discord: the Church was given control of all Byzantine civil laws concerning marriage. Third marriages, while allowed under certain circumstances, were considered questionable and fourth marriages were condemned outright. *Oikonomia* was invoked to legitimatize both Constantine Porphyrogenitus himself and the Euthymian clergy, who were allowed to remain in office. In AD 923, Nicholas restored the communion with Rome. There were some, though, who still refused to accept this *Tome* for nearly another 25 years.

Because of the fourth marriage affair of Leo VI, the Byzantine Church codified its response to the suspicious sexual relationships of second, third, and even fourth marriages. Second marriages, seen as problematic since the second century, were begrudgingly approved, if the man performed the required seven years penance followed by severe limitations on how often he might receive Holy Communion. But, following the precedent set by Constantine VI and the Moechian Schism, the couple was allowed to perform the penance without separating from each other. Third marriages were now seen as a very morally dubious but legitimate recourse for those who seeking companionship or sexual expression, again so long as the appropriate penance of four or five years was undertaken and the same ongoing restrictions on receiving Holy Communion observed. Fourth marriages, even for widows and widowers, were condemned in absolute terms. As a result of this codification and qualified acceptance of second-third marriages, a new rite developed to bless these relationships that were still considered inappropriate but legal. This "Blessing for a Second-Third Marriage" differed from the "Blessing of a Marriage" in several ways in order to make clear to everyone participating in such a wedding that it was clearly a "second best" relationship.

The Conversion of the Rus

Vladimir, the grand duke of Kiev, decided in AD 987 that it was time for his people—the Rus—to join the rest of the "modern world." This meant, in part, abandoning their traditional paganism and embracing one of the "modern" religions: Latin Christianity, Islam, or Byzantine Christianity. He sent envoys to investigate these religious options. On their return, they reported that among the Germans (i.e., western Christians) there was no glory and that among the Muslims there was neither joy nor alcohol. Vladimir exclaimed that neither was a viable option! But among the Byzantines? The envoys had gone to Constantinople and evidently seen the splendor of the patriarch celebrating the Eucharist in Hagia Sophia and reported to Vladimir, "We do not know whether we were in heaven or on earth. We only know that we have never seen such beauty … and that God dwells there among men.… We can never forget that beauty."

The Emperor Basil II sent envoys from Constantinople to Kiev, at Vladimir's request, to teach Byzantine Christianity to the Rus. The envoys arrived late summer AD 987 and negotiated that Vladimir would be baptized with his people and that the Russian church would be organized as an autonomous unit under the metropolitan of Kiev although ultimately subject to the patriarch in Constantinople, that the emperor's sister Anna would marry Vladimir, and that the Rus would receive military aid from Constantinople.

(Just before this, in AD 986–987, the Bulgarians had negotiated for Anna to marry the Bulgarian khan and the Byzantines had sent a different woman, pretending to be Anna, to wed the khan. The truth was discovered and the bishop who had acted as the chief negotiator of the Byzantines was burnt at the stake for lying.)

Vladimir was made a catechumen on Christmas, AD 987 and baptized on Epiphany, AD 988. Crowds of the Rus were baptized in the River Dnieper outside Kiev at Pascha (April 8) and at Pentecost (May 27). The idol of the former god Perun was toppled into the river. Anna arrived in Kiev during the summer of AD 988.

Vladimir apparently took his duties as a Christian prince seriously.

Vladimir listened also to the words of Solomon: "He that giveth unto the poor lendeth unto the Lord" (Proverbs 19:17). When he heard these words, he invited each beggar and poor man to come to the Prince's palace and receive whatever he needed, both food and drink, and marten-skins from the treasury.

With the thought that the weak and the sick could not easily reach his palace, he arranged that wagons should be brought in, and after having them loaded with bread, meat, fish, various fruits, mead in casks, and kvass [a popular alcoholic beverage made from rye bread], he ordered them driven out through the city. The drivers were under instructions to call out, "Where is there a poor man or a beggar who cannot walk?" To such they distributed according to their necessities.[5]

SUGGESTIONS FOR FURTHER READING

Francis Dvornik, *The Idea of Apostolicity in Byzantium and the Legend of the Apostle Andrew.* Harvard University Press, 1958.

Francis Dvornik, *Byzantine Missions Among the Slavs: SS. Constantine-Cyril and Methodius.* Rutgers University Press, 1970.

Francis Dvornik, *Byzantium and the Roman Primacy* (Trans. E. A. Quain). Fordham University Press, 1979.

The Russian Primary Chronicle: Laurentian text (Trans. S. H. Cross and O. P. Sherbowitz-Wetzor). Medieval Academy of America, 1973.

11

Divisions, the Crusades and Reunion

Roman claims and Byzantine claims of jurisdiction continued to plague the eastern Mediterranean area and southern Italy. It was Leo of Ohrid, the archbishop of Bulgaria—a region already known for trading loyalty between Rome and Constantinople—who wrote a letter addressed to one Latin bishop of southern Italy but meant for them all, including the Pope, in AD 1053 complaining about Roman liturgical customs. At issue were especially the Latin practice of fasting on Saturdays during Lent and the use of unleavened bread in the Eucharist.

Leo probably wrote his letter at the suggestion of Michael Cerularius, his friend and patriarch of Constantinople, in response to Pope Leo IX's order that all the Greek-speaking parishes in southern Italy adopt Latin liturgical customs. At the same time, Michael ordered all the Latin-speaking parishes in Constantinople to be closed.

Pope Leo IX in Rome wrote his own letter to Cerularius, criticizing the Byzantine affront to his claims of universal jurisdiction by the use of the title "Ecumenical Patriarch" for the archbishop of Constantinople (a title first used in the sixth century to indicate the archbishop/patriarch was part of the imperial system, not a claim to "ecumenical" or universal jurisdiction). The pope based his claim of universal jurisdiction—in part—on the letter known as the "Donation of Constantine." This donation, supposedly given by the Emperor Constantine the Great to Pope Sylvester in AD 333, gave the popes of Rome civil authority over most of Western Europe and supremacy over the churches of Alexandria, Antioch, Jerusalem, and Constantinople "and over all the churches of God in the whole earth." Constantinople denied the authenticity of this letter. (It was an Italian priest in AD 1439–1440 who exposed the Donation of Constantine as a forgery from the eighth century.)

Pope Leo decided it was best to deal with the Byzantines face-to-face, rather than through the cumbersome and awkward, time-consuming process of sending letters back and forth across the Mediterranean because he also needed to ask the emperor for help against the Normans who were invading southern Italy. He chose his friend Humbert to be his legate and representative. (Humbert had been chosen by Pope Leo to be the Archbishop of Sicily but the invading Normans refused to let Humbert into Sicily so Leo made him the cardinal-bishop of a Roman suburb instead.)

Humbert arrived in Constantinople and was warmly greeted by the emperor. Cerularius, however, refused to meet with him. For months. Humbert had been charged to discuss imperial military aid against the Normans, the Byzantine use of the title "Ecumenical Patriarch," and to insist that the Byzantines stop criticizing Latin customs. He got nowhere. So, on Sunday July 16, AD 1054, Humbert stormed into Hagia Sophia as Cerularius was celebrating the Divine Liturgy and threw a decree of excommunication onto the altar-table. He stalked out and back to Rome. Cerularius excommunicated the cardinal in retaliation.

This mutual excommunication is often cited as the definitive act breaking the Roman Catholic and Orthodox Churches into two distinct and independent institutions. But the pope, Leo, had died in April so Humbert's authority to act had died with the pope who had appointed him. Also, the excommunication of Humbert only mentioned Cerularius and specifically exempted the emperor and faithful people of Constantinople. The excommunication issued by Cerularius only mentioned Humbert. The whole affair was largely ignored by everyone everywhere.

What was noticed was that Humbert did not bring back any military aid against the Normans. So the popes began to negotiate directly with the Normans themselves, often against imperial interests. The hostility and tensions over titles and liturgical customs continued to fester in the west just as they did in the east. It was as if Humbert's mission had never happened.

When Humbert got back to Rome, he became the librarian of the Roman Curia (papal administration) and is said to have designed the decree of AD 1059 that the popes were to be exclusively elected by the college of cardinals (the leading clergy associated with the most prominent parishes in Rome and its vicinity). This move was to insist that no civil interference or ratification was allowed or needed for a new pope to be selected or enthroned.

The Filioque

The Council of Constantinople in AD 381 had amended the Nicene Creed to include statements regarding the Holy Spirit, who was proclaimed to "proceed" from the Father alone although he was worshipped and glorified with the Father and the Son together. But in the kingdoms of the Goths in Spain, where the Christians were all Arians, there were a series of councils that added yet another clause to the Creed. As the Arians embraced mainstream Orthodoxy, their theologians wanted to underline that the Son and the Father share the same divinity. One way to do this was to proclaim that the Holy Spirit proceeds from the Father and the Son together. This phrase, "and the Son," is one word in Latin: *filioque.*

These councils in Toledo (AD 447, 589, 675, and 693), Merida (AD 666), and Braga (AD 675) oversaw the conversion of the Arian Goths to Orthodoxy and inserted the Filioque into the Creed to underscore the divinity of the Son. Pepin, the father of Charlemagne, had it inserted into the Creed in AD 767. It seems to have been used by Latin monks in the Holy Land in the early AD 800s and was debated at Aachen, the capital of Charlemagne, in AD 809. The council at Aachen upheld the use of the Filioque but Pope Leo III refused to use the altered Creed in Rome and had the original text—without the Filioque—inscribed on silver plates which he mounted on the walls of St. Peter's Basilica. But in AD 1014–1015, the Creed with the Filioque was sung in Rome and the addition was upheld again in AD 1215 at the Lateran IV Council.

Photius called the Filioque "the crown of all evils." It became one of the central and most divisive issues between the Latin and Byzantine churches. Every Byzantine list of Latin errors, including the one compiled by Cerularius, included the Filioque.

The Byzantines objected to the Filioque for two reasons: firstly, they said that only another ecumenical council could alter the text of the Creed; secondly, they said that the theology used to justify the Filioque was incorrect.

Some Latins claimed that the Nicene Creed had originally contained the Filioque and that the Greek texts of the Nicene Creed that did not contain the Filioque were incorrect copies of the original! But most Latin theologians admitted that the Filioque had been added to the text although they asserted that the addition was justified because it was true. Latin theologians justified the addition of the Filioque by quoting St. Augustine:

> Therefore the Holy Spirit … is something common to both the Father and the Son. But that communion itself is consubstantial and co-eternal; and if it may fitly be called friendship, let it so be called; but it is more aptly called love. And this is also a substance, since God is a substance, and "God is love," as it is written [*On the Trinity* 6.5:7].

> For if whatever the Son has, he has from the Father, certainly he has it from the Father that the Holy Spirit proceeds from him…. The Son, however, is born of the Father; and the Holy Spirit proceeds principally from the Father and since the Father gives [to the Son all that he has] without any interval of time, the Holy Spirit proceeds jointly from both the Father and the Son [*On the Trinity* 15.26:47].

> Why then should we not believe that the Holy Spirit proceeds also from the Son, when he is the Spirit also of the Son? For if the Holy Spirit did not proceed from

him, when he showed himself to his disciples after his Resurrection, he would not have breathed on them, saying, "Receive the Holy Spirit." For what else did he signify by that breathing on them, except that the Holy Spirit proceeds also from him? [*Homilies on the Gospel of John* 99:7].

The Latin theologians were satisfied that the Spirit proceeded from both the Father and the Son and that the Spirit was, in fact, the bond of love between the Father and the Son.

The Byzantines answered that the Latins misunderstood that the Holy Spirit proceeds from the Father alone in eternity but that the Son sends the Spirit into the world to deal with humanity. The Byzantines said that this distinction between the Spirit's eternal procession from the Father and the Son's sending of the Spirit in time was the correct way to understand the several statements in the Gospels which seemed to contradict each other. Although Jesus had given the Spirit to the apostles on the evening after his Resurrection, saying "Receive the Holy Spirit" (John 20:22), he also said to the apostles at the Last Supper, "But when the Advocate comes, whom I shall send to you from the Father, even the Spirit of truth, who proceeds from the Father, he will bear witness to me" (John 15:26).

It was incomprehensible to the Byzantines why anyone would want to alter the Nicene Creed's statements about the Holy Spirit.

The First to Fourth Crusades

Pilgrimage to Jerusalem had always been an important feature of Christian practice after Constantine the Great decriminalized Christianity. His mother Helen supervised archeological expeditions to uncover holy sites in Jerusalem and around the Holy Land, building great churches and monuments to mark them. A traveler known as the "Bordeaux Pilgrim" wrote notes about his early fourth-century pilgrimage to Jerusalem. The famous woman pilgrim Egeria traveled from Spain to the Holy Land in the late fourth century and wrote a detailed description of the places and services she saw. Pope Gregory the Great of Rome built a hospice in Jerusalem in AD 600 for pilgrims that was popular with Anglo-Saxon travelers.

Muslim Arabs attacked Jerusalem in AD 636 and Sophronius surrendered the city in order to preserve it. Muslim law insisted that cities that surrendered be preserved intact rather than looted and destroyed. The surrendering population was also to be spared massacre and slavery. Sophronius saved the city and its inhabitants by surrendering it. The Christian population was, however, expected to pay special taxes to the Muslim conquerors and were subject to a variety of social discriminations. But they were allowed to remain Christians, one of the "peoples of the Book" in the eyes of Muslim authorities.

Muslim persecution of Christian pilgrims to the Holy Land seems to have begun in AD 1009.

Then, in AD 1070, the Seljuk Turks—a different Muslim tribe who were not Arabs—took Jerusalem. They began to attack not just pilgrims in the Holy Land but pilgrims who were en route to the Holy Land from Western Europe. Various western kings, the popes in Rome, and the various Holy Roman emperors began to exchange letters talking about rescuing the Holy Land from the Muslims and protecting pilgrims going there. They were also interested in forcing the Byzantine Christians to acknowledge the supremacy of the popes in Rome and the superiority of Western Christian practices.

A series of military expeditions, each called a "crusade," were organized by preachers and military leaders. The first, in AD 1095–1101, was organized in response to the preaching of Bernard of Clairvaux (a popular monastic leader) who promised that every knight who "took the Cross" by sewing the emblem onto his cloak would be taken directly into heaven by the angels if he was killed during the expedition. The second crusade was in AD 1145–1147. The third, in AD 1188–1192, was led by King Richard the Lion Heart of England; during Richard's absence from his kingdom, it was said that his brother King John robbed nearly everyone with the assistance of the Sherriff of Nottingham while Robin Hood and his band of merry men stole from the rich to give to the poor.

Pope Innocent III was elected in AD 1198. He was a great organizer and reformer. He wanted to centralize all Christianity—Western European and Byzantine—in Rome. One of his major interests was the liberation of the Holy Land. He began to organize a crusade among French and German knights in AD 1199 but he quickly lost control of the project. The French knights decided to attack the Muslims in Egypt, rather than the Holy Land, and signed contracts in AD 1201 with Venice to transport troops across the Mediterranean.

In AD 1202, the dethroned Byzantine emperor Alexius III arrived in Italy and asked Pope Innocent for help to regain the throne in Constantinople. The Crusaders gathering in Venice were unable to pay the agreed on fee for transportation to Egypt; the Venetians offered to accept the money the Crusaders did have available and take them to Dalmatia, a much quicker trip, instead. The knights accepted this offer and seized a Greek city on the coast when they landed.

Pope Innocent wrote to the Crusaders and urged them to make their way down the eastern coast of the Mediterranean to the Holy Land. But the Crusaders also received an appeal from Alexius III to help him. They made a treaty with him: in exchange for restoring him to the throne in Constantinople, he would restore communion with Rome, he would pay the Crusaders 200,000 gold pieces, and he would provide additional troops to join the Crusaders when they moved on from Constantinople to the Holy Land.

The Crusaders attacked a suburb of Constantinople in July, AD 1203. Alexius fled the battle. The residents of Constantinople refused to honor the "treaty" the Crusaders had struck with the now-missing Alexius. The Crusaders had nowhere to go and no money to go anywhere; so they stayed. Weeks, then months, passed. Tension built.

In March of AD 1204, the Crusaders and the Venetians made a deal between them to evenly share the spoils and plunder of Constantinople and in April, the Crusaders attacked the royal city. Constantinople fell on Good Friday. For three days the Crusaders ran wild, plundering, raping, and slaughtering the people. Witnesses reported that the Crusaders installed a prostitute on the throne of the patriarch in Hagia Sophia and that the streets ran ankle-deep with blood. It was clear that the Western Europeans no longer recognized the Orthodox of Constantinople as fellow Christians of any sort.

The breakdown of the one Church into Roman Catholic and Orthodox was not a dramatic one-momentous-event over one singular all-important issue but a process of gradual estrangement and alienation for a multitude of reasons. The cultural differences between Latin-speakers and Greek-speakers were evident from the beginning of Latin-speaking Christianity across the western Mediterranean region; even in the book of the Acts of the Apostles we can see the ethnic hostilities between Gentile Christians and their Jewish-Christian or "Hebrew" co-religionists and those human dynamics continued to play out over time. There were the theological differences that arose between the early Latin-speaking congregations that were primarily Gentile converts in the West and the Greek-speaking congregations of Jewish-Christians in the East, perhaps seen most clearly in the dispute over the date of Pascha and its relationship to the Jewish Passover (the *Quartodeciman* or "Fourteenth-ers" controversy). There was the estrangement that grew up as each region of the Mediterranean gradually became more exclusively monolingual, functioning only in Greek or Latin. There was the different world views of early theologians who were mostly converted Latin-speaking lawyers as opposed to the Greek-speaking theologians who were poets. There was the overwhelming predominance of Augustine's theology in the West as it was his books that the monks kept with them as they fled the Norse or barbarian incursions and destruction of what remained of Roman culture in Western Europe. The breakdown of the Church into exclusive Eastern and Western segments was a process in which the events of AD 1054 were negligible at the time but which was definitively over when the Crusaders sacked Constantinople in AD 1204.

In May, a Latin (western) emperor of Constantinople was elected by the invaders. In Rome, Pope Innocent expected the Latin occupation of Constantinople to provide vast new resources for the Crusade against the Muslims in the Holy Land but the Latin "empire" of Constantinople was too precarious and too busy struggling to survive to send any assistance to Rome.

Innocent protested the Crusaders seizing church property and goods, to no avail. He also fully expected the clergy and people of Constantinople to accept his primacy and the primacy of Rome in all church business. In exchange, he was willing to allow them to retain their usual services in Greek—rather than Latin—but the ultimate goal was that they would also eventually adopt Western European liturgical rites and use Latin. He completely underestimated the Greek-speaking Orthodox!

The Byzantines regrouped in the nearby city of Nicea and formed the "Nicean Empire" while the Crusaders occupied Constantinople itself. Theodore I was proclaimed emperor of Nicea. But the Byzantines had few resources and had to rely on the pope in Rome to curb the Crusaders' aggression throughout the Mediterranean and Aegean Seas; in order to win the pope's cooperation in trying to control the Crusaders, the Byzantines in Nicea kept promising to work on Church reunion projects.

Genghis Khan swept across the steppes and conquered the Rus in AD 1241. Then he attacked Poland. Western European Christians were fighting on two fronts now and bickering among themselves. Genoa and Venice fought each other for control of various territories in the Middle East. Genoa struck a deal with Michael VIII (Palaeologos), the emperor of Nicea, and together the Genoans and Byzantines were able to retake Constantinople in AD 1261. The Crusaders were driven out. To avoid any future crusade against Constantinople, the emperor Michael promised the pope in Rome to keep working towards reunion of the Orthodox and Roman churches.

The Byzantines were back home. Constantinople was theirs again. But they had only 25 percent of the pre–1204 population. Large areas inside the city walls were now empty fields. No great artists, scholars, or writers remained. Few service books remained in the churches. Most of the people that returned to Constantinople were poor. Monks took on responsibility for holding services in the parish churches because they were the only ones to still have service books and so the liturgical life of the city became increasingly monastic. The great choral tradition of Byzantine churches was replaced by small choirs and individual cantors because there were no music books and—more importantly—so few singers.

The attempts at church reunion collapsed in AD 1268. Latins attacked Constantinople again but failed to take it. And in AD 1291, the Muslims took Jerusalem back from the Crusaders who had occupied it since AD 1099. Michael VIII remained interested in church union as a way to further his own goals and aims. So when Pope Gregory X was elected in AD 1268 and announced in AD 1272 that he wanted to call a council together in AD 1274 in Lyons to heal the schism with the Orthodox Byzantines, the Emperor Michael was happy to cooperate.

Gregory was probably one of the most spiritually-minded popes of that era and was sincere in his wish to overcome the divisions between Eastern and Western Christianity. But the Byzantine bishops and theologians refused to attend. Michael VIII imprisoned several of his leading opponents, offering to release them in exchange for supporting the council in Lyons. Some of the jailed theologians did finally agree that saying the Holy Spirit proceeds "from the Son" (the standard Western *filioque* clause) could be understood as meaning the same thing as the Holy Spirit proceeds "through the Son" (a typical Orthodox formulation); some apparently honestly believed in this equivalency while others were simply browbeaten to accept it.

Byzantine envoys eventually agreed to attend the council but the council opened in May before the Byzantines arrived. The Byzantines did get there— on June 24!—and signed documents already prepared; they agreed to commemorate the pope in the Eucharist and other services, that papal primacy gave the popes ultimate authority in church matters, to accept Roman teaching and practices (such as the use of *filioque* in the Creed, the use of *azymes*— unleavened bread—for the Eucharist, the Latin understanding of transubstantiation, and the Latin understanding of purgatory), as well as accepting Latin canons on a variety of issues (such as marriage).

The participants all celebrated the Eucharist and received Holy Communion together on June 29, the feast of SS. Peter and Paul.

Purgatory, Azymes, Transubstantiation and So On

The Byzantines loved to make lists, especially of Latin Christian religious errors. The lists varied considerably from each other in their length and the number of errors listed, how these errors were or were not categorized, and which errors were deemed most important. Several items appeared on almost all of these lists and thereby seem to be among the most important issues dividing Eastern from Western Christian practice.

Fasting on Saturday was surprisingly important to the Byzantines. Eastern Christian practice had always considered the Sabbath an honored day, second only to the Lord's Day (Sunday) in importance. (The four most important liturgical days of each week were the fasting days of Wednesday and Friday with Sunday and Saturday, the two Eucharistic days.) The Eucharist was traditionally celebrated on Saturdays as well as Sundays, even during Great Lent (when all weekday celebrations of the Eucharist were replaced with the service of the Presanctified Liturgy, in which Holy Communion was distributed from the Holy Gifts reserved from the previous Sunday). It seems that sometime during the fifth century the Roman practice stopped fasting on Wednesday and extended the Friday fast to include Saturday.

The Byzantines objected to the Latins eating "unclean foods" (meat with blood still in it and animals forbidden in the Old Testament, such as beavers, jackals, and bears). Everyone agreed that the New Testament had forbidden "blood" (Acts 15) or meat offered to idols. But offering meat to idols was no longer a common practice in the Mediterranean region, although even the popes sometimes declared that Christians should not eat foods associated with pagan practices among the barbarians of northern Europe. European diets—including the forbidden animals—differed from Byzantine diets partly because different foods were more or less easily available in different regions. Eastern Christians understood the injunction against blood in Acts 15 to forbid the consumption of blood. Most early western Christians had understood the prohibition of blood in Acts 15 to be a prohibition of murder rather than a command to follow certain ritual food prescriptions.

Bread without leaven (*a-zymes*) at the Eucharist was one of the earliest distinctions between Latin and Greek liturgical practice. The Greek-speaking Orthodox saw the yeast in the bread that they used as a sign of the Resurrection. They saw the use of unleavened bread—the same as that used by Jews during Passover—as an embrace of Jewish faith and practice as well as the rejection of Chalcedon (as the Armenians, who rejected Chalcedon, used unleavened bread in the Eucharist). Many councils had repeatedly issued canons forbidding Christians to fast or celebrate holidays with the Jews because Christ and Christian practice had superseded the previous covenant God had made with the Jews. Byzantine Christians saw the Latin use of bread without yeast in the Eucharist as a betrayal of everything right-believing Christians ought to embrace.

Latins insisted that parish priests ought not to marry. Byzantines expected parish priests to be married but to abstain from intercourse with their wives the night before they celebrated the Eucharist. Among the Byzantines, their standard liturgical calendar meant a priest would celebrate the Eucharist once or twice—rarely three times—a week and so would abstain from conjugal relations the night before these celebrations. But western Christians—who had originally followed this same practice—had developed the custom of parish priests celebrating a simplified version of the Eucharist every day. If they were still expected to abstain from conjugal relations with their wives the night before the Eucharist but celebrated the Eucharist every day, what was the point of being married at all? This difference of liturgical practice was ignored and the Latin insistence on clerical celibacy was seen as a condemnation of marriage itself.

Byzantine and Latin practices during Lent were another point of dispute. Latins counted Saturdays as fasting days although the Byzantines did not. (The Byzantines not count Saturdays as fasting days because they still celebrated the Eucharist on Saturday morning even if they did not eat meat or other certain foods.) The Byzantines also had a week of preparatory fasting before Lent itself actually began and then counted Holy Week as a separate fasting period, not simply the last few days of Lent as the Latins did. So, all together, the pre–Easter fast of Lent—as a broadly generic term—was much longer among the Byzantines than among the Latins. Byzantine fasting discipline expected the people to follow a fairly vegan diet that included no animal products of any sort, in addition to no oil or alcohol, during the fast; fish was allowed on a few particular feast days. Latin practice, on the whole, was much less strict.

Also among the divergent practices discussed at Lyons were the Latin teaching about purgatory and transubstantiation. Although both Latin and Greek-speaking Christians had long believed in the value of prayers for the dead and that the departed are engaged in a process of further growth and purification after death before they are capable of entering the presence of God, the Latins had developed a much more codified theology of what they now called "Purgatory." They taught it was a physical place in this world and that it involved flames and suffering not unlike hell itself but that the suffering of Purgatory was temporary rather than eternal. The practice of offering "indulgences" to reduce the time a dead person spent in the fires of Purgatory began. The Byzantines refused to use the name "Purgatory" or assign the dead to a physical location as they experienced purification, growth, development. The Byzantines did not want to describe this process in terms of flames and suffering. They objected to the use of indulgences. In general, the Byzantine Greeks preferred to say as little as possible about this process of growth and purification of the dead.

Another concept that the Greeks and Latins originally agreed on was the presence of Christ in the Eucharist and that the Holy Gifts of bread and wine became his Body and Blood. Over time, the Latin theologians also codified this in ways that struck the Greeks as inappropriate. Using the philosophy of Aristotle, the western Church enshrined the doctrine of transubstantiation in AD 1215 to explain how the bread and wine of the Eucharist become the Body and Blood of Christ: the "accidents" or outward appearances of bread and wine remain but their inner "substance" is replaced by that of Christ himself. The Latins taught that the priest's recitation of the Words of Institution—quoting Jesus' statements at the Last Supper, "This is my Body.... This is my Blood"—are the means by which this occurs. The Greeks preferred to say that the priest asking the Father to send the Holy Spirit to change the Holy Gifts into the Body and Blood of Christ was the critical moment during the Eucharist and refused to endorse any particular explanation beyond that of how the transformation was accomplished or explain how it operated.

A variety of other issues—clean-shaven priests, the Latin understanding that marriage was a contract that dissolved when one of the couple died, the allowance of certain degrees of relatives to marry or not marry, Latin postponement of confirmation for several years after baptism, as well as other liturgical practices at odds with the Orthodox—also angered the Byzantine theologians and canon lawyers.

Byzantine Reception of the Council of Lyons

The envoys returned to Constantinople from Lyons in late autumn. The patriarch abdicated in protest at what the envoys had agreed to and no new patriarch was found until the next May. Michael VIII was willing to settle with the Byzantines' refusal to implement anything the envoys had agreed to, as long as his private imperial chapel was allowed to live up to the council's agreements.

There was deep division in Byzantine society based on whether people thought they should or should not accept the changes agreed to at Lyons. Some that wanted to implement the reunion with the West simply expected material benefits from the Europeans as a result; others seem to have been honest in desiring Christian reunion. The pope began to demand that the liturgical changes agreed to at Lyons be implemented, first in Hagia Sophia and then throughout all Byzantine parish churches. Michael VIII tried to pacify both the popes in Rome and the anti-unionists in Constantinople.

A synod was called in Constantinople in AD 1277 to resolve the tensions between the unionists and anti-unionists. Each faction excommunicated the other. Papal envoys arrived in AD 1279 and the Byzantine anti-unionists refused to even meet with them. Michael VIII grew stricter in his demands for conformity with imperial policy and persecuted the anti-unionists with increasing cruelty. In AD 1282, Pope Martin IV excommunicated Michael as a schismatic as Michael had supported Martin's rival in papal politics.

Michael died in December AD 1282 and although he received the Last Rites as an Orthodox Christian, he was thereafter denied the liturgical commemoration and prayers for the dead that were customary for deceased emperors. The imperial pro-union efforts were dropped.

SUGGESTIONS FOR FURTHER READING

Tia M. Kolbaba, *The Byzantine Lists: Errors of the Latins*. University of Illinois Press, 2000.

Jacques LeGoff, *The Birth of Purgatory*. (Trans. A. Goldhammer) University of Chicago Press,1984.

Miri Rubin, *Corpus Christi: The Eucharist in Late Medieval Culture*. Cambridge University Press, 1991.

12

Gregory Palamas, the Council of Ferrara-Florence and the Fall of the City

Gregory Palamas was born in AD 1296 to an aristocratic family in Asia Minor who were forced to flee to Constantinople because of the Turkish invasions. Gregory grew up in the imperial court of the Emperor Andronicus II, who was a patron of scholars and the arts. (Andronicus was a devout intellectual but only a mediocre politician.) Gregory studied the philosophy of Aristotle, with plans for a career at the imperial court. But when he was 20 years old, his father died and he suddenly decided to become a monk. He placed his mother, sisters, and servants in monasteries in Constantinople and set out with his two brothers for the monastic settlements of Mount Athos (a mountain peninsula in north-eastern Greece on which monasteries had been built since AD 1000).

Having arrived on Mt. Athos, also known as the "Holy Mountain," Gregory lived in solitude and only joined the monastic community on feast days. When one of his brothers and their teacher died, Gregory and his remaining brother moved into the Great Lavra (the principal monastery on the mountain); Gregory became the choir director there. He began a pilgrimage to the Holy Land and to Mt. Sinai but got no further than Thessalonica. He was ordained a priest in Thessalonica and established a hermitage nearby.

Gregory returned to Mt. Athos in AD 1331 due to the danger from Serbian raiding expeditions around Thessalonica. Back on Mt. Athos, he became a hermit again. He was briefly made the abbot of one of the monasteries on the mountain and was responsible for 200 monks but he was regarded as too strict and the monks became antagonistic towards him, resisting his instructions. So he retired from that position and returned to his hermitage.

It was in his extensive hermitage experience on Mt. Athos and at Thessalonica that Gregory became familiar with the practice of *hesychasm* ("quiet"). The hesychasts practiced a form of prayer which has come to be known as the "Jesus Prayer," because it was based on the brief petition "Lord Jesus Christ, Son of God, have mercy on me a sinner." (This prayer and a variety of hesychasm appropriate for non-monastic Christians was popularized in Russia by *The Way of the Pilgrim*, an anonymous text published in 1884 describing the experience of a layman who wandered across imperial Russia saying the Jesus Prayer. *The Way of the Pilgrim* and the Jesus Prayer are also important in *Franny and Zooey* by J.D. Salinger.)

The original motivation of the hesychasts was to live according to the injunction of the Apostle Paul to "pray without ceasing" (I Thess. 5:17). The hesychasts would sit quietly and bow their heads slightly, slowly and quietly reciting the phrases of the Jesus Prayer in rhythm with their breathing. Although most hesychasts would pray with their eyes closed, their opponents accused them of staring at their navels because of their bowed heads. The hesychasts hoped to make the Jesus Prayer so much a part of their existence and so connected to their breathing that they would be able to continue the prayer in the back of their minds as long as they were awake and breathing, even if they were engaged in some other task.

While reciting the Jesus Prayer, the hesychasts were to practice mental discipline and stop their mind from wandering or focusing on anything other than the Jesus Prayer. The words of the prayer were to fill the consciousness of each hesychast and his mind would eventually be united with his heart. By praying with their mind in their heart, the hesychasts would be constantly aware of the presence of Christ and avoid any distracting mental images. The most experienced hesychasts claimed that they had been granted a vision of the uncreated light of God's glory, the same light which the apostles had seen at the Transfiguration of Christ on Mount Tabor (Matthew 17:1–8, Mark 9:2–8, Luke 9:28–36, II Peter 1:16–18). The vision of the uncreated light was understood to mean that the monk had acquired the Holy Spirit.

The hesychasts stressed that each practitioner should be under the guidance and direction of a spiritual father because it was too easy for a beginner or even a moderately advanced hesychast to delude himself about the nature of his experiences while praying. Rigorous self-examination and confession were necessary aspects of hesychasm, as were the regular liturgical services. A practitioner had to always check his own subjective experience against the greater experience and teaching of his spiritual father and confessor as well as the objective teaching expressed in the liturgical hymnography.

Meanwhile, a Greek from Italy named Barlaam arrived in Constantinople in AD 1338. Barlaam saw himself as a loyal Orthodox Christian. He liked the writings of Pseudo-Dionysius and the emphasis on apophatic theology, disliking the Roman efforts and claims to know God so well that they felt comfortable with insisting on the Filioque. So he left Italy as he "loved piety" and all the Greeks in Italy were, de facto, under the jurisdiction of Rome and so forced to abide by the union of Lyons. Barlaam then became an instructor in the university at Constantinople and taught the theology and writings of Pseudo-Dionysius.

As he immersed himself in the apophatic theology of Pseudo-Dionysius, Barlaam became convinced that truly apophatic theology meant that no one could know the truth of the Spirit's procession, whether it was from the Father alone or from the Father and the Son together. Based on this conclusion, Barlaam announced his conviction that it would be possible for the Roman and Byzantine churches to reunite.

Palamas heard about Barlaam's announcement and wrote in response, "Yes, but God does reveal himself and has revealed that the Spirit does only proceed from the Father." Palamas cited not only the Scriptures but also the mystical experience of the monks who practiced hesychasm. Intrigued by Palamas, Barlaam wanted to experience what the hesychasts claimed to have experienced, so he went to live with hesychasts in both Thessalonica and Constantinople.

Barlaam was shocked at what he found.

> I have been initiated by them into monstrosities and in absurd doctrines that a man with any intelligence or even a little sense, cannot lower himself to describe, products of erroneous belief and rash imagination. They taught me almost marvelous separations and reunions of mind and soul, the relations of the demon with the latter, the differences between red and white lights, the intelligible entrances and exits produced by the nostrils while breathing, the shields around the navel and, finally, the vision of Our Lord with the soul that is produced within the navel in a perceptible manner with full certitude of heart [*Letter V* to Ignatius].

Barlaam mocked and derided the hesychasts. He was appalled by the breathing exercises the hesychasts practiced as they prayed. Their "navel gazing" was a waste of time. Their descriptions of the descent of the mind into the heart sounded like nonsense. The claim to have seen the uncreated light sounded like blasphemy. Palamas wrote his *Triads in Defense of the Holy Hesychasts* in response and then went on to write his *Hagiorite Tome* ("Book/Letter from the Holy Mountain") in AD 1340. The *Tome* was addressed to Barlaam and signed not only by Palamas but by all the abbots and monks on Mt. Athos.

Hesychasm, Theosis and the Energies of God

Prayer, in the experience of the early monks and the monastic hesychasts, led to the knowledge of God. But those same monastic fathers would insist that God is in himself unknowable. They fell back on the apophatic theology of Pseudo-Dionysius, certain that is was safer to say what God was not—ineffable, invisible, incomprehensible—rather than what he is. Words not unlike the four negative adverbs of Chalcedon: without confusion, without change, without division, without separation. The knowledge and presence of God which the hesychasts encountered was so filled with the overwhelming divine presence that is was a blinding brightness, a divine darkness in which it was only certain what God was not.

This bright darkness was identified as the glory of God which was eternal and uncreated. This eternal glory was, however, distinct from the unknowable essence of God (Palamas, *Triads* 3.2.13). God communicates himself to the apostles, to the monks, to all baptized Christians who truly seek him

> in mingling himself with each of the faithful by communion with his holy body and since he becomes one single body with us (cf. Ephesians 3:6) and makes us a temple of the undivided divinity, for in the very body of Christ dwells the fullness of the Godhead bodily (Col. 2:9), how should he not illuminate those who commune worthily with the divine ray of his body which is within us, lightening their souls, as he illuminated the very bodies of the disciples on Mount Tabor? For, on the day of the Transfiguration, that body—the source of the light of grace—was not yet united with our bodies; it illuminated from outside those who worthily approached it and sent illumination into the soul by the intermediary of the physical eyes; but now, since it is mingled with us and exists in us, it illuminates the soul from within [Palamas, *Triads* 1.3.38].

Even as Christ gives himself to the faithful in Holy Communion, he remains transcendent and unknowable in his divine essence. He communicates his power, his energy to humans so that each member of the faithful can become by grace everything that Christ is by nature. This process was also called *theosis* ("deification"). The energies of God, his attributes which can be experienced or known by humans, are eternal and uncreated, just as the innermost essence of God is; in the *Triads* Palamas cited Maximus the Confessor: "There was never a time when virtue, goodness, holiness, and immortality did not exist" (Palamas, *Triads* 3.2.7). This distinction between the essence of God—the unknowable inner reality—and the energies of God—which were uncreated but knowable and communicable—was never understood or accepted by Barlaam and the Latin theologians of the west. For Barlaam and his supporters, only the essence of God could be uncreated and therefore the energies of God had to have been created.

One aspect of hesychasm that especially shocked and offended Barlaam was the hesychasts' insistence that the apostles had seen the uncreated and eternal glory of God on Mt. Tabor when they witnessed the Transfiguration of Christ. Barlaam insisted that the apostles could not have seen this eternal and uncreated glory with their physical eyes. But, the hesychasts replied, just as the faces of Moses and Stephen were too bright to look at because of their proximity to God (Exodus 34 and Acts 6), the glory of the Transfiguration permeated the mountaintop. The energies of God are both accessible to the intellect and yet transcend it; some energies are perceived as spiritual light or intellectual light and yet others are capable of being perceived by physical perception (Palamas, *Triads* 3.2.14–16). "They saw it with their corporeal eyes but with eyes that had been opened so that, instead of being blind, they could see … they contemplated that uncreated light which, even in the age to come, will be ceaselessly visible only to the saints" (Palamas, *Triads* 3.3.9). What Palamas is describing here might be recognized as the light of the Eighth Day described by Basil the Great in his *Hexameron* sermons.

Palamas and the hesychasts agreed with Maximus the Confessor that human passions were not to be eradicated but transformed by ascetic effort and participation in the divine energies; in other words, by *theosis*. It is the passionate aspect of our souls that enables us to love God, Palamas wrote. With our passion

> we love or else turn away [i.e., love something other than God], that we unite ourselves [to God] or else remain strangers [to God]. Those who love the good thus transform their power [i.e., the passionate aspect of their soul] and do not put it to death … they activate it towards the love of God and their neighbors—for, according to the Lord's words, 'on these two commands hang all the Law and the prophets' [Matthew 22:40; Palamas, *Triads* 3.3.15].

Byzantine Response to Barlaam and Palamas

There were two councils—in June and August of AD 1341—held in Constantinople to resolve the dispute. In the end, Barlaam was condemned and as a result he moved back to Italy where he was made a bishop and eventually taught Petrarch how to read Greek.

This dispute between Barlaam and Palamas was one aspect of a larger tension between Byzantine culture and the Western European Renaissance. But Barlaam's opinions were only problematic because so many Byzantines agreed with what he said. In the Byzantine context, the dispute was between a secular versus a church-oriented world view. The secularists wanted to marginalize the Church in order to deal with the new, expanding cultural world while many of the more church-oriented wanted to prioritize church teachings and many seemed satisfied to simply repeat old formulas as an adequate response to new questions.

Palamas had a disciple, a man named Akindynus, who had acted as a go-between with Barlaam. The councils also condemned Akindynus as he had thought the "old formulas" were enough and disliked the Palamite distinction between the essence and the energies of God.

The Emperor Andronicus III was pro–Palamas and presided himself at the June council but died four days later, before he could sign the official documents. He and his wife Anne had a baby boy, John V, who was acclaimed emperor with his mother Anne as regent. But Anne was inept at politics. Soon the Patriarch John and the Grand Duke Alexis were facing off on her behalf against John Cantecuzenos (the "right hand" of Andronicus and the real ruler of the empire). Cantecuzenos presided at the August council, which condemned Akindynus.

Just after the August council, Cantecuzenos began open hostilities and a civil war for the imperial crown. Palamas condemned the coup d'état but refused to get any more involved than that in imperial politics. The Patriarch John became angry, wanting Palamas to support the patriarch and the Grand Duke against Cantecuzenos. He ordered Palamas arrested in AD 1343 and added heresy to the arrest warrant to support the political charges against Palamas. Akindynus published a refutation of Palamas and Palamas replied, beginning a "tract war" with his former disciple. John the patriarch excommunicated Palamas and his followers in AD 1344 and ordained Akindynus as a priest.

The Empress Anne did not support the patriarch's theological ideas. She admired Palamas as a theologian and feared him as a politician. She had the patriarch deposed in AD 1347 just before Cantecuzenos won the civil war and was crowned emperor.

In May AD 1347, Palamas was made archbishop of Thessalonica and in July AD 1351 another council condemned another foe of Palamas, Nicephorus Gregoras. Politics continued to be volatile and explosive but Palamas managed to navigate the political conflicts, becoming an outspoken preacher and ardent advocate of social justice.

It was on a trip to Constantinople for church business that Palamas was on a ship attacked by Turkish pirates and held hostage for a year until the Serbian Orthodox were able to raise the ransom the pirates demanded to free him.

Palamas finally died in Thessalonica, November AD 1359. He was canonized almost immediately by his friend, the Patriarch Philotheos in Constantinople. The second Sunday in Lent was made the principal feast day of Palamas in AD 1368. Palamas' teaching about the essence and the energies of God is still celebrated on the second Sunday of Lent as the "second triumph of Orthodoxy," just as important as the triumph over the iconoclasts.

The Council of Ferrara-Florence

Thessalonica fell to the Turks in AD 1429. The Emperor John petitioned the Latins for aid and the Pope Eugene IV responded that the reunion of the

Byzantine with the Roman church was the prerequisite for receiving any assistance against the Turks.

The emperor insisted that the Byzantines were so desperate for assistance that they could not afford to attend the council unless the pope supplied the fleet of ships to bring them. The pope was so eager to reunite the Byzantines to the Latin church that he agreed to this demand. The pope and the emperor then agreed that the Italian city of Ferrara was an acceptable place for the council of reunion and the council opened there in January AD 1438.

But the Byzantine delegation of 700 people—including the Emperor John, the Patriarch Joasaph, the Archbishop Mark of Ephesus, Isidore of Kiev, and support staff—were not there yet! They only arrived in Venice during February and did not get to Ferrara until March.

Now that the Byzantines had arrived, the work of setting the agenda could begin.

The pre-conciliar commission was made of ten Latins and ten Byzantines. The Byzantine members included Mark, archbishop of Ephesus, and Isidore of Kiev together with representatives of the patriarch of Antioch. The emperor had instructed them to keep azymes and the Filioque off the agenda. He did not want these, the most divisive issues, to be discussed at the council. So purgatory became the primary issue scheduled for debate. But "purgatory" included the whole Roman system of indulgences, the teaching that the dead in purgatory suffered in a material fire, that the Church could dispense rewards from the "treasury of merit" accumulated by the saints, and that Requiem Masses could be sold and then offered to release the dead in purgatory from their suffering.

The Patriarch Joasaph seems to have sincerely thought a meeting of good will with his brother-patriarch, the pope of Rome, would lead the Romans to embrace Orthodoxy. Mark of Ephesus thought the emperor's instruction was an attempt to avoid the real issues but responded to the Latin teaching about purgatory as requested.

In his response to the Latins about purgatory, Mark wrote that the punishment of the dead was internal, not external. The dead suffered from sadness, conscious shame, and remorse, as well as their uncertainty about their future. According to Mark, even the biblical descriptions of eternal fire and worms in Hell were to be taken as allegories rather than as descriptions of external physical punishments and suffering. Mark insisted that the true suffering of the damned was the ignorance of God.

Mark tried to go home to Constantinople but was caught by the emperor and forced to stay.

The full sessions of the council finally began in October AD 1438 and the Filioque quickly became the chief concern of the open debate.

Meanwhile, the city of Florence—nearly 150 kilometers away—was agitating to host the council and their efforts included large-scale bribery. They were interested in hosting the council because of the huge profits involved in housing and feeding such an enormous gathering. Pope Eugene IV needed the cash—having paid all the Byzantine travel expenses—and so he accepted the offer, i.e., the bribes, of Florence. The Byzantines agreed to the move because the plague was beginning in Ferrara. So the last meeting of the council in Ferrara was in January AD 1439 and the first meeting in Florence was a month later.

The primary topic was still the Filioque. Isidore of Kiev was in favor of the Byzantines accepting the Latin theology while Mark of Ephesus opposed this plan.

During the sessions of the council the Byzantines were sitting in the back of the meetings. The Medici family, so important in the politics of Florence, were all pro-papal and pro-union and made their opinions known with financial gifts. One of the Byzantine delegates—a theologian from Georgia—upset at the way the Latins did theology by constantly referring to pre–Christian philosophy, complained, "Aristotle, Aristotle! Why all this Aristotle? We should be referring to Saints Peter and Paul, Basil the Great, Gregory the Theologian, and John Chrysostom, not Aristotle!"

Pope Eugene IV made a public promise to the Byzantines that he would send an army and financial aid to them once they agreed to the union. So in June AD 1439, the Byzantine delegation accepted the reunion with the Roman church. The proclamation of union declared that the Byzantines accepted that the Holy Spirit proceeds from both the Father and the Son, the use of azymes in the Eucharist, the teaching of purgatory and the practices associated with it, the primacy of Rome and the pope "as before the schism," and that the Institution Narrative ("Take, eat.… Take, drink") was just as important in the Eucharist as the Epiclesis ("Send down thy Holy Spirit to sanctify these Holy Gifts").

On June 10, just after signing the agreement, the Patriarch Joasaph died. He was buried in the Dominican church of St. Mary the New in Florence. Mark of Ephesus presided at the funeral.

But Mark and several other members of the Byzantine delegation had refused to sign the agreement. The Byzantines who had signed it insisted that they had simply signed it as a statement of their own personal opinions and that any true reunion needed to be ratified by a meeting of Byzantine bishops in Constantinople. Nevertheless, on July 6 the union of the Roman and Byzantine churches was proclaimed in Florence although the Latins refused to allow a celebration of the Byzantine liturgy as part of the reunion celebrations even as the Byzantines were all leaving to go back to Constantinople.

Chaos erupted when the delegation arrived back in Constantinople. The emperor was stricken with grief as his beloved wife died just as he was returning and in his distraction, did not publish the decree of reunion. The delegates who had signed the agreement all renounced their signatures in the face of widespread discontent and mounting public anger at their having signed.

When Isidore returned to Kiev, the union was repudiated by the Russians and he was deposed and imprisoned. After two years, he was able to escape and fled to Rome. The pope made him a cardinal and sent him with 200 soldiers to Constantinople to negotiate the implementation of the union.

The Emperor John died in AD 1448 and his brother was crowned Constantine XI. Constantine, desperate for the aid promised by the pope in the face of ongoing Turkish incursions, tried to convince the public to accept the reunion of the churches. The anti-unionists saw the Latin insistence on everything related to purgatory as an implied repudiation of theosis and hesychasm; they wrote to the pope suggesting a new council be held, this time in Constantinople. Even the pro-unionists angered the pope by still calling him "brother" of the patriarch in Constantinople, rather than "father," and their ongoing refusal to make any of the changes in the Eucharist or the Creed that they had agreed to; all they did was add the pope's name to the list of those prayed for at the Eucharist.

The army and financial aid which had been promised never arrived.

The Turks attacked the imperial capital and after a protracted siege the city of Constantinople fell on what came to be called "Black Monday," May 29 AD 1453. The emperor attended church that morning, hoping to convince heaven to spare the city. As the walls of the city were breached, it is said that a priest, celebrating the Eucharist in Hagia Sophia as negotiated by Isidore, was able to escape with the Holy Gifts at the moment of consecration into a miraculous opening in the cathedral walls; people expected that when Constantinople was freed from the Turks that that same priest would emerge from the wall to continue the Eucharist and give the people Holy Communion from the chalice that he still held.

Isidore, still in the city, dressed a corpse in his cardinal robes to escape execution and was himself sent into slavery with a number of other "insignificant" captives. He eventually escaped slavery and made his way back to Rome again.

The Sultan Mehmed II, "the Conqueror," appointed Gennadios Scholarius, a student of Mark of Ephesus and a leading anti-unionist who had been in Ferrara and Florence, as the new patriarch. The bishops of the Orthodox Church throughout the Turkish empire were appointed as judges and civil magistrates for the Christians in their areas.

The Byzantines expected Christ to return and the world to end when the earth reached its 8,000th birthday (i.e., the end of the seventh millennium of its existence). The new patriarch, Gennadios, calculated that—based on this expectation—that the world would end on September 1, AD 1492. Just as the fall of Rome in AD 410 had seemed to signal the end of the world to many people, many now saw the conquest of the imperial city and the devastation of the Byzantine Orthodox Christians as simply the last of the birth pangs of the End, the signs of the coming apocalypse and Last Judgement.

But the world did not end. So in AD 1510, the monk Philotheus of Pskov claimed that the Russians had inherited the mantle of Byzantium when he wrote: "Two Romes have fallen. A third [i.e., Moscow] now stands. There will never be a fourth!"

Conclusion

History did not end on September 1, AD 1492. It has still not ended. The journey of the People of God through time continues. New issues arise. New disputes erupt. Solutions must be found. Resolutions must be hammered out. How might the Byzantine Christian experience shape these solutions and resolutions?

In his study *Benedictine Maledictions*, Lester K. Little noted that "liturgy by its nature is conservative; even as it maintains an aura of timelessness, at certain moments it needs updating to remain effective, but its effectiveness can be harmed by changes seen as radical departures from the familiar. A middle way of adaptation and barely perceptible modification is best suited to changes in liturgy." This is as true of theology as it is of liturgy. Any theological response to contemporary issues has to be seen as a natural development of previously held positions. These solutions might be innovative but they cannot be "original" or be perceived as the rejection of prior proclamations or consensus.

A crucial element of these prior proclamations and the Byzantine theological consensus was the role of imperial support in calling councils or promulgating the conciliar decisions. While theology has continued to develop among Byzantine Christians since the collapse of the imperial system, there have been no new councils or resolutions to long-standing contemporary issues. There is widespread doubt among many in the Eastern Orthodox world that the Orthodox Church, which identifies itself as the conciliar heir of the apostles, is able to respond to vital issues without an emperor to call or support such councils. No structural vehicle has developed to take the place of the emperors that would enable Eastern Christians to address issues as a pan-Orthodox body. Even the recent "Holy and Great Council of the Orthodox Church" in 2016 was not able to assemble representatives of all the churches who mutually recognize each other as "Orthodox."

The geographic location of the Orthodox in "the diaspora" and the growing presence or increasing influence of theologians who are converts not raised in the Byzantine Christian milieu must also be acknowledged. The theological backgrounds of these converts cannot help but shape their current thinking; how might these backgrounds shape—or warp—theological developments in the world of Eastern Christianity?

But how much of the Byzantine experience is fundamental to Eastern Orthodoxy? How much is its own cultural baggage or holdovers from bygone ages that must adjust to new political and geographic realities? Remembering how the term *homoousias* was first rejected as an adequate description of the relationship between the Father and the Son but later endorsed as the only acceptable term, we must ask how might prior Byzantine theological statements change in new situations so that the fundamental message remains unaltered?

The great early and later Byzantine theologians—Basil the Great, Gregory Nazianzus, John of Damascus, Mark of Ephesus, and the rest—would be the among the first to insist that those who profess to remain loyal to their teaching must do exactly what they did: that is, modern theologians must not be afraid of actively engaging with the world and society in which they live. Even Mark of Ephesus thought it worthwhile to attempt discussing issues with Western Christian theologians. It was that engagement with the world in order to discover how to adequately express the relationship of the Divine mystery to that world that gave Byzantine Christianity its vibrancy and the flexibility to develop as it did.

We have seen so many heresies, so many schisms—both great and small—throughout the course of our narrative. Are such divisions something to be feared? We see such divisions arising among the earliest Christian communities even in the Acts of the Apostles in the New Testament. Cultural and linguistic differences led to pastoral crisis, such as the ignoring of certain needy widows in the distribution of food and aid that is described in Acts 6. Such divisions may be inevitably human in some ways. But the fear of conflict should never shut down discussion. The conflicts we have explored in these pages—with the Arians, the Pneumatomachoi, the Nestorians, and the others—may have had cultural or linguistic or political components but they have all been vital growing experiences as the Church furthered the understanding of God's relationship to his world.

It is the vitality of that relationship that is at the bottom of all the disputes we have encountered. It is the vitality of that relationship that is at the root of any disputes that may be faced currently or that may arise in the future. The controversies and the councils all sought to protect and deepen the understanding of that relationship. It is that relationship that is at the root of all parish life, whether in traditionally Byzantine territories or in "the diaspora." It is that relationship that will sustain the faithful in their struggle to live a life "worthy of… the cup of thy Christ, for resurrection to eternal life of soul and body in the immortality of the Holy Spirit..." (prayer from the *Martyrdom of Polycarp*).

SUGGESTIONS FOR FURTHER READING

St. Gregory Palamas, *The Triads. Apology for the Holy Hesychasts: Selections* (Trans. N. Gendle) Paulist Press, 1983.

John Meyendorff, *The Byzantine Legacy in the Orthodox Church*. St. Vladimir's Seminary Press, 1982.

John Meyendorff, *St. Gregory Palamas and Orthodox Spirituality* (Trans. A. Fiske) St. Vladimir's Seminary Press, 1998.

John Meyendorff, *A Study of Gregory Palamas*. St. Vladimir's Seminary Press, 2010.

Chapter Notes

Chapter 1

1. Jostein Ådna, ed., *The Formation of the Early Church*, Mohr Siebeck, 2005, p. 342, n. 4.

2. The four gospels were written AD 55–115; the epistles of St. Paul were written AD 49–67; the other epistles were written AD 45–150.

3. Tertullian, a slightly younger contemporary of Hippolytus from second-century North Africa, mused on all the ways in which the world would change if Caesar, i.e., the emperor, were to be baptized. But he concludes his daydream by reminding himself that all these longed for changes can never happen "for if Caesar were to be baptized he would cease to be Caesar!"

4. *Pascha* is the Greek form of *Pesach* ("Passover") and the term by which Christians referred to the celebration of Christ's Passion, Death, and Resurrection.

Chapter 2

1. The title "pope" is a variation on the word for "father"; the bishop of Rome and the bishop of Alexandria are both traditionally called Pope. In many Orthodox countries, the parish priest is still called "pop" or some version of "pope" and his wife is called "popadija" or a similar word, derived from "pope" as well.

Chapter 3

1. See the discussion above of Basil himself composing prayers for use at the Eucharist.

2. Sunday was commonly called "the Lord's Day" and many languages still call it by a version of that title.

3. Gregory of Nazianzus, *On God and Christ: The Five Theological Orations and Two Letters to Cledonius*, trans. Lionel Wickham and Frederick Williams, p. 151.

Chapter 4

1. In fact, "that which restrains" the Antichrist only completely collapsed in 1917–1918 with the fall of Astro-Hungary in the West and imperial Russia in the East as these were the last two governments representing themselves as the continuation of the Roman empire.

2. These masks often also included a kind of megaphone around the actor's mouth to magnify the words he spoke so that the audience could hear and understand him.

Chapter 5

1. An abbot of a monastery outside the walls of Constantinople; he was responsible for 300 monks who lived there.

2. The diptychs were small notebooks made of two panels connected by a hinge. The names of important church officials would be inscribed in such notebooks to be read aloud during the intercessory prayers of the Eucharist. To be either included or removed from the diptychs indicated whether the person was or was not a member-in-good-standing of the Church. In addition, sometimes a pair of icons might be attached with hinges and called diptychs as well.

3. Cyril himself had written: "And so we unite the Word of God the Father to the holy flesh endowed with a rational soul, in an ineffable way that transcends understanding,

without confusion, without change, and without alteration, and we thereby confess one Son and Christ and Lord. The same, one God and Man" (*Epistle* 45).

Chapter 6

1. Preamble to Justinian's *Novella*, cited by John Meyendorff, *Imperial Unity and Christian Divisions*, p. 209.
2. Leontius of Jerusalem, *Adv. Nestorius* V.28, cited in John Meyendorff, *Christ in Eastern Christian Thought*, p. 54.
3. Leontius of Jerusalem, *Adv. Nestorius* V.29, cited in John Meyendorff, *Christ in Eastern Christian Thought*, p. 54.

Chapter 7

1. Dean A. Miller, "Byzantine Sovereignty and Feminine Potencies" in *Women and Sovereignty*, ed. Louise Fradenburg, Edinburgh University Press, 1992, p. 256.
2. Constantine Tsirpanlis, "Aspects of Maximian Theology of Politics, History, and the Kingdom of God" in *Patristic and Byzantine Review* 1, no. 1 (1982), p. 8.
3. Maximus the Confessor, *Ambigua* 41, in Migne, *PG* 91:1309–1312C.
4. Lars Thunberg, *Microcosm and Mediator*, p. 378.
5. Maximus the Confessor, *Commentary on the Our Father*, in *Maximus Confessor, Selected Writings*, p. 107.
6. Lars Thunberg, *Microcosm and Mediator*, p. 381.
7. Lars Thunberg, *Man and the Cosmos*, p. 84.
8. Maximus the Confessor, *Mystagogy*, in *Maximus Confessor, Selected Writings*, pp. 21, 24.

9. Lars Thunberg, *Man and the Cosmos*, p. 89.
10. The condemnation of Pope Honorius by the ecumenical council proved problematic in 1870 when Vatican I proclaimed the popes infallible when he speaks *ex cathedra* ("from the throne," his seat as bishop of Rome) on faith and morals.

Chapter 8

1. See A. Jeffery, "Ghevond's Text of the Correspondence Between Umar II and Leo III" in the *Harvard Theological Review* 37 (1944), pp. 269–332.
2. John of Damascus, *On the Divine Images*, 1.16
3. Daniel J. Janosik, *John of Damascus: First Apologist to the Muslims*, p. 144.
4. Kenneth Parry, *Depicting the Word: Byzantine Iconophile Thought of the Eighth and Ninth Centuries*, p. 163.

Chapter 9

1. Catherine Roth, *On the Holy Icons: St. Theodore the Studite*, p. 16.

Chapter 10

1. *Life of Constantine* (*Vita Constantini*), chapter 18.
2. Steven Runciman, *The Byzantine Theocracy*, Cambridge University Press, 1977, p. 110.
3. Joan Hussey, *Orthodox Church in the Byzantine Empire*, p. 104.
4. Nicholas Mysticus, *Ep. 32*, in Joan Hussey, *Orthodox Church in the Byzantine Empire*, p. 105.
5. *Russian Primary Chronicle*, pp. 121–122.

Bibliography

Primary Sources

Augustine, *The City of God*. (Trans. H. Bettenson) Pelican Books, 1972; reprinted by Penguin, 1984.

Basil the Great, *On the Holy Spirit*. (Trans. Stephen Hildebrand) St. Vladimir's Seminary Press, 2011.

Chrysostom, John, *On Virginity, Against Remarriage*. (Trans. Sally Rieger Shore) Edwin Mellen Press, 1983.

Chrysostom, John, *On Wealth and Poverty*. (Trans. Catherine P. Roth) St. Vladimir's Seminary Press, 1984.

Early Christian Writings: The Apostolic Fathers (Andrew Louth, ed.) Penguin Classics, reprinted 1987.

Eusebius, *Ecclesiastical History*. (Trans. C.F. Cruse) Hendrickson Publishers, Updated edition, 1998.

Gregory of Nazianzus, *On God and Christ: The Five Theological Orations and Two Letters to Cledonius*. (Trans. Lionel Wickham and Frederick Williams) St. Vladimir's Seminary Press, 2002.

Patrologia Graeca (J.-P. Migne, ed.) Paris, 1857.

Procopius, *The Secret History* (Trans. R. Atwater). University of Michigan Press, 1961.

Pseudo-Dionysius the Areopagite, *The Divine Names and Mystical Theology* (Trans. J. D. Jones). Marquette University Press, 1980.

The Russian Primary Chronicle: Laurentian text (Trans. S. H. Cross and O. P. Sherbowitz-Wetzor). Medieval Academy of America, 1973.

St. Athanasius. *On the Incarnation*. (Preface by C.S. Lewis; trans. and introd. John Behr) St. Vladimir's Seminary Press, 2011.

St. Gregory Palamas, *The Triads. Apology for the Holy Hesychasts: Selections*. (Trans. N. Gendle). Paulist Press, 1983.

St. John Climacus, *The Ladder of Divine Ascent*. (Trans. C. Luibheid and N. Russell). Paulist Press, 1982.

St. John of Damascus, *Three Treatises on the Divine Images*. (Trans. A. Louth). St. Vladimir's Seminary Press, 2003.

St. John of Damascus, *Writings*. (Trans. F. H. Chase, Jr). Catholic University Press, 1958.

St. Leo the Great, *Sermons*. (Trans. J. P. Freeland and A. J. Conway). Catholic University of America Press, 1996.

St. Maximus the Confessor, *Maximus Confessor, Selected Writings*. (Trans. G. C. Berthold). Paulist Press, 1985.

St. Maximus the Confessor, *On the Cosmic Mystery of Jesus Christ*. (Trans. P. M. Blowers). St. Vladimir's Seminary Press, 2003.

St. Theodore the Studite, *On the Holy Icons*. (Trans. C. Roth). St. Vladimir's Seminary Press, 1981.

The Way of a Pilgrim and A Pilgrim Continues His Way. (Trans. O. Savin). Shambhala, 1991; reprint 2001.

Secondary Sources

Adna, Jostein, ed., *The Formation of the Early Church*. Mohr Siebeck, 2005.

Anderson, Gary, *The Genesis of Perfection: Adam and Eve in Jewish and Christian Imagination*. Westminster John Knox Press, 2002.

Aulen, Gustaf, *Christus Victor: An Historical Study of the Three Main Types of the Idea of Atonement*. Macmillan, 1969.

Brown, Peter, *The Rise of Christendom*, 2nd edition. Blackwell, 2003.

Chitty, Derwas, *The Desert a City: An introduction to the Study of Egyptian and Palestinian Monasticism Under the Christian Empire*. St. Vladimir's Seminary Press, reprinted 1977.

Dvornik, Francis, *Byzantine Missions Among the Slavs: SS. Constantine-Cyril and Methodius*. Rutgers University Press, 1970.

Dvornik, Francis, *Byzantium and the Roman Primacy*. (Trans. E. A. Quain). Fordham University Press, 1979.

Dvornik, Francis, *The Idea of Apostolicity in Byzantium and the Legend of the Apostle Andrew*. Harvard University Press, 1958.

Hussey, Joan, *Orthodox Church in the Byzantine Empire*. Clarendon Press, 1990.

Janosik, Daniel J., *John of Damascus: First Apologist to the Muslims*. Pickwick Publications, 2016.

Jeffrey, Arthur, "Ghevond's Text of the Correspondence Between Umar II and Leo III" in the *Harvard Theological Review* 37 (1944).

Kelly, J.N.D., *Golden Mouth: The Story of John Chrysostom—Ascetic, Preacher, Bishop*. Baker Books, 1995.

Kolbaba, Tia M., *The Byzantine Lists: Errors of the Latins*. University of Illinois Press, 2000.

LeGoff, Jacques, *The Birth of Purgatory*. (Trans. A. Goldhammer). University of Chicago Press, 1984.

Little, Lester K., *Benedictine Maledictions: Liturgical Cursing in Romanesque France*. Cornell University Press, 1993.

McGuckin, John, *Saint Cyril of Alexandria and the Christological Controversy*. St. Vladimir's Seminary Press, 2004.

McGuckin, John, *St. Gregory Nazianzus: An Intellectual Biography*. St. Vladimir's Seminary Press, 2001.

Meinardus, Otto F. A., "Paul's Missionary Journey to Spain: Tradition and Folklore" in *The Biblical Archaeologist* 41, no. 2 (June 1978), pp. 61–63.

Meyendorff, John, *Christ in Eastern Christian Thought*. St. Vladimir's Seminary Press, 1975.

Meyendorff, John, *Imperial Unity and Christian Divisions*. St. Vladimir's Seminary Press, 1989.

Meyendorff, John, *St. Gregory Palamas and Orthodox Spirituality*. (Trans. A. Fiske). St. Vladimir's Seminary Press, 1998.

Meyendorff, John, *A Study of Gregory Palamas*. St. Vladimir's Seminary Press, 2010.

Miller, Dean A., "Byzantine Sovereignty and Feminine Potencies" in *Women and Sovereignty* (ed. Louise Fradenburg). Edinburgh University Press, 1992.

Morris, Stephen, *When Brothers Dwell in Unity: Byzantine Christianity and Homosexuality.* McFarland, 2015.

Parry, Kenneth, *Depicting the Word: Byzantine Iconophile Thought of the Eighth and Ninth Centuries.* Brill, 1996.

Robinson, Thomas A., *Ignatius of Antioch and the Parting of the Ways: Early Jewish-Christian Relations.* Baker Academic, 2009.

Rubin, Miri, *Corpus Christi: The Eucharist in Late Medieval Culture.* Cambridge University Press, 1991.

Runciman, Steven, *The Byzantine Theocracy,* Cambridge University Press, 1977.

Russell, Norman, *Cyril of Alexandria.* Routledge, 2000.

Sahas, Daniel J., *John of Damascus on Islam: The "Heresy of the Ishmaelites."* Brill, 1972.

Tarasov, Oleg, *Icons and Devotion: Sacred Spaces in Imperial Russia.* Reaktion Books, 2002.

Thunberg, Lars, *Man and the Cosmos: The Vision of St. Maximus the Confessor.* St. Vladimir's Seminary Press, 2012.

Thunberg, Lars, *Microcosm and Mediator: The Theological Anthropology of Maximus the Confessor, second edition.* Open Court, 1995.

Tsirpanlis, Constantine, "Aspects of Maximian Theology of Politics, History, and the Kingdom of God" in *Patristic and Byzantine Review* 1, no. 1 (1982).

Vasileios, Marinis, *Death and the Afterlife in Byzantium: The Fate of the Soul in Theology, Liturgy, and Art.* Cambridge University Press, 2017.

Wessel, Susan, *Cyril of Alexandria and the Nestorian Controversy: the Making of a Saint and of a Heretic.* Oxford University Press, 2004.

Winslow, Donald, *The Dynamics of Salvation: A Study in Gregory of Nazianzus.* Philadelphia Patristic Foundation, 1979.

Wybrew, Hugh, *The Orthodox Liturgy: The Development of the Eucharistic Liturgy in the Byzantine Rite.* SPCK, 1989.

Index